BEYOND THE
LADIES LOUNGE

BEYOND THE LADIES LOUNGE

Australia's Female Publicans

CLARE WRIGHT

MELBOURNE UNIVERSITY PRESS

MELBOURNE UNIVERSITY PRESS
An imprint of Melbourne University Publishing Ltd
PO Box 1167, Carlton, Victoria 3053, Australia
mup-info@unimelb.edu.au
www.mup.com.au

First published 2003
Text © Clare Wright 2003
Design and typography © Melbourne University Publishing Ltd 2003

Cover illustration: Hotel exterior, West Wylong, NSW, 1997
Author photo: Virginia Cummins

Designed by Lauren Statham, Alice Graphics
Typeset in 11pt Apollo by Syarikat Seng Teik Sdn. Bhd., Malaysia
Printed in Australia by McPherson's Printing Group

National Library of Australia Cataloguing-in-Publication entry

Wright, Clare Alice.
   Beyond the ladies lounge: Australia's female publicans.

   Bibliography.
   Includes index.
   ISBN 0 522 85071 5.

   1. Women—Hotelkeepers—Australia—History. 2. Hotels—Licenses—Australia—History. I. Title.

647.9494

To Damien
for the big picture
And Ruth
who beholds the detail

Contents

PART IV 'SHE KNOWS WHAT SHE'S ABOUT'
Controlling the Public House

Illustrations

Preface and Acknowledgements

This book has been a long time coming. It began its life as a Bachelor of Arts Honours thesis, completed at the University of Melbourne in 1991. My fledgling research was inspired by the drinking customs of the crowd with whom Damien, my then boyfriend (now husband), and I gathered at his outer suburban football club. I was particularly drawn to the gender and spatial implications of the weekly post-game performance in the social rooms: the way that alcohol divided the room, with men standing in huddles around the bar, drinking beer, and the women sitting around tables on the opposite side of the room, sipping 'girlie drinks'. As the evening progressed, and conviviality turned to drunkenness, the two off-field teams slowly merged; the women were finally able to approach their partners—enter the masculine territory—if only to drive their limper halves home. Public drinking rituals revealed an institutionalised gender division where women, it seemed, were forever consigned to a marginal social position, both in space and in worth.

But I wanted to write history—not sociology or ethnography—and I wanted my original contribution to an already hackneyed feminist theme to be the collection of oral history. And so I advertised in the daily press for women who had worked or drunk in pubs from the 1940s to the 1980s. I had many responses. I talked to a dozen women and asked them earnest, if somewhat inane, questions. They answered me respectfully, honestly, humorously, wisely. And they told me things I didn't know. They told me stories I'd never heard. They talked about their lives in ways I'd never imagined. They introduced me to theories—of work and play and politics and identity—that could not be ignored or repressed or denied. These women loved pubs.

I am indebted to my original interviewees for turning me around, passing me a piece of lemon slice, and pointing me in a new direction. The excursion has been all the more compelling and rewarding for seeking possibilities instead of restraints, opportunities in place of obstacles. Where my initial premise had been an anatomy of lack, they told me a tale of plenty. My BA Honours thesis—Real Women Do Shout: Narratives of Female Pub Culture—was the story the women themselves wanted to have heard. Its themes were empowerment, pleasure, community and connection.

Real Women was warmly received by my academic mentors. But it was the wider public response which encouraged me to pursue the topic of female pub culture beyond the limited scope of undergraduate research. For the following two years, Damien and I travelled around Australia in a veteran Land Rover, working, fishing and exploring our vast, beautiful continent. Three months of our trip were spent living at The Australian Hotel, my mother-in-law's family pub in the western Queensland town of Murgon, which is now run by Damien's aunt, Jill Tiernan. Whenever I discussed my previous research with people we met in the pub or on the road, I encountered the same response: 'Well, it's about time! You must talk to my cousin Margaret. She had the pub at Innisfail for years.' Or 'How fascinating. My grandmother ran a hotel in Sydney after her husband was killed in the war.' Or the most common reply—almost a mantra —'Have you heard of Ma Ring of Billinudgel?' Ma Ring, the centenarian hotelkeeper, is to the late twentieth century what Isobel Gray, 'the Eulo Queen', was a century before: a legendary figure, the subject of affectionate anecdote, tall story and true.

By the time we arrived back in Melbourne in 1995, I knew I was on to something. I worked for a year for the then Federal Member for Wills, Phil Cleary. Always quick with a yarn, Phil regaled me with tales of the La Franchi sisters who ran the Swiss Mountain Inn in central Victoria, where his Irish ancestors had settled in the nineteenth century. Old-timers in Phil's working-class inner city electorate fondly recalled female publicans from the 1940s and 1950s. And down at the Edinburgh Castle on Sydney Road, Mary ruled supreme—selling beers, organising political forums, catering the local football functions.

By 1996, I had reached critical mass. Female publicans to the right, female publicans to the left. Town and country. Past and present. With a postgraduate scholarship to temper the plunge back into student life, I embarked on the doctoral thesis which is the bedrock of this book. I spent the best part of that first year of postgraduate research in the musty bunker that was the old Victorian Public Record Office in Laverton, my head buried in the huge leather-bound volumes of liquor licensing records. I was barely able to turn the pages in front of my by-now heavily pregnant belly. It was a race to see which would be delivered first: the baby or the burgeoning list of female licensees' names. The plot was getting thicker.

Though the focus has shifted from a history of women and pubs generally, to a history of female publicans specifically, the story of Real Women has been re-told in new and complementary and sometimes contradictory ways by the women interviewed for this book: Kath Byer, Gloria Fry, Eileen Clatworthy, Carmel Cooper, Eliza Faull, Anne and Janet Parr, Lillian and Margaret O'Connell, Edna Jory, Nancy Reis, Eileen O'Hanlon, Pam Sleigh-Elam, Lynne Cox, Samantha Gowing and Amy Robson. Though my time in the archives has been precious, it is the view from inside the hotel that primarily informs the study. The language, ideas and inflections of these women have been central to this project. It is the resonances and recurrences in the interviews that have formed the basis of my research strategy. They are the clues and questions with which I armed myself when scouring the documentary sources—liquor licensing records, parliamentary debates and royal commissions, legislation and court reports, daily newspapers, trade journals and temperance publications, literary magazines, popular novels and folksongs—moving from the individual and experiential to the structural and ideological.

The life stories of female publicans and their daughters have presented the means for an intellectual journey, one both personal and academic in scope. I am grateful to these truly hospitable women for their time, patience and encouragement.

Writing this book would not have been possible without the generosity and sustenance of many people. My doctoral research was undertaken with the assistance of an Australian Postgraduate Research Award; the transition from thesis to book has been aided by a University of Melbourne Publication Grant, the Geoffrey Serle Award (sponsored by the Australian Historical Association) and support as a Research Fellow at The Australian Centre at the University of Melbourne. I am especially appreciative of the hard work and devotion of the women at the Melbourne University Family Club Child Care Centre.

My deep thanks go to David Goodman and Kate Darian-Smith, whose diligent guidance and belief in the worth of the project have been a blessing. I have enjoyed the expertise and advice of Chris McConville for over a decade. Patricia Grimshaw nurtured the ambition of a wide-eyed Honours student. Christina Twomey and Deborah Rechter offered profound intellectual support, and other gifts besides. Fiona Capp, Robin Gerster, Teresa Pitt and Janet Mackenzie provided precious clues in the evolution from thesis to book. Jenny Darling and Margaret Barca took my hand and showed me a new way forward. The companionship of Rhyll Nance, Michael Cathcart, Graham Willett, Gwenda Tavan, Jan Clohessy, Ros Bandt and other members of The Australian Centre made all the difference to my time as a student there.

I would particularly like to acknowledge the passion and judgement of several of my postgraduate colleagues: Helen Doyle, Maria Tumarkin, Rachel Hughes, Barry O'Mahony, Tony Birch, Perrie Ballantyne and Anna Clark. My dear friends Kate Doherty and Sarah Tomasetti have been vigilant benefactors of humour, concern and unconditional acceptance. Alice Garner fell gracefully into both camps.

My family network is large and giving and has been essential in providing the respect, support and faith I needed to accomplish this project. My father, Richard Perry, has always encouraged me to do what makes me happy and has unflaggingly embraced my choices. John Goldlust fuelled a democratic temper and a love of history from an early age. My grandmother, Alice Leonards, counselled me to trust my instincts. Rachel Goldlust, Madeleine and George Wright, Sister Philomene Tiernan and Dermot Tiernan have all contributed to my well-being. Many other friends and family members have asked all the right questions and made all the right noises.

Finally, my deepest gratitude is reserved for those closest to home. My mother, Ruth Leonards, is an angel. If not for *her* work, my work would have ground to a crashing halt years ago. She has cared for my children, transcribed my interview tapes and made chicken soup on demand —always with a smile on her face. I am indebted to her energy and kindness. My sons, Bernie and Noah, were conceived and grew with this project. Without them, my work would have progressed in a more rational fashion but with infinitely less wonderment and meaning. I cherish you.

And to Damien, who has been there from the beginning. Thank you. With your courage, intelligence and love, anything is possible.

A Note on Terminology and Spelling

In Australia, the word *hotel* is used as a generic term for a public house. 'Hotel' applied equally to inner-city working-class pubs, grand metropolitan establishments whose function was largely residential, and both humble and majestic country inns.

In this book, *female publican* and *female hotelkeeper* denote a woman who ran a hotel. In particular, I focus on the *female licensee*: the woman who held the licence for a hotel. Although it is now common to use the word 'woman' as an adjective ('woman publican', 'women licensees'), I have rejected this practice as both grammatically incorrect and inequitable: we would never speak of a 'man publican'.

The noun *licence* often appears as *license* in direct quotes from older texts.

I have chosen to spell *hotelkeeper* as one word, along with *innkeeper* and *saloonkeeper*, and the verbs *hotelkeeping, innkeeping* and *saloonkeeping*. This was the most common usage in the nineteenth and early twentieth centuries and is followed by most modern scholars in the field of alcohol studies.

I have deliberately used the term *public housekeeper* to describe someone who keeps a public house and also someone who is a housekeeper to the public. The act of *public housekeeping* is thus wilfully framed in terms of the commercial operation of domesticity.

A Colonial Pub Crawl

IT IS 1889. YOU ARE TIRED, thirsty and in search of a congenial place to rest your feet amidst the hurly-burly of the boom-time metropolis of Melbourne. You walk through the front door of the two-storey, rough-cut bluestone hotel in Franklin Street, near the Victoria Market. The building has a simple hipped roof, french windows either side of the door and two symmetrical brick chimneys. Unusually, the public house is not located on a corner, but 'in the middle of a line of street'.[1] You have heard of Mac's Hotel, famed for being the coaching terminus from which eager prospectors set off for the Victorian diggings, gold dust in their eyes, and the place to where they returned, more often unsuccessful than not (see Plate 1). Built in 1853 for publican John McMillan, Mac's Hotel—with its array of discreet parlours and rowdy public bar downstairs, six bedrooms upstairs and one hundred horse stalls outside—welcomed the dreamers and the disaffected alike. But you have no time for history. You are thirsty and tired. You walk up to the bar and are greeted by your host, Mrs Margaret Tobin. You are not surprised to discover that the publican is a woman. Margaret has been the licensee at Mac's since 1887, and if you were to return to the hotel six years later, you would still find her name hanging above the front door.

Replenished, you go on your way, as so many before you have, and will continue to do; hotels specialise in human traffic. Perhaps you, or your fellow riders, wander east and then down Swanston Street. At the corner of Swanston and La Trobe Streets, you come to the Travellers Home Hotel, built in 1850. Ten of its twenty-three licensees have been women; Mrs Kate Foster holds court there now. Further along Swanston Street is

1. *Mac's Hotel, Franklin Street, Melbourne, c.1933.*

the Strangers Home Hotel; the current publican, Mrs Nightingale, is one of eighteen women to hold the licence for these premises. Next to St Paul's Cathedral, on the corner of Flinders Lane, is the Cathedral Hotel, under the eleven-year reign of Mrs Maria Thompson. Down to Elizabeth Street now, and the Golden Fleece Hotel. Licensed Victualler: Mrs Maria Graham. Further west along Elizabeth Street, you come to the Sportsmen's Club Hotel, where Mrs Annie Robertson plays 'mine host'.

Once on Bourke Street, you have fifty-four hotels to soothe what ails you. Why not try Miss Annie Mulligan's Excelsior Hotel? In 1854, the leader of the gold diggers' rebellion at Eureka, Peter Lalor, took refuge in the attic here, when the hotel was known as the National. Or Mrs Hampden's Rose of Melbourne or Mrs Pasquin's Foley's Hotel. The long-serving Mrs Annie Bulgaer of the Farmers Club Hotel is sure to please; there's not much she wouldn't have seen in her eighteen years as a publican. At the American Bar Hotel, you'll find Mrs Haines and her lavish 'Yankee' bar fittings, which have been a feature of the better-patronised goldfield hotels since the mid-1850s.[2]

But if you are looking for a real treat, a lush banquet of European opulence peppered with colonial hospitality, you must stop for a while on the hill at the corner of Bourke and William Streets. You have arrived at the legendary Menzies Hotel, built in 1867 for Archibald Menzies (see Plate 2). With its five storeys, eighty bedrooms, grand dining room, two large billiard rooms, eight private sitting rooms, music room, drawing room, lounge and public bar, kitchen, laundries and servants' quarters, the Menzies was lauded as the finest hotel in the colony to that time. Step inside, take a deep breath, and appreciate the 'unheard-of display of rich panelling, carved stairways, glittering gas chandeliers, resplendent curtainings, thick carpets, and elaborate furniture'.[3] Sample the 'rich exotic food', prepared under the direction of a former Buckingham Palace chef, and then seek out the manager of this empire of salutation: you want to thank her. Mrs Catherine Menzies descends from her residential wing upstairs. She took over the licence from Archibald almost ten years ago, and will oversee the hotel's trade for another decade. You are a humble patron indeed, compared to the list of rich and famous who have sought her custom, but she graciously accepts your accolades and wishes you well on your journey.

You are at the business end of town now, where the other half drinks. At the Four Courts Hotel on the corner of William and Little Collins Streets, Mrs R. Clifford is the licensee. And then there is the competition: the Law Courts Hotel, corner William and Little Bourke, where you will find Mrs Wishart hosting the legal eagles. These women would have heard some tales in their time, but perhaps none so sad as the story

2. *Menzies Hotel, Bourke Street, Melbourne, c.1870.*

of the Shamrock Hotel, just up the road on Little Bourke Street. This hotel was built in 1862. In 1868 the licence was taken by Michael O'Brien, who ran the business with his wife, Ellen, until his death on 28 February 1870. Not a month later, on 9 March, the widow Ellen buried her only child, Catherine, who had also died at the hotel. But Ellen stayed on at her public house, despite its horrors, and continued with the business until 1874, when the licence was transferred to Michael Walsh. In 1882, the records show that a Mrs Ellen Walsh took the licence; she ran the hotel until 1890. Could this be the same Ellen, married to a second Michael and living with her ghosts in the same hotel for twenty-eight years? Perhaps you could ask her, if dutch courage prevails.

Or maybe you could ask another widow what it is like to reside in the same city hotel for over three decades. Up on the corner of Queen and Little Bourke, at the Harp of Erin, you will meet Mrs Bridget Stapleton, who ran the hotel with her husband Stephen from 1868 to 1889 and then took on the licence by herself for another ten years. Kitty-corner, at the Sorrento Hotel, built by Mrs Marion Lane in 1876, the licensee is now Mrs Annie Coffin, morbid by name, not by nature.

This is how I imagine a pub crawl in central Melbourne, 1889, might proceed. The list of female publicans running city hotels in this year is representative, but not exhaustive. The tour could equally have taken place in Collingwood, or Carlton, or Sydney, or Hobart. The picture is the same—women at the helm of hotels whose names bear the weight of Australia's history, symbolism and identity: shearers and sportsmen, patriots and sycophants, elitists and commoners, church and state, the possessive and the dispossessed, the homesick and the homespun. The names tell the stories—the National, the American Bar, the Golden Fleece, the Menzies, the Four Courts, the Strangers Home, the Shamrock, the Harp of Erin, the Cathedral, the Sportsmen's Club, the Farmers Club, Foley's, Mac's—but the story can often belie the name of the proprietor behind the bar. We do not think of nineteenth-century women as authority figures in the realms of politics, pastoralism, religion, sport and patriotism, yet their influence was beyond question in the law and custom of hotelkeeping.

If Margaret Tobin at Mac's represents the close-up vision of the woman as publican, the wide-angle view is just as compelling. Far from being a 'male domain', where all women were relegated to the pitiful margins of public drinking space until the liberating 1970s, the Australian hotel has in fact been an enduring site of female control and independence. In 1853, women comprised only 2 per cent of the licensees for metropolitan Melbourne. However by 1876, after the boon to the liquor industry that was the Victorian gold rush, this figure had risen to 22 per cent. By 1889, the year of our imaginary pub crawl, 30 per cent of Melbourne's city and suburban hotels were licensed to women. And by the first decades of the twentieth century, over half of Melbourne's hotels had a female licensee. In some districts in this year, particularly the inner city, working-class (and notably Irish) suburbs of Collingwood, Footscray and South Melbourne, the proportion of female publicans was as high as 58 per cent, 62 per cent and 68 per cent respectively. Rates in regional centres such as Ballarat and Bendigo were just as great at the turn of the century. Women continued to represent between 40 and 50 per cent of Victorian licensees until the 1950s.[4] A tired and thirsty traveller might have enjoyed his drink in the company of men, but he was odds-on to be entering the house of a woman.

Although this trend is apparent in other Australian states, my research focuses on Victoria, where liquor history is particularly noteworthy for many reasons: the goldfields impetus leading to a boom in regional centres and then, by 1900, a scattering of wayside pubs with little population around them; the dense concentration of hotels in metropolitan and suburban Melbourne with an intensely local community focus; the strength of the Methodist–Presbyterian anti-drink movement and an equally significant Irish Catholic tradition of hotelkeeping; and the fact that for sixty or so years after the gold rushes, Melbourne and Victoria set the pace culturally, economically and demographically for the rest of Australia.

As licensees, women were not merely passive front-persons to a social and commercial institution otherwise controlled by men. Of legal necessity, they were the proprietors of their own separate businesses, whose autonomy could not be disputed by court or community. While a great many female publicans in the late nineteenth and early twentieth centuries were widows, taking over the licence to the family business after the death of their husband, this was by no means the only route to hotelkeeping for women. Unmarried daughters, spinster sisters and married women unrelated to the previous licensee all successfully applied for the valuable property of a liquor licence. Female publicans often transferred the licences for their hotels to other women, and there were many hotels that saw an unbroken string of up to a dozen women holding sway behind the bar. Clearly, networks of women conspired to pass on the privilege of selling alcohol.

In the late nineteenth and early twentieth centuries, women were not only numerically prominent in the occupation of hotelkeeping, but the hotel itself owed much of its political survival to values that were associated with *female* sex roles: domesticity, respectability and maternal restraint. As the no-nonsense head of the public house, Australian women in hotels have enjoyed a unique social visibility. In the liquor trade journal, the *Vigilante*, a reporter noted in 1930 that 'Rarely a sitting of the Licensing Court passes in Melbourne at which licences are not granted to women'.[5] Indeed, the history of female publicans runs counter-intuitively to our expectations of 'woman's place' in the pre-modern era. As 'public housekeepers', female licensees performed normative womanly work within the discordant context of a mercantile enterprise.

The traditional authority of female publicans is evident in the faded photographic images that commonly line today's pub walls. Nineteenth-century publicans were particularly fond of using the new technology of photography to immortalise their status as proprietors and community leaders. And there, taking up her rightful position in the foreground of the picture, stands the female hotelkeeper, flanked by staff, children and a smattering of mostly male customers (see Plates 3–6). You can often identify the licensee by her seemly attire, as much by her position as the leader of the communal household. The hotel itself looms large in the background; the human territory is clearly claimed by the woman up front. As was law, the licensee's name hangs above the front door: a sign of possession, a symbol of status, a statement of power.[6] By reconstructing the hotel as a 'female domain', we can begin to appreciate the pub as an intricate, heterosocial space which has historically relied on the labour, initiative, personalities and devotion of women—as well as the patronage of men—for its founding and continuity as an iconic cultural institution.

One aspect of this complexity is reconciling the pub as the arche-typal Australian male social institution with the female publican as the archetypal Australian matriarchal figure. From Henry Lawson to Thea Astley, several generations of literary raconteurs have used the figure of the female hotelkeeper to depict fortitude, resilience, humour, integrity and charm. Given the legendary strength of their spirit, it is no wonder that female publicans have been central figures in many dramatic rep-resentations of Australian community life.[7] Most recently, we have the example of Meredith Monaghan in the ABC's runaway hit, *SeaChange* (1999–2001). The omniscient manager with a finger in every pie, Mere-dith's character resonated with such a wide national audience precisely because Australians are imbued with a social memory of her kind and

3. Women and children first. Australian Hotel, Clark's Hill, Victoria, c.1890.

4. Pieper's Hill Hotel, Bendigo, n.d.

5. *Acott's Hotel, Bendigo, n.d.*

6. *Blue Bell Inn, Bendigo, n.d.*

calling. Female publicans have always stood in close proximity to Australia's cultural epicentre.

As proprietors of the principal colonial social institution, female publicans have also been witnesses to many of Australia's defining historical moments. When Edward Hargreaves found gold in the hills behind Bathurst in 1851, thus sparking the New South Wales gold rushes, the first person to whom he reported his discovery was Susan Lister, the licensee of the Wellington Inn where he was boarding. Mrs Bentley, wife of the publican at the Eureka Hotel, was tried for her part in the fracas which led to the famous goldfields rebellion in 1854. The Glenrowan Hotel, where the legendary bushranger Ned Kelly made his 'last stand' in June 1880, was licensed to Ann Jones, an English widow supporting three children.[8] Many would know that, in more recent times, Dawn Fraser and Cheryl Barassi have worked as publicans, and this seems fitting: the larrikin Olympic swimmer and outspoken footballer's wife are formidable women. Ambitious, frank and forthright, they are late-twentieth-century embodiments of the stereotypical frontierswoman of our colonial past.

Unearthing the numerical prevalence of women as publicans raises two important questions. First, why were conditions so agreeable for women to be keeping hotels in the late nineteenth and early twentieth centuries? How can these arresting figures be explained? And second, why has this tale not been previously told, particularly given the oft-cited significance of public drinking culture to Australia's core values and identity? Clearly, some historical accounting is called for when the records reveal a situation so antithetical to the representations of pub culture that have been central to our national story—a boys' club which privileged men's fantasies over women's dignity.[9]

Neither madonna nor whore, female publicans have mastered the interior territory of the pub with decency and integrity while commanding respect in the broader public sphere for their achievements and status. By challenging the notion of the hotel as anti-home and a place of 'sexual apartheid', it is possible to acknowledge the pub as a place where women have historically lived, loved, worked and taken their leisure; a complex environment that could, as we are so often told, be hostile to women, but could also, as we are less frequently encouraged to believe, be supportive of women's needs and aspirations. By going inside the hotel, and asking to speak to the boss, this book goes where no Australian historian has yet ventured: beyond the Ladies Lounge.

'Likely to Keep Orderly Houses'

Female Publicans
and the Law

A Monument to Her Enterprise

LIKE MANY IRISH GIRLS of her generation, Anastasia Banks left her Kilkenny home in 1852 in order to better her prospects. Anastasia's quest took her to Victoria and ultimately, in 1871, to the Stockyard Creek diggings in South Gippsland. Here she met and married William Thornley, who exchanged single life for a liquor licence to operate one of the twenty public houses in the booming township of Foster. When Thornley died two years later, his 47-year-old widow decided to keep the licence. Under Anastasia's management, Thornley's Exchange Hotel became famous throughout Gippsland in the 1880s and 1890s. Just months before her death in 1906, the octogenarian hotelkeeper supervised an extravagant refurbishment of the licensed premises she had occupied for thirty-four years. As Anastasia's eulogist remarked, 'the handsome structure now stands as a monument to her enterprise'.

Anastasia Thornley's wealth, flair and goodwill were not expended on her hotel alone. She bought 318 acres of land in Meeniyan, financed a local goldmine and, when bush fires ravaged Foster in 1898, she turned the hotel's bedrooms into hospital wards as an expression of her 'sincere fellowship with suffering humanity'. After Mrs Thornley's death, the town returned the favour. A funeral procession of twenty vehicles, fifty horsemen and a hundred on foot turned out to farewell 'Foster's oldest and best friend'. At her grave—still the largest and most ornate in the Foster cemetery—the massed crowd heard the publican eulogised as a 'heart and soul in sympathy with district and people' (see Plate 7).

Almost a century later, the holiday visitor to Foster can enter the district's Historical Museum and feel the wellspring of sentiment still

7. *Anastasia Thornley's grave—in 2002 the most prominent headstone in the Foster Cemetery, Victoria.*

reserved for Thornley. An entire display wall is devoted to her life, including a huge framed portrait of the woman, dressed in decorous widow's weeds, a Mona Lisa lilt to her firmly set lips, a flicker of mischief in her eye. The sepia tones belie her flaming red hair (see Plate 8). The museum's accompanying text reinforces the image of determination and calm resolve: 'the active controller of her prosperous business . . . she made for herself a name and position for honest purpose, integrity of character and whole-hearted generosity which stood her in good stead at every turn on Fortune's wheel'. As I stare up at her compelling portrait, I become aware of a kindred observer, lightly touching my elbow. 'Are you interested in Anastasia?' asks the elderly local historian, Rosie Crawford. She smiles conspiratorially. 'She's our town pet, you know.'[1]

Kath Byer and I sit together in the commodious lounge at the Notting Hill Hotel in the outer Melbourne suburb of Clayton, Kath's home and business

8. *Anastasia Thornley, c.1870.*

premises for over sixty years. When she married Sidney Byer at the age of eighteen, he had the licence for a hotel in Bacchus Marsh, where Kath was born and raised by her father Stephen Shea, a barber, and her mother Florence, a shop proprietor. Two of Kath's three brothers became publicans. In 1936, Kath and Sidney bought the Notting Hill Hotel and Kath became the licensee in 1942. Kath leans towards me and explains:

> Sidney wasn't really a publican. He was entertaining, mainly! I could see that I had to take the pub over if it was going to be clean and all that sort of thing. So that's it. I just did it from the day I got married. There was no agreement. It was the way it was. Sidney was interested in all the decisions. But I was the publican ... No, I've never considered any other vocation for myself.

'The Nott', under Kath's reign, has remained a constant force—a symbol of durability to the three generations she has served—while the immediate surroundings have transformed from market gardens to factories to university precinct to office buildings. Her customers have included farmers and professors, process workers and journalists. From white collar to blue, she has advised, consoled, served, donated, employed and amused. As the hotel's 'Reverend Mother', she has ministered to the needs of her community, and been rewarded for her efforts. Financially, yes, but also socially and emotionally: 'You've got to get respect as a publican. That's the story. As a woman, you can get more respect in a hotel than you get out on the street ... but you've got to be pretty strong. And you've got to like it. You see, I love it.' There it is again: the humble yet self-satisfied smile. And that gentle, defiant twinkle in the eye.[2]

Spanning almost one hundred and fifty years, the stories of Anastasia Thornley and Kath Byer delineate the long tradition of female hotelkeeping in Australia. Their success in running hotel businesses challenges the prevailing historical wisdom that women's opportunities for self-employment 'disappeared almost entirely' by the mid-1800s, with domestic service, teaching and prostitution remaining 'almost the only paid employment available to women' until World War II.[3] The legal framework that regulated the trade in liquor in Victoria was in fact distinctly favourable to the participation of women as licensees. This positive legal climate existed even though there was barely any other public issue that had been the subject of so many legislative measures as the sale of alcohol. Indeed, between 1835 and 1908, there were thirty-six acts that regulated the sale and distribution of liquor in Victoria, equating to changes in the law at least every two years.[4] There was certainly nothing *laissez-faire* about the regulation and administration of the liquor trade in Australia. Female publicans did not, therefore, surreptitiously slip in the back door of commercial hospitality. So why, when women reached the legal threshold of licensing arrangements, was their entrance rarely hindered?

We commonly assume that the legal subordination of women in the nineteenth century severely restricted their opportunities to engage in the public sphere of commerce and the professions. As one labour historian has noted, 'legislation generates a knowledge of sexual difference through its power to set boundaries and proscribe transgressions'.[5] Thus approved notions of femininity have assigned 'appropriate' social roles for women, a process that has generally limited the range of women's human possibilities. In the case of public housekeeping, however, women's sexually prescribed tendency to 'keep orderly houses' was precisely the key that afforded them entry to the official liquor trade. In a relationship of mutual benefit, the presence of women legitimated the industry while the industry afforded women a legitimate vocation.

A close examination of some of the key pieces of licensing legislation, as well as many judicial cases that applied and interpreted those acts, reveals that—contrary to our expectations—the law privileged female licensees' rights as commercial traders over their sexual identities as women.[6]

The early acceptance of female licensees within the formal legal structures that were designed to regulate the sale of alcohol in the colonies was fundamental in establishing a cultural tradition of female hotelkeeping. The legal legitimacy of this customary practice protected later generations of liquor-selling women from the more restrictive notions of 'true femininity' which were part of the late-nineteenth-century gender order: dependence on a male breadwinner, restrained distance from the world of work, and exclusive attention to the private concerns of being a good wife and mother. Indeed, female licensees enjoyed an unprecedented legal and economic independence; even after the married women's property reforms of the 1870s, most married women remained in a more dependent state than many married women who had held liquor licences in earlier colonial times.[7] Female publicans were legally certified boundary-crossers.

If Anastasia Thornley could confidently sell you a beer at her reputable establishment, it was because she had the weight of a century of legal authority behind her.

Traditions: From 'Shebeen'
to 'He or She'

BY THE 1790S, WHEN EUROPEANS began to call the new penal settlement of New South Wales their home, the practice of women selling alcohol for a living was nothing new. In the Middle Ages, married women dominated the production and seasonal sale of beer in England and Ireland, an occupation that was considered to be a domestic craft. This situation began to alter in the 1600s, when brewing became a large-scale, centralised activity, run by men. British historian Judith Bennett has argued that by the seventeenth century, anxieties about the drink trade 'were displaced from *all* brewers onto *female* brewers alone'.[1] Male regulators blamed the excesses of alcohol consumption and abuses in the liquor trade on female moral weakness, an association that won female liquor sellers a reputation as being disobedient, disruptive and sexually degenerate. The guiding assumption of law-makers was that 'when women sell liquor, disorder and promiscuity will result'.[2]

Magistrates began to ban alehouse licences to women between the ages of fourteen and forty, presumably the years when female sexual activity was at its height. Licensed victualling was thus effectively restricted to widows, who enjoyed a protected status in most male trades as they carried on their husbands' businesses and kept themselves off parish relief. In Ireland, unlicensed liquor selling by widows through 'shebeens', or kitchen-bars, became a significant feature of the trade but was largely condoned by authorities as a form of communal charity.[3] As the majority of female licensed victuallers prior to the sixteenth century were widows in any case, the intent of legislation against un-widowed women running alehouses appears to be more ideological than practical:

the law reinforced the notion that women working independently of men posed a threat to the patriarchal order of society.

While authorities and social commentators may have associated female ale selling with disorder, drunkenness and sexual impropriety, women persistently turned to alehouse-keeping to make their livings. With limited opportunities for women in Tudor and Stuart England, running an alehouse 'provided one of the few avenues for achieving social recognition and possibly advancement'.[4] Besides providing social status and recognition, ale selling required no specialist training and was not controlled by guilds; a private home could be easily and legally converted to a tippling den; no large capital investment was needed; there was a prospect of reasonable profit; and female ale sellers were 'something of a catch in the marriage market'.[5] Thus there were many pull factors that motivated women to sell liquor; they were not merely pushed by financial necessity. Women's perseverance in entering the trade, despite the negative 'cultural memory' of their calling, was evidently worth the effort.

The situation with regard to British inns was significantly different from alehouses. In the eighteenth and nineteenth centuries, when most legal and some social distinctions between inns, taverns and alehouses had narrowed, the traditional class divide largely remained: the inn was home to the landed, professional and mercantile aristocracies, and the alehouse was a place of 'lower order' communion. Alehouse-keepers rarely became innkeepers, reflecting the fact that most publicans were drawn from the ranks of respectable servants, farmers, sportsmen or former bar attendants, where innkeepers were often wealthy property owners and gentlemen.[6]

Although there is no doubt that the women of these dynastic inn families would have played a pivotal part in the day-to-day management of the establishment, it seems that few women held licences to run inns in their own names. Thomas Burke, in his 1943 history of English inns, contends, 'Though innkeeping closely touches domesticity, the women innkeepers were few'.[7] Burke does note, however, that there have been some 'famous female innkeepers', all widows and 'comely old gentlewomen' who have kept up the 'dignified calling' of innkeeper.[8] Other references to innkeepers' wives generally confirm Burke's picture of the gentlewoman/helpmeet whose place in the business venture and good reputation are assured by her relationship to the family unit. She is not 'disorderly' for she knows her station.

The colonial authorities in the penal colony of New South Wales were thus presented with two conflicting models for female victualling:

the unruly, permissive alewife or the dignified, matronly innkeeper. Quite clearly, they chose the latter. Determined to stamp out the illegal trade in spirits, authorities actively promoted the supply of beer as a defence against drunkenness.[9] And from the late 1790s, licences were issued to women as part of this purposeful campaign, regardless of their marital status or convict origins. This is significant, given the claim of some historians that female convicts and early female immigrants prior to the 1840s 'were expected to be, and were treated as, whores, and this label was applied indiscriminately to virtually all women in the colony'.[10] Whereas in England, the primary concern of licensing laws for over five hundred years had been 'the maintenance of public order', in Australia the legislative focus was on the control of traders, no doubt reflecting the colony's origins as a penal settlement. Women were kept out of the English liquor trade precisely because trade problems such as drunkenness and cheating were directly attributed to their presence. In Australia, on the other hand, women of good character were considered part of the solution. What is surprising about the early Australian experience, then, is not that women pursued liquor selling as a means of self-employment, but that the colonial authorities chose to disregard both the depraved reputation of female ale sellers and the social background and age of female convicts (not in the least 'comely old gentlewomen') in awarding women the legal status of licence holders.

The colonial authorities had a blank slate for designing the sort of liquor trade they wanted to establish. Indeed, successive governors were so eager to create a respectable, fully regulated and deliberately constituted liquor industry that they even built a government brewery at Parramatta in 1804. Moreover, Australia was, from the outset, 'a modern commercial economy rather than a traditional, household economy'.[11] Colonial authorities were thus in a position to institute calculated trade practices rather than tinker around the edges of custom and its ingrained prejudices. It is hard to sustain the claim that Australia's first women were indiscriminately branded as whores when, by 1815, twelve out of the ninety-six licences issued for the Sydney area were held by women. It is also clear that authorities were prepared to condone hotelkeeping by young, single women. Sarah Bird, the first woman to hold a liquor licence in Australia, was a 27-year-old, unmarried convict when she hung out her sign for The Three Jolly Settlers in 1797. The following year she wrote a letter to her father in England claiming to have 'met with tolerable good success in the public line'.[12]

The significant break with British tradition, therefore, lay in the practice of granting licences to women other than widows, with the expectation that the government's best hopes for a reputable liquor trade rested as safely in the hands of the colony's enterprising women as with its mercantile men. Key pieces of licensing legislation from the early colonial period reveal just how intimately women were drawn into those deliberate plans for a modern commercial economy.

'Fit and proper': The measure of repute

Licences to sell alcohol in the colony of New South Wales were first issued in 1792 but legislation regulating the supply of licences was not enacted until 1825.[13] A Publican's General Licence was issued by the Colonial Treasurer after an applicant had received a certificate, signed by a Justice of the Peace, a minister of the Church of England, the chief constable and 'three respectable housekeepers residing within the district'. This certification process was designed to ensure that the applicant was 'a person of good fame and reputation, and fit and proper to keep a public house'.[14] In the official investigation of character, marital or ex-convict status was not at issue; rather, authorities wished to know that an applicant had not obtained the money for a house by 'immoral means'.[15]

Sarah Bird's letter to her father gives some indication as to how single women may have accumulated the capital to finance their business venture. The innovative young convict woman acquired small quantities of commodities such as tea, sugar, needles and snuff on her passage to New South Wales and sold these items for vastly inflated prices in her new home. And so, surmises J. M. Freeland, 'hard-headed Sarah worked herself into a position which restored to her many of the privileges of freedom'.[16] Through her access to property and legal status, Sarah had indeed made a sea change of miraculous proportions.

Many accounts of Australia's early convict period point to the 'tolerable good success' of women in obtaining the necessary certificates and recognisances to be issued a licence to retail alcohol from their homes, either as pardoned convicts, convicts' wives, widows or, from the late 1820s, free women.[17] After a recognisance was entered into, the licence was valid for one year at an annual fee of £30. Thereafter a licensee could only lose their privileges if 'he or she' breached the recognisance. Once a licence was approved, the victualler's house was legally constituted as a 'public house' or 'licensed premises', as the licence pertained to the place, not the person.[18] This situation reversed the British model, which licensed the person, not the house. As we shall see, this divergence later became important when the emphasis of licensing turned from character appraisal to property rights.

Throughout the early decades of the 1800s, the proportion of female licensees appears to have been approximately 5 to 25 per cent of all victuallers' licences. The prospect for these women to achieve some financial security and public esteem was significant in a time when women's economic and social options were otherwise tightly bound by law and convention.[19] Ex-convict women, who had 'scarcely owned the very clothes they wore when committed for trial in Britain', could right-fully obtain leases for land, build houses and conduct businesses—in their own names.[20] The effect was cumulative. The first generation of native-born white Australians—'colonial lasses'—were afforded oppor-tunities for social improvement far beyond what they ever could have imagined in England.[21] Women who applied for liquor licences were therefore advantaged over their British forebears in that, if they could raise their own finance by morally acceptable means, they were not dis-qualified from participation by virtue of their gender, marital status or class background. The 'fitness' of their character was demonstrable, not presumed.

That women were frequently recognised as being 'capable' by the colonial authorities, and had established a significant presence as hotelkeepers, is manifested in the very wording of the earliest licensing legislation. In a peculiar use of gender-neutral language, the legislation consistently refers to 'he or she' and 'his and her' when speaking of the licensed victualler: for example, 'in his or her house', 'any person applying to have his or her license renewed', 'his or her executors or administrators or trustees'. Even the *pro forma* licence application makes provision for 'he (or she)'.[22] This is noteworthy given that it was conven-tional to use generic male terminology in nineteenth-century legislation.

Apart from its explicit inclusion of women in the pool of potential licence holders, the early colonial legislation made another significant break from British tradition. Where in England the rationale for granting licences to women was based on notions of charity to widows, in Aus-tralia the emphasis was on enterprise and accomplishment—perhaps a reflection of the youthful character of the colony's inhabitants. The con-ditions that an applicant needed to fulfil in order to obtain certification were weighted towards public performance in a small community. If an applicant was not of 'good fame and character', it was expected that the licensing officials would know about it: 'It shall . . . be lawful for the said Justices to grant licenses to such persons only as, in their judgment upon the said certificates and upon other information before them, shall be entirely unexceptional and likely to keep orderly houses'.[23] The gender-inclusive terminology and the emphasis on judicial discretion indicate that the law was encoded to reflect the social practice of female hotel-keeping. The test of keeping an 'orderly house' on the recommendation of other 'respectable housekeepers' created a legal climate that encouraged the continuation of early colonial traditions.

Subsequent amendments through the early nineteenth century continued to stress the importance of peer esteem. A good reputation was the key element in achieving character certification. Although some female licensees, like their male counterparts, no doubt engaged in disreputable trading practices such as selling adulterated liquor and harbouring gamblers, convictions against the licensing act were a distinct mark against 'fitness'. It was thus a publican's public behaviour, rather than gender, which was most at issue in the early colonial period. However, given the customary associations between women, alcohol and disorder, it was probably more important that a female publican keep her nose clean.

A superior reputation could be earned, but a woman's standing could also be achieved by more conventional means. Marriage was not a prerequisite of licence holding, but it was an orthodox sign of respectability. The licensing law recognised the special moral status of married women. For example, the laws that prohibited convicts under sentence from being employed in a public house made an explicit exception in the case of 'the lawful wife of any licensed person, although under sentence as aforesaid'.[24] However, reputation and respectability were not the same thing. Legislation in Victoria never expressly barred unmarried women from the trade, as was the case in some other states. The annual registers of licensing courts, with their handwritten lists of every licence granted, transferred or renewed every year, dutifully record hundreds of women as 'Miss'. Evidently, marital status was but one of the discretionary criteria available to a licensing magistrate in considering the character of an applicant.

If the legislation was content to leave the matter of a publican's 'fitness' up to the discretion of community and court, it was far more prescriptive on the requirements of the public house itself. The domestic nature of the business of selling alcohol in the colonies was formally enshrined in early legislation in New South Wales. According to the 1838 *Licensed Victuallers Consolidation Act*, a publican was compelled to continuously occupy the licensed premises as 'his or her usual place of residence'. This responsibility to live 'on premises'—which remained in force in Victoria until 1968—was certainly a practical arrangement, given that opening hours could be from 4 am to 9 pm. No publican could legally refuse lodgings and victuals to a traveller. Thus a licensed premises was bound to provide—apart from the bar-room—two sitting rooms and two sleeping rooms 'actually ready and fit for public accommodation', in addition to a residence 'occupied by the family of the publican'. The legislative requirement to offer accommodation apart from the publican's residence separated 'public' and 'private' space in the hotel, thereby instituting another layer of moral integrity into commercial hospitality. Unlike private residences at the time, the licensed public house was also required by law to supply 'a place of accommodation, on or near the premises, for the use of the customers thereof, in order to prevent nuisances or offences against decency'.[25] Thus a coy but sanitary concession was made for the principle that what goes in must come out.

Civility was further catered for by the imperative to offer 'wholesome and usual provender' to customers: a hot meal to complement the warm bed. Even horses would appreciate the gesture made in the statutory compulsion to provide stabling for at least six of their species. Such domestic provisions constituted the Australian public house along the lines of an inn, privileging the notion of 'home comforts' above mere public drinking. Reading the statutory requirements as a whole, it was clearly the government's intent that the trade in liquor be conducted in as civilised a manner possible; peopled with upstanding folk and sheltered in creditable dwellings. It was their vision that, in establishing a commercial hospitality trade, women and their families would be significantly included in this domestic industry profile. This point is underscored by the fact that women were rarely granted other varieties of liquor licence, such as a wine licence or grocer's licence. Unlike the Publican's General Licence, these other permits came with no service and accommodation requirements.

When the first permanent European settlement was officially commenced in Victoria (formerly the Port Phillip District of New South Wales) in 1835, a tradition of female hotelkeeping had already been established, both in law and practice. When Victoria assumed responsible government and began enacting its own legislation in 1851, this custom was recognised in the form and substance of the new statutory arrangements for liquor licensing. The *Wine Beer and Spirits Sale Statute Consolidating Act* of 1864 primarily affirmed the New South Wales legislation, requiring accommodation of not less than six rooms, plus the licensee's family residence. The public nature of the licence application process was reinforced by the requirement that one copy of the application form be posted on the front door of the licensed premises and one copy be published in a newspaper. References to convicts were omitted, but otherwise the licensing system as it had been established—annual licensing, with the onus on the community to object to an applicant on the basis of unsuitable character and reputation—remained in force. Again, the early Licensing Acts in Victoria did not deem it necessary to comment on the eligibility of any applicant on the basis of their gender, age, marital status, or any other demographic feature. The spirit of the legislation, however, was clearly the pursuit of good houses with good keepers.

Character judgement: Applying the law

Definitions of 'goodness' and accusations of deviance, particularly sexual deviance, are one of the key ways in which women's lives have been circumscribed and their femininity assessed.[26] Historians have pointed to the role of the state in regulating sexual morality and setting boundaries for acceptable womanly behaviour. Some argue that the law has principally worked to maintain a gendered social order that scrutinised women's sexual conduct and curtailed their freedom to autonomously participate in the public world.[27] We might therefore expect that the most subjective assessment of women's fitness to be licensees would appear in the judicial interpretation of the 'good fame and character' clause—a matter over which the courts exercised 'enormous discretion'.[28]

Steeled to find overt gender bias in the discretionary assessment of the 'fame and character' of liquor-selling women, we are astonished to discover that, for the most part, the learned judges did not view female licensees as transgressing boundaries in their occupation of public space or their activity as liquor sellers. A detailed investigation of law reports of the nineteenth and early twentieth centuries reveals that female publicans were, on the contrary, primarily regarded as respectable businesswomen with an equal right to trade within the confines of the law. Rather than the gender order, it was the commercial order—which in the case of the liquor trade relied on a reputable, responsible, sober custom—which the courts sought to maintain through their interpretation of the licensing acts. To this end, and not surprisingly, a strict code of behaviour was rigorously applied: drunkards, bankrupts and 'lunatics' need not apply. The unconventional wisdom to be gleaned here is that the standards appear to have been no harsher on women than on men.

The official perspective on how a woman's reputation affected her ability to be granted the privilege of a liquor licence is demonstrated in a prominent case in Victoria. The 1886 trial of *Albrecht v. Patterson*, set before the Full Court of the Supreme Court, was in fact an action of slander, not an appeal against a decision of the Licensing Court. The undisputed facts of the case were that Miss Albrecht, licensee of the Harp of Erin Hotel, was accused by Mrs Patterson of having adulterous relations with her husband, of going away to have his child and of being a 'kept woman' in her hotel. Mrs Patterson threatened to use such allegations against Miss Albrecht should she apply to have her licence renewed. The Full Court was asked to decide, as a point of law, whether the words uttered 'touched her [Albrecht] in her trade or business as a licensed victualler and hotelkeeper'. Counsel for Miss Albrecht argued that, in keeping with the legislative requirements that a licensee be of good fame and character, 'It is certainly injurious to a woman who carries on the business of hotelkeeper, to say of her "she is a kept woman in that hotel". No person would allow a respectable woman to stay at an hotel, the proprietress of which was notoriously a "kept woman".'

The court rejected this reasoning in its finding that Mrs Patterson's accusations 'did not touch her in her trade, for they were not spoken of her with reference to her trade'. The court disagreed that Miss Albrecht's future ability to get a licence would be compromised by the present allegations, as 'chastity was not part of the plaintiff's duty as a publican'. Justice Holroyd expanded on this noteworthy statement:

> To have imputed to the plaintiff that she kept a disorderly house would have been very different from charging her with adulterous intercourse. Such an imputation would have reflected directly on her behaviour in conducting her business. Accusing the plaintiff of having been a kept woman in the hotel was treated by her counsel as almost if not quite equivalent to representing her house as the resort of prostitutes ... we do not believe that the words amounted to more than an impeachment of the plaintiff's morality.

Although not expressly called upon to do so, the court made a notable distinction in its interpretation of the 'fame and character' provision of the licensing legislation. A woman's moral character could be assessed in relation to the manner in which she ran her hotel, but her sexual conduct could not in itself be scrutinised.[29]

As far as their public status was concerned, the role of female licensees was thus confined to their professional, not personal, behaviour. An earlier New South Wales decision suggests that this principle had long been followed by the law lords. When publican Mary Knight applied to the Licensing Court at Singleton for the renewal of her licence to the Albion Hotel in 1866, the local police sergeant objected on the grounds that she had delivered an illegitimate child and was therefore an 'unfit person'. His gripe was ignored and Knight's licence was granted.[30] Thus, in a significant departure from the traditional taint of promiscuity that persistently haunted other women associated with the hotel industry—notably barmaids—female licensees remained immune from sexual stigma when it came to assessing their suitability to control and manage public houses.

Ultimately, judicial interpretations of the law in the late nineteenth and early twentieth centuries supported the right of women to engage in business, concentrating on their performance as publicans rather than any notional impropriety associated with their engagement in the liquor trade. This legal landscape provided unique opportunities for economic and social participation that many women eagerly grasped.

Property and Marriage:
An Unholy Alliance

IN 1876, THE VICTORIAN LICENSING LEGISLATION received an overhaul. The voluminous findings of the 1867 Royal Commission 'upon the operation and effect of the *Wine and Spirits Sale Statute 1864*' had delivered a resounding verdict on the state of the colony's liquor trade: an excess of 'dirty, incommodious and unfurnished drinking shops' had flourished in the previous decade, thus polluting the commercial atmosphere for the 'respectable hotels' which carried out the worthy and important business of 'the entertainment of guests' and 'the accommodation of travellers'. To this end, the commissioners recommended that 'The privilege of selling should be accompanied by such conditions as would preserve to licenced houses the character of places for the reception of guests'.[1] The focus of the new Licensing Act was therefore to place statutory restrictions on the number of new licences being issued, to police the quality of liquor being sold, and to minimise the competition to 'respectable hotels' by 'beer shops', 'licensed grocers' and 'low-class public-houses'. The effect of these legislative changes was to emphasise the 'privilege of selling' as it related to property holding, rather than the earlier attention to character assessment.

To understand the social circumstances that led to the outbreak of 'low houses', 'shebeens' and 'dancing parlours' that so offended the public sensibilities of the 1870s generation of law-makers, we need to look back to the changes wrought by the extraordinary period of demographic, social and moral flux that was the gold rushes. The high incidence of wife desertion and female destitution during this time of upheaval, as well as a reform impulse towards promoting 'domestic associations' as an antidote to masculine irresponsibility, ultimately favoured the participation of women in the hotel industry.

The discovery of gold in Victoria had an immediate, if inherently contradictory, effect on the liquor trade. Authorities reacted to the mass exodus of men to the goldfields by placing a total ban the sale of alcohol on the diggings. This prohibition, which lasted until 1854, was intended to keep the restless and often frustrated contingent of male miners at a distance from the demon drink. But of course, the ban on hotels on the diggings did not stem the flow of alcohol: illegal 'grog shops' flourished, along with crime, drunkenness and prostitution. The gold rushes thus augmented the profitability of liquor as a prized commodity while also increasing the illegality of its selling. Contemporary observers and temperance leagues expressed anxiety about the state of lawlessness and moral inversion on the goldfields where 'strong men fell and blooming maidens met a fate worse than death'.[2] Conversely, a more radical element of society valued the independence and freedom from socio-political constraints that frontier life could offer.[3] One product of the unfettered space of the goldfields was the predominance of unlicensed liquor shanties where 'All attentions were given to the diggers at these places, mostly run and staffed by women' (see Plate 9).[4]

Often operating out of a canvas tent or bark hut, 'sly-groggers' were able to make substantial winnings without ever picking up a pick or pan. Sly-grogging also had an advantage over licensed victualling for women in that little capital was required to start trading. In a cultural climate that condoned a certain degree of reckless disregard for authority, local notoriety—ever a good business asset for a publican—could also be secured. Mother Jamieson was renowned for lending her dishes to diggers to pan for gold. Mrs Bunting carried pistols on coach journeys to protect prospectors from bushrangers; by contemporary account, 'nothing could exceed her dignity and bulk'. Charlotte Edwards, a shantykeeper at Creswick, claimed to have found the first gold in the district. Whether this was true or not, the legend was no doubt good for publicity.[5]

The culture of the gold rushes thus threw up two conflicting images: the picture of bacchanalian disorder that reflected a fear of moral decline, and the image of the gallant, independent frontiersman and woman.[6] But apart from the cautionary or folkloric aspects of these tales, contemporary accounts of life on the diggings can also give us an inkling as to the motivation of the women who took to sly-grogging. Neither

9. *'Diggers at a sly grog shop warned of the approach of a commissioner.'*

debauched nor heroic, their needs were often distinctly prosaic. In 1853, the goldfields chronicler William Howitt related an incident involving the Inspector of Police on the Bendigo diggings and a female sly-grogger:

> A poor Irishwoman was left a widow with several children, the youngest of which was only a few days old. [Inspector] Hermsprong discovered that this poor woman sold grog. When he charged her with the sale of grog, she did not deny it, but said that her husband being killed by an accident, her countrymen had advised her, as her only means of support for herself, and little children, to sell grog, promising to give her their custom; and the poor woman said piteously, 'What, your honour, was I to do?'

The Inspector was evidently not as moved by the woman's plight as her fellow countrymen were. The sly-grogger lost everything when the notoriously corrupt and vicious policeman torched her tent, with all her belongings and some of her children still in it.[7]

Early widowhood was a feature of life in colonial Australia; the particularly high incidence of wife desertion during the gold rushes has also been well documented.[8] Opportunities for employment were scarce for women left to support themselves and their families. Self-employment, especially if it could be carried out from a home base and in conjunction with child-care, was thus a lifeline for many destitute women. As Howitt's account suggests, the traditional charitable support for liquor-selling widows continued to be an attribute of colonial life, particularly among the Irish.

Sly-grogging could be a short-term response to the cessation of income from a male breadwinner, but it could also lead to an ongoing interest in the hotel industry. Some women made themselves enough profit to build hotels on the roads to the diggings, for which they could then receive a licence and become legitimate, respectable traders. Matilda Field, for example, opened the first hotel in Walhalla, the Reefers Arms, in 1863. This process has been linked with the increasing settlement of the goldfields, after the initial rush had tapered off. With the granting of liquor licences on the diggings after 1854, hotels were built in town streets where miners settled with their wives and children, thus making 'a more normal type of living possible'.[9]

This tempering of the excesses of exclusive male companionship through licensed public houses—again, often run or staffed by women —was no accident. Colonial reformers made a conscious effort to promote female immigration to Victoria, believing in 'the doctrine of the beneficial social effects of women, of the power of domestic life to soften and ameliorate the harshnesses of gold-rush society'.[10] If policy makers sought to harness men's energies to private home life, the logic also held for public houses. As hotelkeepers, women were to be the agents of control. They could govern the behaviour of men from within the preferred masculine environment of the public house, just as they did within the 'ideal' haven of the family home. Indeed, many female publicans did endeavour to exert a 'woman's touch' over their hotel interiors, providing such accoutrements as fresh flowers, soft furnishings, pianos and framed photographs (see Plate 10). Many single men and uprooted diggers responded positively, preferring the warmth and homeliness of hotels to their flimsy tents flapping in the wind. Hotels fostered a domesticated backdrop to masculine enterprise and endeavour, providing home-cooked hot meals and warm, dry beds at the end of a hard day's digging.

10. *'A Relic of the Gold Days—The old Bar of the Glasgow Arms Hotel now delicensed, at Talbot, Vic.'*, Age, 12 September 1933.

At the same time, hotels became the focus of a vast range of community activities in the rapidly expanding diggings townships. Apart from accommodation, goldfields hotels provided a place for business dealings, judicial duties, mining exchanges, land sales, and public services such as newspaper and library holdings. Of course, not all social intercourse was so high-minded. Hotels with accompanying dancehalls, bagatelle rooms and theatres also flourished during the gold rush years, winning the entire liquor industry a reputation for debauchery and exploitation due to the propensity of young men and women to mix at these venues. As a response to the high incidence of sly-grogging during the gold rush era, legislation that made licences easier to obtain was introduced in Victoria in 1864. The *Wine, Beer and Spirits Statute* simultaneously reduced licence fees, extended trading hours, allowed hotels on the goldfields, and lowered building requirements regarding accommodation provisions and building materials. The result was that many illegal shanties and dram shops effectively became licensed shanties and dram shops.

But it was the exponential population growth during the gold rush years that was the most compelling source of the industry's swelling fortunes in the mid-nineteenth century. In 1851, just before the first rush, Victoria had 77 000 inhabitants. By the 1854 Census, this figure had reached 237 000, and by 1857, Victoria had a population of 410 000. In 1861, the total had grown to 540 000, or half of the entire population of Australia. Of this number, about one-quarter resided in metropolitan Melbourne and most of the remainder on the goldfields.[11] Due to the vast demand for hospitality services required by this flood of immigrants, and the emphasis on 'domestic associations' to make a simmering, excitable population 'governable', women who may have begun their lives as illicit liquor sellers were readily absorbed into the expanding hotel industry. Anxiety over the liquor trade was not displaced onto female traders alone—a discriminatory process which, as we have seen, characterised the British response to liberal licensing laws in the sixteenth century. Rather, the focus of reform agendas turned to the burgeoning number of public houses and their ever-diminishing quality.

Cleaning up after the rush

By the time of the 1876 legislation the tide of opinion had well and truly turned against mass licensing. Authorities were determined to halt the surging stream of liquor trading but, despite the testimony of many witnesses to the 1867 Royal Commission (including other publicans) that single women should be debarred from holding licences, neither the commissioners nor the subsequent Licensing Act suggested a connection between 'low houses' and women, single or otherwise. Instead, the major plank of the new legislation was that no new publican's licences were to be granted for three years, except for hotels with more than thirty rooms. After that time, it would be ratepayers who would determine how many (if any) new licences were to be issued. Thus the system of 'local option' was instituted.

Henceforth, the only way to receive a licence was through the provision for licence transfer or renewal. Importantly, the 'objection model' replaced the public certification process, and local councils could authorise any person to object on behalf of ratepayers. Licensing Inspectors were empowered to investigate breaches of the Act, and could pose their own objections to licence transfers or renewals.[12] The emphasis on ratepayers, as opposed to the 'housekeepers' of the earlier system, was an indication of the growing civic culture of the colonies.

That women did not participate as taxpaying or voting citizens at this time—and thus were excluded from a certification process that formerly embraced them—was similarly reflected in the language of the licensing legislation. Publicans were no longer referred to as 'he or she', but exclusively in masculine pronouns (although the language on the licence form itself remained gender-neutral). The 1876 legislation did not explicitly disqualify a woman from holding a licence, but ominously, a clause was inserted that would be the subject of much controversy and judicial interpretation in later years. Section 50 of the Licensing Act stated: 'In the case of the marriage of any female being a licensed person, the license held by her shall confer upon her husband the same privileges and shall impose on him the same duties obligations and liabilities as if such license had been granted to him originally'.[13] A woman was only afforded the same treatment if her licensee husband was committed to a lunatic asylum. For the first time, a female licensee's legal position appeared to be different from that of her male counterparts.

Traditionally, married women were implicitly favoured by the licensing legislation because marriage fitted the profile of colonial respectability. Although it is difficult to quantify the proportion of married to single female licensees from the licensing registers, due to the fact that a marital signifier (Mrs/Miss) is not always recorded, it is apparent that in the metropolitan area married women outnumbered single women by a ratio of 3.5:1 and in rural regions by 6.5:1.[14] 'Married women' here includes widows. In the later decades of the nineteenth century, the legal consequences of the act of marriage itself—and particularly its effects on property ownership—became a central concern of Western jurisprudence more generally. This was partly in response to first-wave feminist agitation around legal issues relating to the dependence of wives, who had 'no entitlement as of right' to personal or family property, including custody of their children.[15]

In English common law, a husband and wife were one person. A married woman was a *feme covert*, a woman covered or hidden by her husband in law—a status which, all too commonly, was reflected in social practice also. On marriage, a woman's money, goods, income and lands became the property of her husband. She could not incur debts, nor could she sue or be sued in court, except with her husband's permission and in both their names. For these reasons, a married woman could not enter into a contract in her own name, for the ability to be held accountable in a court of law was central to contractual freedom. A married woman's ability to engage in business dealings was therefore, in theory, severely curtailed. On the other hand, a single woman—a *feme sole*—had the same rights as a man; it was 'marriage that disabled a woman'.[16] Underpinning this mode of social organisation was the assumption that a married woman did not require any independent legal status, for being at one with her husband, his status held and protected—indeed, covered —her. Financial and legal independence were unnecessary for a married woman's safe passage through life.

If this theory was only remotely connected to women's life experiences in England, it was even more abstracted from colonial Australian realities. A highly transient workforce, vast distances and frontier opportunities colluded to ensure that 'till death do us part' was but one means of the likely separation of married couples. And death might well do the parting. With high mortality rates in the nineteenth century, many women could expect to lose their husbands while they still had children growing up. Desertion, wife beating and lunacy were notable features of colonial family life, with women left to fend for themselves and their children in the absence of their husbands. In response to local circumstances, Australian officials often turned a blind eye to legal niceties, allowing colonial wives to issue and receive promissory notes, sue debtors and trade in their own names. By local custom, wives could hold property, including land, as part of their own separate estate. This situation ensured that married women in the early colonial period had a much greater degree of practical and legal freedom than in England.[17]

The civil courts' propensity to allow married women to trade in their own names, coupled with the licensing legislation as it was expressly written, affords a compelling explanation as to why a hardy tradition of female hotelkeeping grew up in the Australian colonies. When the laws were tightened up in the latter part of the century, and judicial discretion yielded to a mood of 'imperial orthodoxy', there was already a deeply embedded cultural context and legal precedent for women to run their own independent businesses as publicans. Part of the respectability and acceptance of their trade has always called upon this long, stable tradition.

Australia's legal distinctiveness, and the resulting tradition of married women running their own independent businesses with the implicit sanction of law, was particularly significant in times of great social upheaval. In the gold rush era, and again during the 1890s depression, married women's unique vulnerability was brought to the fore. The combination of legal subordination and social confinement meant that the cessation of income from a male breadwinner, whether through death, desertion, disability or unemployment, left whole families in destitution and wives 'trapped in appalling situations'.[18] Prostitution was a time-honoured survival strategy; on the other end of the moral spectrum, taking in lodgers provided income for women who were fortunate enough to own their own homes. Hotelkeeping was one of the few legitimate, public avenues that luckless women could pursue to provide the shelter and support that were otherwise in scant supply.

Knowledge of the desperate circumstances of many women who became publicans did not escape the powers-that-be. In debating the 1885 licensing amendments, David Gaunson, Member for Emerald Hill (an electorate which included South Melbourne, a suburb with a high density of hotels), noted that 'It is well known that a number of public-house licences are held by wives who have obtained protection orders against their husbands or who are living apart from them without any protection at all'.[19] Mrs James Cleary fitted this profile. With five children and a protection order against her drunkard, publican husband, Mrs Cleary built and ran the Courthouse Hotel in rural Kyneton. In a press report of the death of James by suicide, Mrs Cleary was credited as a 'much-respected and very industrious woman'.[20] David Gaunson was particularly well-placed to understand the plight of such embattled women. As Ned Kelly's defence attorney in 1880, he would have been familiar with the widowed Mrs Kelly's recourse to sly-grogging to support her large and impoverished family. Gaunson later became a legal adviser to the Licensed Victuallers' Association.

Female publicans were not only legally enabled to own the valuable property of a liquor licence, but also, by the 1880s and 1890s, they had the important advantage of being able to obtain financial backing from the brewing companies that had effectively 'tied' the majority of hotels in Melbourne, Ballarat, Bendigo and Castlemaine.[21] It is important to recognise that, unlike Mrs Cleary, the majority of publicans (male and female) did not own the freehold of their licensed premises, particularly in the city and large regional centres. Rather, they paid an 'ingoing' sum for the lease, licence, furniture, stock and goodwill of the hotel. Where banks were not prepared to take the risk of lending capital to women whose legal status was annulled by marriage, brewers were ready and willing to see married women take the leases of their hotels in exchange for exclusivity contracts which bound the licensee to sell that brewery's product. This reciprocal arrangement is likely to have been well-established in Australia, given that the tied-house system was operating widely by the 1820s and brewers often stood as sureties for licensees as early as the

1790s.[22] While a protection order returned married women to the legal status of a *feme sole*, it was ultimately the lack of employment opportunities and access to business capital that made separated women so economically vulnerable.

Were female publicans dummies?

Although the Married Women's Property Acts, which were initially introduced in Victoria in 1870, went some way to affording women a 'theoretical equality' in the eyes of the law, most commentators agree that the potentially revolutionary laws did little to change the economic, legal and social subordination of women because the right to own property did not equate with the ability or opportunity to accumulate wealth.[23] The majority of women continued to work for very low wages in a sex-segregated market or to labour in their own unpaid, dependent domestic territory. It was thus the *ability* to acquire separate property—rather than the right—that was married women's ticket to economic and social entitlement.

It has also been pointed out that many couples exploited the Married Women's Property Acts to avoid creditors by transferring property from a liable spouse to the other, legally unaccountable spouse. While there may have been instances in which wives were the 'active agents ... manipulating new statutory rights to their own advantage', most cases involving the fraudulent transfer of property between spouses benefited the husband, who used it as a tactic in managing his independent property.[24]

Could such methods account for the increased number of female licensees in late-nineteenth-century Victoria, as wives created separate estates in times of financial difficulties by transferring their husbands' property—the licence—to their own name so that creditors could have no redress? Was the female licensee wife just a legal front—a 'dummy' in licensing parlance—for a publican husband who really managed the affairs of the business, received the takings and called the shots from behind the bar? Were most female licensees merely the nominal heads of public households?

While isolated instances may have slipped through the net of licensing inspection, there are several key legal stipulations that would militate against such fraudulent practices being the norm in the Victorian hotel trade. Most obviously, dummying was illegal. It is ingenuous to suggest that because there was a law against it, it did not happen; but the sham transfer of licences is not sufficient to explain the predominance of women as licensees at an industry-wide level in the late nineteenth and early twentieth centuries. Moreover, my detailed investigation of licence-holding patterns in Victoria does not commonly reveal the transfer of licences from husband to wife, except on his death. The lists of successive licence holders for hotels in urban, suburban and country Victoria show that the majority of licences obtained by women were transferred either by other women or by extended family members, or on widowhood. There are no recorded legal cases in Victoria involving the fraud or insolvency of a male publican attempting to avoid his responsibilities by transferring the licence to his wife.

A common reason for attempting a licence transfer from husband to wife was if a male licensee was in danger of losing the licence for multiple infringements of the Licensing Act. This too was prohibited by law: if, after any licensee had been twice convicted of offences, such licensee procured the transfer of the licence 'to his or her wife or husband (as the case may be)', the offences were imputable to the transferee.[25] Licensing Inspectors, who were able to post objections to transfers and frequently did, were well aware of the organisation of the hotels they policed and were suspicious of applicants who might be attempting to evade the law. Again, corruption in the inspection system might account for some exceptions to the rule, but not enough to explain the overwhelming numbers of female licensees. It was more likely, in fact, that many male licensees were only nominally in charge of their licensed premises, the day-to-day management of clientele, staff and business affairs being the domain of a 'helpmeet' wife. A married woman, on the other hand, had to hold an independently constructed estate to which the profits of the business flowed in order to prove that she was in operative control of her licensed enterprise. The sovereignty and integrity of women who held liquor licences is borne out by both law and practice.

The concept of 'beneficial interest', integral to the workings of licensing legislation, was important in protecting the autonomy of the licensee and in preventing spurious licence-holding. A central tenet of the licensing system in Australia is the idea that 'a publican's license is a personal right attached to a particular place'.[26] A licence conferring the 'privilege of selling' was definitely an estimable asset. A liquor licence had a material value (it could be bought and sold) as well as a moral value (it made an act lawful which without it would be unlawful).[27] Common to the various Licensing Acts was a provision making it an offence for a licensee to carry on his or her business for the benefit of any person other than the person whose name was recorded on the licence.

The fact that the right of a licence was an individual entitlement was embodied in a physical sense. By law, the licensee's name had to appear in large lettering above the door of the licensed premises, and the publican was required to produce her licence in the presence of a Licensing Inspector if requested. Put simply, 'The general control of the house must be in the hands of the keeper'.[28] Thus the legal and pragmatic concept of 'beneficial interest' made it an offence for anyone other than the licensee to carry on the business for their own benefit, even with the knowledge and consent of the licensee.

There are no recorded court cases involving dummying in Victoria, but a Queensland example involving husband and wife illustrates the sort of situation the law aimed to prevent. In the case of *Kinnane and Chiconi v. Gay*, a licence transfer was refused on the grounds that the transferee was 'unfit to hold a license'. The facts were that Mr Kinnane applied to transfer his licence for the Royal Hotel to Mrs Esther Chiconi. Mrs Chiconi's husband, Thomas Chiconi, was the freehold owner and licensee of the Tattersell's Hotel, located 500 yards from the Royal. While the legal test was one of fitness, the case did not turn on the character of the unsuccessful transferee, Mrs Chiconi. In fact, the court made a special point of noting that its judgement was not based on Mrs Chiconi's 'fitness or otherwise' regarding her capacity 'to conduct properly the license of the Royal Hotel, owing to the rough class of persons who frequented those premises'. Furthermore, Justice Lukin made it clear that neither was Mrs Chiconi denied the licence on account of her being a married woman, given that 'It is well known that . . . it had been the practice to grant licences to married women of well-known respectability living apart from their husbands, and under such circumstances as gave them absolute control of the house in respect of which the license was granted'. Rather, the court concluded that, on evidence, Mrs Chiconi was 'a mere nominee and dummy' because she was still living with her husband and had no separate estate or bank account of her own. Without these indicators of independence in place, it could not be concluded that the licence was 'for her own sole benefit': 'She would not have absolute control of the premises, but would be subject to the interference of her husband [as] the passive agent of her husband in so far as the method of control and the management of the business of the licensed premises were concerned'. This being the case, Mr Chiconi would effectively hold the interest in two licensed premises, which was unlawful.

The strict maintenance of the beneficial interest clause achieved two related ends. First, because of the concurrent stipulation that a person could not have a beneficial interest in more than one licence, the legislation ensured that the trade could not be monopolised or cartelised by absentee landlords, in the way that Mr Chiconi was attempting. True to the ambitions of the original colonial licensing system of community accountability and recognisance, the business of hotelkeeping was regulated to stay local, personal and discrete—and thus presumably easier to control. This situation put the hotel industry at odds with the mid-nineteenth-century trend in other retail and trading activities where 'individual entrepreneurs (male and female) were being overshadowed by partnerships and corporate formations'.[29] Clearly, the licensing legislation's anachronistic tendency to favour individuals over more 'modern' business models indirectly encouraged the participation of women, who had less access to corporate management structures. The hospitality industry's reliance on 'old-fashioned' business principles was still being noted in the mid-twentieth century.[30] A second effect of the clause was that, by making the licensee the direct beneficiary of the business as well as directly responsible for licensing infringements, it created a pecuniary motive for the publican to maintain a reputable establishment whose internal lines of control and authority were clearly vested.

That women could and did lay claim to that authority—the personal right of a publican's licence—thus put them at odds with the common law position on women's property for most of the nineteenth century. If a female licensee married, by right of coverture, her husband became an overnight beneficiary of her business—a situation that contravened the licensing law. The presence of married women was so much part of the status quo of the industry that when the dependent position of married women in other aspects of society became the focus for political, legislative and judicial debate in the late nineteenth century, the Licensing Act was amended to clarify its position on coverture. Rather than making marriage an impediment to receiving a licence—a disqualification that could have been easily and clearly inserted—the legislators chose to inscribe the murky, equivocal Section 50.

Whether a single female publican in Victoria chose to transfer the licence to her husband upon marriage depended on the circumstances of the business. It is clear that many married women continued to be the genuine keepers of their public houses, managing the day-to-day operations of the enterprise, while their husbands worked in separate occupations. Although, in accordance with licensing regulations, the family might live at the hotel, the male partner was not required to be involved in the daily management of the premises or control of the business. He might help out by serving in the bar—and very likely by 'entertaining' guests on the other side of the bar—but the responsibility for the running of the enterprise was squarely placed on his wife's shoulders.

This arrangement was acknowledged both publicly and privately. When Mrs Ann Rosina Follett applied for a licence for the Pioneer Palace Hotel in the seaside resort of Torquay in 1890, the licensing court reporter commented that 'the house was a splendid one, nearly all the rooms being very large, well ventilated and altogether of a superior kind ... The application was granted'.[31] It was casually noted that Mrs Follett's husband, James, ran his own coaching business but the court privileged the outstanding features of the licensed premises over Mrs Follett's marital arrangements. Mrs Esther Blake built the Grand Hotel at coastal Airey's Inlet in 1889 and ran the establishment with her son's assistance until 1900, when the premises were gutted by fire. Mrs Blake's husband was an overseer on an outlying station and had no active role in the business, though he evidently played an active part in the marriage, returning to Airey's Inlet on horseback every weekend. Esther Blake was remembered in the district for 'her capacity to draw corks with her teeth', a skill that won her the title of 'the woman of the iron jaw'. Presumably, Mrs Blake's genuine control over her enterprise was not in question.[32]

Regardless of whether the couple lived together in the hotel, it was this question of how the business was constituted—who was in financial and physical control—that was critical to licence holding. In situations where a couple ran the hotel together in a joint venture, the husband invariably held the licence. In this case, their property was deemed to belong to the husband, as the law—even after the passage of the Married Women's Property Acts—took 'no account of the family as an economic unit' and thus made no provisions for joint ownership of assets.[33] But in cases where the business was the wife's independent endeavour—she held the purse strings, signed the papers and was liable for debts and contracts—her legal sovereignty was not compromised by marriage.[34]

Court cases give us a fair indication of how the provisions against dummying worked themselves out in social practice. Again, judicial interpretation of the law—at least at the higher echelons of the justice system—favoured the rights of female publicans as commercial traders over a narrow construction of their prescribed roles as women. For example, in the 1897 case of In Re Martin, the Full Court of the Supreme Court of Victoria determined that a husband did not acquire a beneficial interest in a liquor licence merely because that licence was held by his wife. An 'interest', the court held, meant something which a person might enforce in his own right at law: 'The fact that the wife allows the husband to sleep, etc., in the house, does not give the husband any interest'. 'Interest', the judge declared, 'does not mean a bounty'.[35]

Female publicans had access to valuable property rights that were denied to other nineteenth-century women, particularly married women. Even when all women received 'theoretical equality' through the Married Women's Property Acts, their legal entitlements were worth little in the face of wider structural and ideological impediments to accessing and accumulating wealth. Female publicans, on the other hand, enjoyed a customary acceptance of their socially valued and legally constructed role within the hotel industry. This legitimacy was supported by a raft of judicial interpretations of the Licensing Acts which, through the endowment of legal rights and responsibilities, ultimately rejected many of the presumptions and proscriptions that fashioned womanhood as a state of incapacity. When we decipher the legal apparatus and judicial decisions on which women's ability to hold a liquor licence hinged, we appreciate just how seriously female licensees were regarded. They were neither trivialised, demonised nor silenced. The cases that were brought against them as traders, and that they brought against others as appellants, set precedents which male publicans were bound to follow. Moreover, authorities had ample opportunities to crack down on sham licence holding by wives should they have seen fit. In the eyes of the law, female licensees were anything but dummies.

Person or Woman?

IF THERE WERE MANY REASONS WHY a woman might be pushed into hotelkeeping in the late nineteenth century, it is also clear that the liquor industry exerted a considerable pull on female energies and aspirations. Indeed, the exponential growth in the proportion of female licensees in the last decades of the nineteenth century, and extending well into the twentieth, cannot be comprehensively explained by the financial perils of wife desertion, economic depression and social dislocation. If this were the case, we would expect to find that in periods of economic prosperity and stability, the rate of female hotelkeeping would drop back to baseline levels (perhaps 10 per cent to 15 per cent, the proportion of women— mostly widows—running English alehouses between 1600 and 1900).[1] Instead, the proportion of female licensees in Victoria rose from approximately 30 per cent in the 1880s (a period of great economic expansion) to over 50 per cent by the turn of the century, then did not drop below 40 per cent for the next fifty years. Undoubtedly, the fact that legislation did not expressly disqualify any women by virtue of their marital status in itself widened the pool of women potentially drawn to hotelkeeping. Structurally, the licensing law in Victoria empowered women to act independently of men. And women, judging by the numbers, capitalised on this opportunity to forge their own professional identities within the hotel trade.

Public housekeeping provided more than just a temporary meal ticket in times of crisis. If women merely turned to hotelkeeping as a survival strategy then, presumably, their tenure in the industry would have been short-lived, or perhaps cyclical, depending upon how long it took to regain their economic equilibrium. Certainly, many women only hung their name over a hotel door until the next annual licensing meeting, when they transferred their privileges to another eager contender. Yet it is also clear that many women used hotelkeeping as a vocational outlet, pursuing their business and related activities for many decades, and certainly well beyond 'retirement' age.

Apart from women who had a family connection to hotelkeeping—a distinct feature of the trade—there were notable others who appeared to pursue their business independently of kith or kin. Miss Catherine Reynolds, for example, held the licence to the Commonwealth Hotel in Elizabeth Street, Melbourne, for twenty-seven years. Miss Margaret Mulhall was the licensee at the Templemore Hotel, La Trobe Street, for twenty-four years. Miss Teresa O'Malley kept the Sydney Hotel for twenty-four years, while Miss Annie Hurley ran the Tower Hotel, Hawthorn, for twenty-one years. Other women ran a string of hotels over equally long time spans: among hotels in the central business district of Melbourne, Mrs Ellen Rahilly held the licences for three over thirty-four years, Mrs Annie Horton Crundall for six over thirty-one years, Miss Sarah Oliver for eight over thirty years, and Miss Daisy Cunningham for five over fifty years.[2]

There is evidence that women who started their careers as leasehold publicans in working-class Collingwood ended their days in private residential freeholds on the other side of the river in leafy Kew. Of course, affluence and social mobility were not every woman's experience of hotelkeeping; the vast disparities in hotel size, location and clientele, as well as an individual woman's suitability to the job, prevent generalisations about the 'success' of women's enterprises. Valuation records give some indication of annual income. In the country town of Ararat, Jane Gilchrist earned an average net profit of £522 per year for the period 1903–05 from her Scott's Hotel, while Mary Jane Battye earned an average of £327 from her Shire Hall Hotel over the same period. (Fellow publican Antonio Leopold averaged £353 from his Commercial Hotel and Alexander McDonald earned £124 at the Terminus Hotel.) In central Melbourne, Margaret Commins of the Coopers Arms Hotel, Little Bourke Street, claimed a net profit of £157 in 1905. Her gross takings of £975 were derived from three boarders, two lodgers, casual meals, casual beds (seven per week) and sales of beer, wine and spirits; her costs included three employees, rent of £144 per annum, food, liquor, cigars and cordials.[3] When Norah Flannery died in March 1913, she left an estate of £2900 realty and £2809 personalty to her children.[4] Mrs Elizabeth Ralph, who died at her Junction Hotel in the outer metropolitan suburb of Preston in October 1930, left an estate of £20 154 realty and £17 485 personal property to her children.[5] Such assets amount to more than just survival in the absence of a male breadwinner.

There is no doubt that, while some women turned to hotelkeeping to keep their heads above water, others were attracted to the hotel industry because it offered them material and career prospects that were sorely lacking in other fields of female endeavour, particularly for women with little education for whom teaching and nursing were not an option.

The last major piece of Victoria's licensing legislation of the nineteenth century, the *Licensing Act* 1885, provides another clue to the positive motivations of women entering the liquor trade. This statute, passed after the enactment of the Married Women's Property Acts, stipulates in its terminology section that a 'person' shall include a *feme covert*. According to J. F. Rahilly's 1890 guide to the legislation, Section 151 of the new Act was passed for the express purpose of 'legalising the position of married women who held licences under the repealed statute'. Rahilly's text particularly mentions that Section 3 'includes women in the term "person"' and that, in all other respects, 'the masculine gender shall include females'.[6] This article finally enshrined, beyond reasonable doubt, the social reality and legal recognition that married women could hold (and always had held) liquor licences. Furthermore, Section 81 provided that, when a female victualler married, she could opt to transfer her licence to her husband. The new situation created by the Married Women's Property Act meant that such a transfer was now a matter of a woman's choice for her separate estate on marriage, rather than a legal *fait accompli*. Under the former Licensing Act 'the simple fact of her marrying' entailed rights and responsibilities on her husband. Now, the licensing court had to determine whether the husband, should he apply for his wife's licence, was a fit person under the Act. In an odd twist, by making women's position with regard to the law more just, men were subject to increased restrictions on their freedom. A husband now had to pass the same fitness test as his wife, or any other male applicant for a victualler's licence.

By incorporating all women in the designation of personhood, the act also conferred a form of social citizenship on female licensees at a time when their sex was otherwise politically disenfranchised. In the eyes of the body politic, women were not fit to vote, but in the interests of free trade, they were entitled to sell liquor as fully fledged commercial entrepreneurs. As an expression of class interest, legislators privileged the creation of a social order compatible with capitalist expansion over a rigidly patriarchal gender order. By enshrining female licensees' person-hood in the 1885 Act, the legislators were, in fact if not by intent, revers-ing the trend towards gender differentiation as a basis for limiting the range of public and vocational activities open to women. Some historians claim that small businesses run by women declined as 'the boundaries imposed by marriage and family ties became sharper and clearer' in the last decades of the nineteenth century.[7] Hotelkeeping by contrast became an increasingly female-dominated occupation.

Keeping house in the age of the 'new woman'

By the turn of the twentieth century, the focus of legislative concern in Victoria had shifted from married women's eligibility to hold liquor licences to the status of unmarried women. In 1906, the Licensing Act was once again subjected to a major overhaul. Standards of respectability shift to reflect the times; what is commendable to one generation is anathema to the next. By the early twentieth century, the emphasis of concern about 'women's place' had shifted from the threat posed by married women who worked outside their homes to the alarming fact that an increasing number of women were eschewing marriage altogether.[8]

In response to the generational preference for independence, public anxiety had focused on youth. More particularly, a strong element of fear surrounded the moral well-being of young women who were not pro-tected by the restrictive eye of home and family. The Woman's Christian Temperance Union was especially concerned to safeguard young, single people from the 'predatory' nature of the hotel: for men, by rescuing them from the deleterious effects of alcohol consumption, and for women, by prohibiting hotel bars as a place of female employment.[9] The guiding assumption here was that singleness was inseparable from youth and desirability, as it was the institution of marriage which sanctioned women's sexuality.[10]

The *Licensing Act* 1906 in Victoria responded to this mood of moral panic over the corruption of youth. For the first time in Victoria's history, the licensing legislation inserted an age restriction into women's eligi-bility for licence holding. Section 53 of the Act prohibited the granting of licences to women under the age of twenty-five 'unless the business has devolved upon her as owner or trustee'.[11] The two-faced nature of licensing law is here perfectly illustrated. On the one hand, legislators acknowledged that it was a common trade practice to 'devolve' licences within extended families—and thus allowed for daughters, sisters or other female relatives of publicans to carry on family businesses. On the other hand, they wanted to be seen to be responding to the concerns of the temperance-affected day. Therefore, only *certain* young women would be allowed to come into contact with the evils of the traffic in liquor: those whose family connections presumably shielded them from moral danger. But the Victorian legislation did not equate youth with single-ness: it never explicitly prohibited, or even made it a 'general policy', to exclude single women from licence holding. The Daisy Cunninghams of the trade—spinsters with life-long careers as publicans—were preserved in their vocational choices.

This focus on age, rather than marital status, is consistent with the other key restriction on women's involvement in Victoria's hotel trade in this era: the now infamous banning of barmaids. This process occurred in two legislative stages: by the 1906 Act, no female under twenty-one years of age, except the wife or daughter of the publican, was permitted to sell, supply or serve liquor in the bar. (It was proposed that the cut-off age be forty, but Premier Bent rejected this on the grounds that 'there was no woman he knew of who was forty years of age'—an interesting reflection on the demographic changes of the era.)[12] In 1916, the age threshold was replaced with a total ban on barmaids, though the veto was not retrospective. However, the 1916 legislation permitted an explicit and broad exception for the wife, sister or daughter of a licensee, the female partner of a licensee or the licensee herself, being a woman.[13] While not denying the presence of sex discrimination in the 1906 and 1916 Acts, it is important to recognise how many practical exceptions were afforded, as well as the way in which some women's authority and opportunities within the trade were being further enhanced.

While young women were being singled out for exclusion—harking back to conventional associations between alcohol, sex and disorder—older, married women and female family members were being explicitly recognised as a legitimate feature of the trade. The tendency of the twentieth-century legislation, therefore, was to distinguish between classes of women, regardless of their character, reputation or proprietorial rights. Previously, a woman was defined as a 'person' and it was left to the discretion of licensing courts to determine the integrity of her person-hood. Neither the new licensing legislation itself, nor the legal practi-tioners who commented upon the law in their texts, give any rationale why young women should now be judged 'unfit' to hold a licence. Parlia-mentary debate at this time, however, reveals a concern that young women might not 'behave themselves' in the public bar or would be exposed to men's unscrupulous behaviour.[14] The age-old insinuation that liquor-selling women might themselves be sexually predatory or sexually vulnerable had crept into the legislation by stealth if not design.

Implicit in the legislation, therefore, was the notion that older women, married women and women with family connections were 'safe' from the hotel's corrupting environment, while young women were in need of the state's protection. Thus the regulation of the Victorian hotel industry became sexualised in a way that did not affect the overall participation rates of women as licensees, but rather, changed the culture of hotelkeeping by intimating that the environment was suitable only for certain 'types' of women.

This new generation of 'reform' legislation can also be seen as a response to the particularly restrictive moral climate during wartime. It was this general mood of deprivation and concern for national honour that ushered in early-closing legislation. Originally intended as a wartime provision when it was introduced in 1916, the *Intoxicating Liquor Temporary Restriction Act* was given permanency in 1919. The 'six o'clock swill'—the relentless crush of heavy drinking in public bars between 5 pm knock-off and 6 pm closing—was to be a Victorian institution for the next fifty years.[15] The laws regulating the traffic in liquor would continue to be amended in small ways over the next half-century but, prior to the radical overhaul of the licensing system in 1968, the hotel industry was in stasis.

Yet the concepts that had shaped licensing legislation, and inevitably hotel culture, were never far from the surface: agency, interest, control, character, fame and fitness. There is no doubt that, despite the sexually discriminatory nature of the early-twentieth-century disqualifications against licence holding, women continued to be central to the idea of what a properly regulated, respectable hotel trade should look like. Ultimately, women—and particularly married women—were enabled to rise to the top of a trade that privileged broad nineteenth-century notions of domestic control and order over more puritanical, restrictive constructions of female sexuality.

Legal status: A comparative view

The legal and social implications of the Australian response to liquor licensing are particularly compelling when compared to the experience of other female liquor sellers internationally. The United States affords the most striking contrast. In his study of workers and leisure in the industrial city of Worcester, Massachusetts, Roy Rosenzweig has documented the process by which the saloon became a public commercial enterprise 'predicated on the growing spatial separation of male sociability from the home'.[16] In Worcester in the 1830s, Irish immigrant widows perpetuated their native tradition of 'unlicensed and home- or kitchen-based liquor sellers'.[17] In 1875, fifty years after Australia began legislating to control the retail sale of alcohol, Massachusetts passed its first comprehensive liquor laws allowing the legal operation of public drinking places. As licences were prohibitively expensive, most 'Irish kitchen saloonkeepers' were effectively forced to continue as illegal operators, which, in time, led officials to view female sellers as 'disreputable and criminal' where previously they had been seen to be performing a harmless if illicit community service. Where in 1875, women comprised 22 per cent of Worcester's saloonkeepers, by 1880 there were only two women graced with a licence.

Rosenzweig's detailed and compelling account of the shift in Worcester women's fortunes as saloonkeepers is supported by wider statistical analysis of the American liquor trade. In 1915, the *American Prohibition Year Book* published an extraordinarily thorough survey of the 'total number of persons engaged in the liquor business' in 1910. The figures are totalled by state, major city and, in a rare gesture to comprehensiveness, gender. Thus we can tell that nation-wide, there were 66 724 male saloonkeepers and 1491 female saloonkeepers; women comprised 2.25 per cent of the trade.[18] Some states of the union had less than 1 per cent of their saloons licensed to women, while eleven states had no female saloonkeepers at all.

The American example provides a stark comparison with Victoria in the same period, where over 50 per cent of hotels were under the management of female licensees. It is significant that the typical American saloon architecture did not include accommodation, and therefore did not have the domestic associations that were important to women's participation in the Australian hotel industry. American women's ability to run businesses and provide for their own independent livelihoods through the retailing of alcohol was restricted to the informal, illegal fringes of a vastly profitable and powerful industry. In Victoria, where women had always been formally brought within the rubric of the licensed trade, female hotelkeepers were at the apex of the industry at precisely the time that the industry was at its most socially, culturally and financially influential.

There has not been enough international research in this field to make definitive comparisons, but we can draw together some informed impressions of how liquor-selling women in other countries fared in an epoch of increasingly restrictive gender roles. In his study of the nineteenth-century Parisian café, W. Scott Haine suggests that the archives of the 1870s to 1890s are 'rich with examples of female café owners indispensable to their businesses'.[19] Although he does not offer any numerical evidence or legal analysis, Haine argues that the proprietorial female presence behind the bar ensured that cafés were not 'ordinary patriarchal spaces'. He also implies that the Parisian situation was somewhat distinctive. Haine cites the fact that couples, widows and single women often ran cafés as a reason why the temperance movement was weaker among the French working class than any other industrial society.[20]

In New Zealand, a country whose colonial history more closely resembles Australia's, it is clear that women played an important role in the legal liquor industry, particularly on the goldfields. Although no statistics are available, it appears that marital status was the key determinant in women's access to liquor licences, with widows forming the majority of licence holders.[21] Women were enough of a presence in the industry to pose a threat to late nineteenth-century ideals of 'women's place': an 1889 court decision went so far as to cancel the licences of married women. The Licensing Act of 1908 went one step further, prohibiting all women except widows from holding a liquor licence; legislation barring single women from licence holding was not repealed until 1952. Interestingly, however, magistrates could refuse a licence to a man whose wife did not live with him on the grounds that it was 'essential for the protection of female servants, and in order that the house might be properly conducted, that the licensee's wife should reside on the premises'.[22] This ruling suggests that, as in Victoria, women's centrality to a respectable hotel industry was acknowledged; but at the same time, and unlike Victoria, the right of a woman to control her own house and business affairs was denied.

Closer to home, it may be the case that Victorian women were afforded more latitude than their liquor-selling sisters in other states. While licensing laws for the eastern colonies flowed from the same initial set of colonial experiences and expectations, by the early twentieth century the particular configuration of local politics (including the strength of temperance agitation) resulted in legal disparities. In South Australia, for example, the Licensing Act 1908 prohibited single women from holding a publican's licence. Remarkably, in 1915, this disqualification was extended to include widows as single women.[23] The practice of female hotelkeeping had certainly been strong in South Australia: in 1908 it was stated in parliament that 'of over 700 hotels in the State more than one-fourth are in the possession of the fair sex'.[24] However, local historian Patricia Sumerling claims that the sexual morality of women applying for a licence 'was under constant scrutiny' as the Licensing Bench was assisted by the police in investigating the moral character of applicants.[25] This situation compares unfavourably to the Victorian decision in *Albrecht v. Patterson*, in which the court determined that a woman's 'private character' could have no bearing on her ability to get a licence.

In New South Wales, according to the *Liquor Act* 1912, no single woman could be granted a new licence; although she could apply for a licence transfer, it was against 'the general policy of the Act' and licensing courts were likely to refuse the transfer.[26] (Single men were similarly frowned upon, unless a 'respectable and capable housekeeper' assisted them.) The Act did not expressly bar married women from licence holding, but it specifically listed the categories of married woman who would be eligible to hold a licence in her own name—divorced and judicially separated wives, those holding protection orders as deserted wives, and women married to legally certified lunatics—suggesting that 'general policy' also militated against female publicans being married. It is clear that such women did in fact hold licences, if not in the same high numbers as Victoria.

Other states had their fair share of female publicans too. One study of Townsville hotels documents that from 1869 to 1890 there was always at least one woman running a hotel in that city, with up to five at a time. After 1900, the authors point to the 'sudden and unexplained rise' in female publicans in Townsville. By 1902, half of the town's hotels were run by women—most widows, some unmarried and some with husbands in other occupations although 'this was not encouraged'. Furthermore, these female publicans were highly respected (if they 'kept their hotels very strictly') and were accepted within Townsville's middle-class social circle.[27]

In Tasmania, a 1902 Act provided that no married woman could hold a liquor licence, and in 1908 this disqualification was extended to all women under the age of forty-five.[28] Female publicans averaged approximately 11 per cent of the total licensees from 1865 to 1914.[29] In Western Australia, an 1880 Act prohibited the granting of licences to any woman 'not the widow of a publican dying while licensed'.[30]

Although this survey of other Australian states is incomplete, it does help illustrate the point that Victorian women may have been in a unique position in terms of their legal authority to participate in the hotel industry. What is undeniable is how central the licensing system itself was in determining women's ability to run their own businesses and, in the process, constituting them as formal agents in the twin processes of commercialisation and colonisation.

Contrary to the experience of female liquor sellers in other countries, by the first decades of the twentieth century female publicans in Victoria had secured a fundamental foothold in the legal structures that regulated the drink trade. Furthermore, their statutory and cultural rights had been upheld by judicial interpretations that favoured the interests of property and the free market over orthodox notions of women's place. Thus for Victorian women, the 'privilege of selling' yielded a distinct freedom. Yet a controversial court case of 1884, which threatened to undermine a century of legal and cultural tradition, was to attest that the franchise of female publicans was intimately tied to the political processes and protagonists of the day. Freedom, like captivity, needs its guardians.

PART II

'The Very Nature of Things'
The Politics of
Public Housekeeping

Minogue's Case

IN 1884, MRS CATHERINE MINOGUE, publican, applied to the licensing stipendiary magistrate of Kyneton for the transfer of a licence for the Clare Castle Hotel. Mrs Minogue had already purchased the furniture, goodwill and licence for the hotel from savings she had made in her previous business at another Kyneton public house. Although Mrs Minogue cohabited with her husband, his work as a contractor compelled him to travel, and the publican was solely responsible for her hotel interests. The licensing magistrate refused to hear Mrs Minogue's application on the grounds that, as a married woman living with her husband, she was automatically prohibited from holding a licence under Section 50 of the *Licensing Act* 1876.

In November 1884, Mrs Minogue took her case to the Supreme Court of Victoria. Her intentions were limited. She requested a finding that would compel the licensing magistrate to determine her original application on its merits. Despite Mrs Minogue's humble claim, the ensuing litigation took an unprecedented turn and resulted in a decision that had dire ramifications for *all* married women holding liquor licences in Victoria. So profound was the court's pronouncement that the action spilled out of the judicial system to rebound finally in the press and parliament. This very public debate about the role of women in the hotel industry ultimately focused attention on a social practice as old as the colonies themselves: female hotelkeeping.

More generally, the Minogue case tested the rights of married women to earn an independent income. As we have seen, the Victorian licensing laws had previously allowed all women to trade as separate business entities, regardless of their marital status. But by the urbanising

1880s, when the mercantile community was consolidating its financial strength with broader political influence, public opinion eschewed the frontier social inversions that often saw women as breadwinners and family heads. In the development of new ideas about appropriate femininity, 'woman's place' was being defined more narrowly.[1]

As the editor of the *Age* argued in support of the Supreme Court's decision to disqualify married women from licence holding:

> We have only to read the harassing details of assaults by husbands on their wives . . . to discover the law only read human nature aright when it held that the wife was under the dominion of her husband . . . It seems to be in the very nature of things—in the different constitution of women, which has a disposition to look up to and depend upon someone stronger than herself.[2]

The curious logic of this position—citing women's 'natural' proclivity towards subordination to deny them the right to act independently of their husbands—says much about the contestation of gender roles in the Victorian era.

The Supreme Court's decision in Minogue's case followed the late-nineteenth-century trend towards the state's restriction of married women's participation in the labour market and, particularly, the professions. One result of this process was the increasing rigidity of the male breadwinner/female homemaker model of social organisation.[3] Judging by the position of the Supreme Court and the *Age*, it appears that it was precisely the autonomy of female licensees, not their voluntary thraldom, which threatened certain people's understanding of the 'very nature of things'. What is remarkable about Minogue's case, then, is that it did *not* act as a catalyst to wider gender discrimination and differentiation in licensing law and judicial practice. Once the heat of the controversial decision died down, the case was effectively relegated to the shelves of court reports while female publicans—married and single—lived to sell another beer.

How did this happen? Why did female publicans not experience the same restricted access to 'cultural capital' as other career-minded women in this era? By the 1880s, when the liquor trade was a boom industry in a boom time, the culture and economy of hotels was steeped in female heritage. By the time Catherine Minogue took her case to the Supreme Court, it could never be asserted that she was a maverick crusader for women's rights. She was simply a businesswoman defending her legitimate claim to conduct her daily enterprise. Like many female publicans before her, she chose to assert her rights in a court of law. Catherine Minogue was not an anomaly, either to her sex or to her trade. The Supreme Court's position, on the other hand, flew in the face of almost a century of judicial and political precedent.

Within a month, however, parliament stepped in to legislate away the repercussions of the Minogue decision, preserving married female publicans' right to continue trading in their own names. If a week is a long time in politics, then the month following Catherine Minogue's defeat was sufficiently protracted to reveal that female publicans in Victoria had powerful allies. Those who could have sacrificed female publicans to the prevailing ideology of temperance chose not to. Indeed, these friends in high places were prepared to rally behind the likes of Mrs Minogue, despite the cultural trend towards the masculinisation of work and merit at the end of the nineteenth century.

Argument in the case of *Regina v. Nicholson, ex parte Minogue* turned on the proper interpretation of Section 50 of the *Licensing Act* 1876 which, as we have seen, conferred on a husband the rights and liabilities of his publican wife's licence 'as if such license had been granted to him originally'.[4] Counsel representing the Crown argued that the proper construction of this clause was that no married woman living with her husband, whether or not she had a separate estate, was permitted to hold a publican's licence. To support this conclusion, he argued that if a married woman living with her husband was able to hold a licence then, by claiming the legal defence of marital coercion, she would be able to avoid the penalties for licensing infringements set out in the Act. Under this reasoning, a wife was powerless to stop her husband from, say, serving alcohol during prohibited hours or gambling on the premises and, it was argued, such an evasion of the law could not possibly be the legislature's intent.

Mrs Minogue's counsel conversely claimed that, by passing the Married Women's Property Acts, the legislature had enshrined a married woman's right to trade independently—as a *feme sole*—in any business she so desired. As to the proper construction of Section 50, her lawyer argued that any prohibition said to exist against a married woman holding a licence 'is at the most a matter of inference. If such an important question of policy had been intended it would have been distinctly expressed —not left to conjecture'. The provision for the transfer of rights and responsibilities from wife to husband was entirely intended for the case of a woman who wilfully relinquished her separate estate on marriage, which Mrs Minogue had not done.

When it came to the judgement, the court was vehemently divided on the matter. In the end, two of the three Justices ruled that a married woman not judicially separated from her husband, whether she had property to her separate use or not, was prohibited from holding a publican's licence. The notoriously austere English-born judge, Justice Holroyd, did not refute the legal right of married women to possess property for their separate use. Rather, he rigorously asserted that a woman had no *moral* right to hold a publican's licence, due to the nature of the occupation: 'Nor do I think that there is any reason why her husband should not be able to prohibit her from carrying on a separate trade against his wish . . . especially when the separate trade is that of a publican'. Holroyd confessed that laws existed which permitted married women to run their own businesses but he insisted that 'the holding of a publican's license is not one of the purposes contemplated by that legislation'. His fundamental assumption was that no reasonable man on the Bondi tram would let his wife run a hotel if he had any say in the matter.[5]

In his dissenting judgement, Justice Higinbotham begged the court to stick to the legal grounds for denying a married woman a liquor licence. He could find none.

> There is nothing in this Act, I think, to prevent a married woman, who has gained a qualified independence by virtue of possessing separate property of this kind, from applying for a license to be issued or transferred to her . . . If the Legislature intended to make coverture a disqualification, that intention would probably have been expressed in briefer and more direct terms than section 50.[6]

As a temperance advocate, a women's suffrage supporter and the 'patron saint' of Victorian liberals, George Higinbotham was perhaps more willing to live with some of the tensions within jurisprudence than his Supreme Court colleagues. As an Irishman, Higinbotham may have had more than a legalistic relationship to women of 'qualified independence'. Historian Patrick O'Farrell has argued that the key to understanding the importance of hotels in the Irish-Australian experience lies in the function of the female licensee: 'Her social role often became that of matriarch, confessor to the community . . . a feature of the Irish life of many a country town, respected and sought out particularly by single men who needed a sympathetic female ear, thought to be experienced and independent'.[7] This insight might help to explain the general judicial acceptance of female publicans given that, in the early to mid-nineteenth century, one-third of Victorian barristers were Irish and many Irish barristers went on to become police magistrates and judges.[8] By 1884, however, it was the English judges' privileging of ideology over law and tradition, driven by their evangelical sense of moral and social danger, which held sway in Minogue's case.

The effect of the majority decision was not, of course, confined to Mrs Minogue's inability to obtain a licence for the Clare Castle Hotel, Kyneton. For the first time in almost a century of female hotelkeeping, the court's unexpected interpretation of the Licensing Act made it illegal for married women to hold a publican's licence. Thus overnight, hundreds of women in Victoria had been effectively deprived of their livelihoods. As licences were renewed annually and expired on 31 December each year, the Minogue decision, passed down on 3 November 1884, meant that married female publicans could hold their licences for less than eight weeks further. Finding transferees within that time for hundreds of hotels was a logistical impossibility. Trying to sell a hotel business without a valid licence (the licence being attached to the premises, not the person) was equally untenable. If they continued in their trade these previously legally consecrated businesswomen would be sly-groggers, a miserable loss in status and respectability. One can only imagine Catherine Minogue's horror: her meagre request to be given another chance to prove her fitness had placed so many of her sister publicans in financial and social peril.

Within a month, however, the Victorian parliament intervened to throw oil on the troubled waters of a hotel industry in turmoil. On 5 December 1884, parliament passed an Amending Act to override the consequences of the Minogue case. The purpose of the amending legislation was to allow married women to renew their existing licences or become transferees for a licence in 1885, 'any construction of the law to the contrary notwithstanding'.[9] As the preamble to the Act stated, this concession would give those female publicans disabled by the Minogue ruling 'a reasonable time by way of notice to dispose of their businesses and be enabled to transfer their respective businesses'. It also explicitly stated that such licensees affected by the Act were to be dealt with 'in the same manner as any other licensee'. Married female hotelkeepers were safe—for the time being.

But why did parliament, not known for its legislative haste in matters of marginal electoral importance or contentious policy, move so quickly to safeguard the livelihoods of women who earned a living by selling alcohol? How those with vested interests in a robust hotel industry came to embrace female publicans as a benchmark of the trade's values and aspirations is a story that will take a few pots to tell.

CHAPTER | 7

The Fallout:
Press and Parliament

BY THE 1880S, HOTELS HAD cemented their primacy as the architectural and cultural landmarks of the flourishing metropolis of Melbourne. In an era of economic prosperity and urban growth, the grand hotels of the 1880s reflected the unprecedented confidence of the times, the faith that the Australian colonies could hold their own among the industrial nations of the Western world. As a paean to their prestige, big city hotels adorned their interiors with 'garlands, grapes, wreaths, leaves, putti, and the whole vocabulary of colour and form ... uninhibitedly strewn with abandon on every available surface'.[1] More noticeable than the flamboyant decor, however, was the sheer number of metropolitan hotels, giving rise to the vernacular incantation of 'a pub on every corner'.

But urban hotels were no longer the primary agents of communication, organisation and advice as they had been in frontier days. In the last decades of the nineteenth century, those informal social roles were being commercialised by transport and finance companies, advertising, public administration and post and telegraph services.[2] Hotels were, however, increasingly important as centres of both gentrified and working-class leisure activity in the metropolis, where public drinking reflected the masculine values of work and reward. Moreover, to a great degree, liquor taxes helped finance the expansion of public administration and infrastructure. Since the foundation of Victoria, the liquor industry had produced one-fifth of the state's total revenue and, as the parliamentarians well knew, 'the hotelkeepers were the collectors of that vast amount'.[3] Hotelkeepers, through their official organ, the Licensed Victuallers' Association, and in line with the growing movement towards professionalism, assumed a civic prominence to match the garlands and wreaths.

Catherine Minogue, as the keeper of a modest country public house, did not threaten the social organisation of interior space in the pub, culturally infused, as it was, with female and family leadership. Rather, as a married woman claiming a legal and professional interest in an influential industry, the assertion of her right to trade independently threatened the economic, political and gender territory of urban commerce. In this calcifying landscape, labour market regulation was directed towards eradicating those other than white, male breadwinners.[4]

The 1880s witnessed the beginning of the decline of the long tradition and respectability of married women's employment in important community institutions such as post offices and telegraph stations, a trend which was cemented in New South Wales in 1895 by the Public Service Act, which barred the employment of all public servants' wives. Conversely, other newly professionalised services such as nursing were feminised as women were posited as 'agents of purification'. 'The woman question', which thrashed out the acceptable avenues to women's self-sufficiency, was central to debates in political economy at the end of the nineteenth century.[5] But if the Victorian Supreme Court's ruling was consistent with broader political agendas of the time, how representative was its opinion that female publicans deserved particular exclusion because of the nature of their trade?

In an era when the traffic in liquor was the pre-eminent moral and social issue of the times, judgement in the Minogue case was newsworthy. The court's verdict, as we have seen, was handed down on 3 November 1884. On 6 November, the first public commentary on the startling verdict hit the streets in an editorial in the notoriously pro-temperance newspaper, the *Age*. The decision of the Supreme Court was, in the paper's view, 'a very welcome one': if there were 'serious reasons' why unmarried women should be debarred from holding licences, there were even 'graver reasons' why married women shouldn't be permitted to be licensees, despite the fact that they were 'always considered capable' under the various Licensing Acts. In a turn of phrase suggesting the editor had just discovered a little-known secret, the article confided that 'In fact, there are a considerable number of licences at the present time held by married women'.[6]

The anti-temperance, pro-free-trade *Argus* reserved its editorial position for a few weeks longer. Then, on 21 November, it reported on the Legislative Assembly's debate of the licensing amendment bill. The paper cautiously reported that the Supreme Court's decision had 'set aside a long-standing practice'. Unprepared to stick its neck out any further, the paper chose to publish a letter to the editor as the voice of community opinion. Henry D. McKenzie of Woodend had written to state 'whatever objection there may be to the principle embodied in the issuing of licences to married women', nonetheless, by refusing a custom whereby 'vested interests have been called into existence', the court's ruling would

> deprive many respectable married women of the means of making a living for themselves and families, and in some instances lead to destitution and want; for it is an unfortunate fact that in most cases where publicans' licences are held by married women, the necessity arises from the inability of the husband, from some cause or other, to maintain his family.[7]

In appealing to nineteenth-century notions of chivalrous masculinity, this concerned citizen's approach was a conventional, if benevolent, one. Pleas to chivalry were routinely used to influence social policy in this era of politics.[8]

These two versions of 'the nature of things' expressed by the journalistic response to the Minogue verdict essentially set the terms for ensuing parliamentary debate on the issue, and ultimately, for the perception of licensed women in the hotel industry. The 'reform' dictum held that it was morally reprehensible for a married woman to be engaged in a calling that debased her sex and compromised her God-given place in society, 'under the dominion of her husband'. The 'conservative' position stated that it was unjust to abrogate the property rights of any individual who had legally accrued them. This economic injustice was even more pertinent when the victim was a helpless but deserving woman. No voice of public opinion was quite prepared to say, however, that there was nothing inherently wrong with married women holding liquor licences.

'Incalculable injury': Debating the *Licensing Act* 1885

This silence is particularly deafening in the parliamentary debate that accompanied the passing of the 1884 Amending Act that preserved married women's right to renew their licences. With characteristic flair, David Gaunson—vociferous opponent of temperance reform and legal adviser to the Licensed Victuallers' Association—railed against the injustice of the Minogue ruling:

> The result of that decision would be that incalculable injury would be done to hundreds of married women who were now holding licences, unless the law was altered ... It was utterly impossible for these licensees to transfer their licences in time to enable them to escape from the desperate and deplorable loss—in fact, complete ruin—which would fall upon them from the decision of the Supreme Court.

Yet even this staunch sympathiser ultimately voiced the same ambivalent support for female publicans as the letter-writing Mr McKenzie: 'However desirable it might be to have the law so that no woman under any circumstances should hold a licence, the fact remained that the Licensing Act made provision for women holding licences, and licences had been held for years by married women in the city of Melbourne'.[9] Perhaps Gaunson, an acclaimed barrister, was merely playing politics by presupposing his adversaries' arguments. But it is equally possible that no politician was willing either to throw these unfortunate women to the lions or to unequivocally champion their rights *as women*. Defending the rights of women along property lines avoided recriminations from press, church and business.

In the same parliamentary session, Premier James Service, a 'classical advanced liberal', land reformer and anti-Catholic, also declared that the Supreme Court's ruling was 'at variance with a long practice' and that 'serious injury was being inflicted upon people who had hitherto been innocent in the eyes of the law'.[10] Service's standpoint may have been influenced by more than mere recourse to legal precedent. He revealed that 'a deputation of women' had waited upon him that morning and voiced their intention to go to the Privy Council in London if justice could not be found in Victoria. The contingent, presumably of irate female publicans, must have argued with some force. Convinced of their plight, Service likened the women's position to squatters being turned off their runs with no notice and no opportunity to sell their sheep. By evoking the credibility and lineage of pastoralism, Service was giving serious economic and cultural credence to these women's predicament. However, in supporting the Amending Act, which would protect them from 'immediate ruin', Service reiterated the now common refrain that 'this question had no reference to the policy of married women holding licences'.

In the late nineteenth century male interests generally determined what was public and political.[11] The post-Minogue debate reveals that the question of married women's licences was certainly not regarded as a 'woman's issue'. Married women's claim to licence holding was male politics because it pertained to the economic right to trade, an entitlement that could not be removed without compensation. In this sense, Catherine Minogue became a pawn in wider political debates between free trade conservatives and protectionist reformers.

The 1884 Amending Act was intended to preserve married women's licences until the end of 1885, by which stage the Licensing Act was slated to be redrafted. A permanent resolution to the conundrum posed by the Supreme Court's decision could then be found, and explicitly stated, in the fresh legislation. That was the theory. As it happened, there must have been a lot of backroom dealing in 1885. When the bill was finally enacted, it registered an unequivocal rejection of the Supreme Court's ruling and an explicit endorsement of the legal and customary rights of married women to hold liquor licences. In the terminology section of the new Act, a licensed 'person' was deemed to include a *feme covert*. Going one step further, the irksome Section 50—the legal leverage used by the Supreme Court to oust married women—was amended to preclude the 'simple fact of her marrying' from vesting a female licensee's rights in her husband.[12]

It is difficult to ascertain the full spectrum of parliamentary or public opinion on this extraordinary departure from the sentiments expressed only a year earlier. The press went silent on the issue. When the Licensing Law Amendment Bill was introduced for parliamentary debate in 1885 only one politician, the ever-gallant Gaunson, discussed the sections relating to married women. He argued:

> It is well known that a number of public-house licences are held by wives who have obtained protection orders against their husbands, or who are living apart from them without any protection at all. What real difference can there be between the commercial status of a married woman practically separated from her husband and that of a widow?[13]

Why no other parliamentarians chose to speak on the 'general policy' of issuing licences to married women is a matter of speculation. The absence of press reporting on the issue during 1885, and the curious lack of temperance opposition to the practice of women running hotels (discussed further in Chapter 15 of this book), suggests that there was not sufficient public support for the Supreme Court's position to warrant any major political consternation.

Married female publicans weathered the post-Minogue storm with their right to trade intact on the strength of two current ideologies: the fiscal protection of mercantile freedoms and the chivalrous protection of vulnerable women. These rights were never significantly eroded, nor even seriously challenged in a public forum, throughout the following turbulent decades of temperance agitation, depression, wartime and post-war conservatism. Female publicans continued to dominate hotelkeeping, even though working women by the early twentieth century were increasingly marginalised from the public world. According to historian Desley Deacon, women working outside the home became social pariahs, 'stigmatized as selfish or unfortunate . . . an anomaly to be pitied, exploited or ignored'.[14] Yet married female publicans, essentially working within their own homes, profiting from their trade in domestic services, apparently did not threaten the advancing system of industrial capitalism and its gender order of male economic supremacy and female dependency. What this situation suggests about the hospitality industry in Victoria, particularly in light of the American example where women were forced out of commercial selling, is that the liquor trade may have furnished a steady flow of state revenue but its 'cultural capital' remained antiquated well into the twentieth century.

Licence reduction: A back door exit for female publicans?

If the official legislative response to the Minogue case did ultimately endorse the policy of female licence holding, was there a less transparent means of discriminating against women's participation in the hotel industry? Desley Deacon has argued that, although the New South Wales Public Service Act of 1895 did not expressly bar married women from employment, unofficial discrimination began to occur through the *administration* of the Act. In a climate of fierce public debate about the participation of women in the workforce, Deacon maintains that it was through the management of state policies that the gender order was truly policed. Thus, for example, contracts that female heads of families had long held for telegraph station or post office supervision were simply not renewed. In an increasingly centralised bureaucracy, men were given such posts on the basis of individual merit, heightening women's need for dependency as merit became masculinised.[15] Was this surreptitious process of professionalisation similarly re-created in Victoria's liquor licensing system?

Certainly, the trend towards increasing state regulation of the hotel trade in the early twentieth century allowed every opportunity for more bureaucratic intervention. In 1906, the Licensing Act entrusted the job of administering the number and quality of hotels and hotelkeepers in Victoria to a new statutory authority, the Licences Reduction Board. The Board was instituted to do something about the indisputable fact that the number, and particularly the location, of hotels in Victoria were totally disproportionate to population size and distribution. As we have seen, the Victorian *Wine Beer and Spirits Statute* 1864 was intended to open up the trade as a response to the high incidence of sly-grogging associated with the gold rush. The result, complained the wine and spirit merchant W. J. White to the 1867 Royal Commission, was that 'Any place can be licensed now. Some of them are very little better than a few packing cases stuck together.'[16] James Jenkins, on behalf of the temperance Order of Rechabites, similarly voiced his concern at the social profile of such packing-case publicans: 'At present no respectable capitalist would invest in the business; and if this goes on the whole trade will fall into the hands of the lowest class of people'.[17]

By 1876, it was estimated that in some areas there was one hotel per thirty people; no district had less than one hotel per 150 inhabitants. By 1885, there were 1046 hotels in metropolitan Melbourne and 4299 hotels in the colony, one-quarter of which provided fewer than six rooms.[18] Late-nineteenth-century licensing legislation was aimed at treading the fine line between encouraging a 'profitably conducted' trade (a trade which ultimately profited the colonial coffers), upholding the property rights of those already licensed, and seeing that only an acceptable 'class of people' were given the privilege of a liquor licence.

But on one issue, no-one at Spring Street could argue: Victoria had an incredible glut of hotels, with most suburbs and country towns far in excess of their statutory quotas.[19] In Collingwood, for example, there were fifty-seven hotels where the allowable number was twenty-eight. Port Melbourne had double its share; rural Daylesford had triple. In Kyneton, Catherine Minogue had vied for the licence of one of thirty-two hotels, eighteen more than the town's quota. While a few districts had less than their ration of licensed premises, the political crunch was whether or how to compensate for the large number of licences that would just have to go.

Proponents of compensation argued along the lines of the civil injustice that would be caused if a property right was extinguished without restitution. But if the principle was economic entitlement, their rhetoric focused on the implications of a government that was prepared to violate basic moral standards. Women loom large in this scenario. Again, it was the code of chivalry that framed the debate. With few prospects for self-help available for economically vulnerable women, many parliamentarians pointed out that it was widows and children who would suffer if hotels were closed without compensation. George Swinburne, Liberal member for genteel Hawthorn and an active Methodist, rejecting the bill's proposal for six o'clock closing, pointed out that 'a number of poor women, or poor men, were depending for their livelihood on the takings in their businesses between six o'clock at night and ten o'clock'.[20] (Swinburne's position also illustrates that politicians didn't always align themselves along classic 'wet' and 'dry' lines; indeed, the 1906 Licensing Act was put to a conscience vote.)

The tactic of offering up decent, impoverished women as the ultimate instrument of moral blackmail was used ten years later when debating the bill to prohibit the employment of barmaids. One parliamentarian argued that the restrictive legislation would be injurious to all humble hotel businesses that could not afford to hire a barman. His evidence?

> There are plenty of hotels in the country which are kept by widows who, possibly, have no daughters old enough to serve in the bar . . .
> In the future they would not be able to call in a [female] servant, or hired help, so that they might obtain a couple of hours' relaxation during the day.[21]

This apparent concern for the well-being of deserving women was not enough to save barmaids, but, in the wash-up of the 1906 debate, parliament did vote for compensation. In the politics of public credibility, conventional ideas about female vulnerability and deservingness collided with a reform agenda which privileged the publican who 'desires to keep a good house'.

If elected representatives used chivalrous posturing to boost their integrity, were the state's administrators equally beholden to this public image? Or was their mandate to ruthlessly weed out the most dispensable hotels wide enough to eradicate female public housekeepers? The official rationale of the Licences Reduction Board, as stated by its chairman, Robert Barr, was to deprive those licences 'not necessary for the convenience of the public or the requirements of the several localities of the said districts'. In all likelihood, Barr cautioned, this would mean that public houses that were 'old, poor and ill-designed [would be] most readily spared'. It is worth examining the licensing reduction process in some detail so as to illuminate how the Board's procedures may or may not have been biased against women.[22]

The Board sent forms to all publicans in the state, requiring them to provide details of their financial dealings over the 'statutory years' of 1903 to 1905. Such details included tax returns, rents paid, income (divided into accommodation, meals and bar trade) and outgoings. Hotel owners were required to provide separate documentation of their capital investments. Where a publican was both licensee and owner, both sets of paperwork had to be completed. This information was necessary for determining, firstly, what 'class' a hotel belonged to, and secondly, how much compensation was to be paid to the owner and keeper of a licence-deprived house. Form letters were addressed 'To Sir or Madame'.

It is interesting to find that most owners of hotels, whether independent freeholders or breweries, secured the services of a solicitor to complete the necessary documentation but very few licensees sought such assistance. Moreover, a great many publicans could not fill out the forms at all, claiming that they did not keep regular books, had 'lost' the necessary information, or had been unable to get the relevant material from previous licensees who had run the business over the statutory years. Publicans were a notoriously nomadic bunch, with many hotels witnessing an annual turnover of licensees. This occupational propensity towards transience can be seen a part of the traditional culture of licensed victualling in Britain, where patterns of mobility suggest that even a five-year stint in one hotel was a long tenure by trade standards.[23] Given the sketchy records left by previous proprietors, many hotelkeepers simply estimated an annual income; most, at least, were able to say how much rent they paid. The archival holdings of the Licences Reduction Board reveal just how 'small-time' the majority of hotel businesses were. In 1913, the Board reported that 80 per cent of the hotels that had been closed throughout the city and suburbs had done a bar trade only.

The Board executed its work with remarkable speed and efficiency. Between 1907 and 1910, it closed 26 per cent of metropolitan hotels (64 of 362), 28 per cent of Bendigo's hotels (54 of 302) and 28 per cent of Ballarat's hotels (39 of 281). In 1916, buoyed by its unprecedented public, government and trade approval, the Board was made permanent, though its name was changed to the Licensing Court of Victoria. By 1920, 1475 Victorian hotels had been delicensed by deprivation or surrender. The average compensation per hotel was £566, although there was a significant difference between country and city properties: of the 414 hotels closed in greater Melbourne, an average compensation of £920 was paid, compared to £425 for the 1037 delicensed country hotels. By 1922, there were only 2008 hotels left in the state, a reduction of more than half on the 1876 figure.[24]

Although this decrease would appear to spell success for the work of the Licences Reduction Board, and the cause of temperance in general, economic historian D. T. Merrett has argued that the reduction of licences 'was more effective in conferring monopoly rents on licence holders than in reducing the consumption of alcohol'.[25] The principal beneficiary of regulation, contends Merrett, was the liquor trade. The Licensed Victuallers' Association supported the Board's work, not least because the regulators were anti-prohibitionists who believed that improving the practices of the trade—rather than abolishing it altogether—would lead to a decrease in alcohol consumption. Those publicans left standing after the Board's process of purification were very likely to gain in social acceptability and financial stability by weeding out the most noxious of the hotel industry's own members. The Board thus 'placed its faith in controlling the licensee' with the aim of forcing the liquor trade to adopt professional, merit-based standards of business activity which were more in keeping with early-twentieth-century criteria for capitalist industry.[26]

So how did female publicans fare through this project of industry improvement? Particularly, how were they affected by the extraordinary attrition rate of hotel licences between 1906 and 1922? If the Licences Reduction Board sought to regulate the liquor industry by controlling the licensee, did such control have particular implications for female licensees—especially married ones who, as we have seen, threatened some people's sense of the natural status of men's dominion over women? Hospitality expert Bronwyn Higgs has claimed that women 'bore the brunt of reductions' under the Board's regime because most hotels that lost their licences were located in the country, and women ran a disproportionate number of pubs in remote rural locations.[27] However, in 1906, over half of Melbourne's metropolitan hotels had a woman as principal licensee; thus, in order for women to have 'borne the brunt' of the Board's purge, mere logistics could not have been the only consideration. The critical issue, then, is whether married women did in fact get shunted out of the industry—and if they did, was it through force of circumstance, structural disadvantage, or sheer malignant will on the part of licensing authorities?

At first glance, we might presume that female publicans were at a disadvantage in the licensing reduction process. Procedurally, the work of the Licences Reduction Board took on all the worst vestiges of an adversarial judicial system. Ominously, a witness could openly attack another on whatever grounds they saw fit in the defence of their own house; the 'character' of a licensee was always open to question, and, one might presume, a woman's character was vulnerable to vexatious claims of sexual impropriety, proven or not. The courts had ruled out 'private character' as grounds for licence disqualification, but the Board was not bound to follow judicial precedent. Many licensees of humble hotels, particularly the owner-occupiers of remote wayside pubs in dying country towns, chose to voluntarily surrender their licence rather than face the bureaucratic barrage, the accusatorial nature of the process, and the inevitable failure of their decrepit buildings to meet the Board's standards.

Mrs Mary Harrington, owner and keeper of the Robin Hood Hotel, Musk Creek (near Daylesford), was one such woman. On 11 November 1914, she wrote to Mr Bennett, the local Licensing Inspector, requesting his assistance in the surrender of her licence. In shaky hand and with marginal literacy, she implored:

> I hope I am not too late as I am in a very bad health I got this neauretessia [sic] lost the use of my legs and hands and as you can see it is no good to me so dear Sir if you could help me to get the compensation and I cannot a servant only my granddaughter.

Mrs Harrington received £225 compensation on 13 November. Perhaps surrendering more than her licence, she died eight days later.

Again, Annie Luke, a widow with one small child, requested the voluntary surrender of her licence to the Railway Hotel, Bullarto, in December 1916. In a letter to the Board she stated:

> I received the forms but I do not quite understand how to fill them in . . . as the inspector of police will tell you the house is not-fit-to live in as the rain pours down in every room . . . I have no one to go to for advice and I have not circumstances to go to a solicitor . . . If I do not get the compensation early in the new year I will have to take a situation until I receive it and that means that I will have to part with my little child and I am not strong enough to take a hard place I have had pneumonia twice since I came to this place and it has ruined my health.

In February 1917, Mrs Luke was paid £45 compensation. The monies were paid to her mother, as Annie had 'left on the 11.30 train'.

The adversarial nature of the Board's project—assessing one hotel's merits over another's—often saw publican pitted against publican. Two country hotels that had previously traded as friendly competitors could suddenly become fierce rivals for the one licence once the Board came to town. Such was the case in the Victorian goldfields town of Costerfield in 1913, where Mrs Mary Ford of the Antinomy Hotel was locked in combat with Mr John Golden of the Costerfield Family Hotel. When the Antinomy retained its licence, Mr Golden appealed. He requested a re-hearing on the grounds that Mrs Ford had run a sweepstakes for 15 shillings during a recent woodchopping competition in her yard. This crime, argued Mr Golden, warranted a licensing conviction but evidence had not been submitted at the deprivation hearing. The Board would have none of it. It held that Mrs Ford's hotel 'was doing considerably more trade in meals and beds, as well as in the bar, and catering more effectively than its neighbour for the mining population'. True to its rationale of ridding the industry of its 'weakest houses', the Board favoured Mrs Ford's estimable track record over Mr Golden's petty indictments.

Although some women without doubt felt the thin edge of the Board's administrative wedge, others received a more favourable reception than we might expect. Certainly, the Board's procedures were skewed against the poorest and least bureaucratically adept publicans. The owner-occupiers of small, remote rural hotels—many of whom were elderly widows—were exceptionally vulnerable to the process and were more likely to voluntarily surrender their licences. Indeed, 32 per cent of delicensed hotels were both owned and run by a woman.[28] The vast majority of these were small shanties in locations that had not been populated since the gold rushes and did little more than beer trade. Many of these licences would have been originally issued at the time when granting women licences correlated with the frontier conditions that led to desertion and early widowhood. By comparison, breweries owned 17 per cent of delicensed hotels. Breweries, it goes without saying, had greater resources to improve their hotel buildings, obtain sound legal advice and 'modernise' their business practices.

The clearest indication of partiality in the licensing reduction process is that tenants were disadvantaged over owners of hotels. Issues of literacy, legal representation and poor record-keeping contributed to the vastly diminished amounts of compensation that licensees received as compared to owners; in most cases, licensees received one-fifth to one-sixth of the sum awarded to owners. Hotels in large towns or suburbs that had owner-proprietors stood the best chance of a licensee receiving more than a cursory compensation. For example, owner-licensee Isabella Carrison, of the Farmers Union Hotel, Horsham, received £1275 compensation when her hotel was closed in 1914. At the time, the average compensation was closer to £375.[29] Despite Isabella's good fortune, the fact that female publicans were more likely to be tenants than freeholders suggests that for women, compensation proved but a token gesture at appeasing propertied class interests, despite the political rhetoric about protecting vulnerable widows and their families. In the end, the proprietorial rights of licence holding were worth far less than those of land holding.

However, the fundamental point that needs to be stressed here is that the plentiful archival holdings of the Licences Reduction Board establish no pattern of overt or oblique discrimination against female publicans on the basis of their gender. In particular, there is no evidence that married women came under more scrutiny than any other category of hotelkeeper. Poverty, illiteracy and isolation were encumbrances that ultimately disadvantaged some women, but so too some men. For every notation in the Board's minute books where a woman was deprived of a licence, there is another case in which a female licensee was favoured over a male rival. The Board clearly interpreted its charter narrowly, making determinations about a hotel's relative merit on the basis of its location, trade and buildings rather than moral judgements about a publican's private character or gender suitability. The sort of reasoning employed by the Supreme Court in Minogue's case, which questioned a woman's capacity to control a business (and her right to make that a publican's business), played no part in the Board's reckoning. It is thus difficult to conclude that the Board pursued an insidious policy of excluding the participation of women in the industry, married or otherwise.

The most tangible evidence that gender bias was not a force in the Board's determinations can be drawn from a statistical overview of the licences deprived between 1906 and 1930. During this period, 53 per cent of the entire number of hotels closed were licensed to women. Unfortunately, it is not possible to gauge the exact percentage of female licensees over this same period for the whole state. But between 1906 and 1923, 50 per cent of metropolitan and suburban hotels were licensed to women and approximately the same number of hotel licences in the Bendigo, Ballarat and Castlemaine regions were held by women. Based on these tallies, it would thus appear that although there may have been a slight disproportion in the number of hotels closed while a woman was running them, the discrepancy is not such as to sustain the conclusion that female licensees 'bore the brunt' of the Board's purge. If the Board *did* wish to control the rate of female participation in the hotel industry through the administration of its reduction powers, it failed. Women continued to represent between 40 and 50 per cent of licensees through-out Victoria until the 1950s.

In the Board's bid to improve the hotel industry and bring it into line with more professional business management models and aspir-ations, certain 'classes' of hotelkeeper were intentionally excised from the trade. Publicans who were poor, illiterate, elderly and otherwise un-skilled in business practices such as bookkeeping were obvious targets for deprivation. Hotels that were unkempt, incommodious and fiscally expendable were similarly ejected. Essentially, this meant that publicans who used their own modest homes as a licensed base to sell liquor lost the 'privilege of selling'. This obviously impacted on a great many women, for whom the trade in liquor had been an important and legal source of income.

However, if one aim of the licensing reduction regime was to 'control the licensee', there is no evidence that the Licences Reduction Board used its administrative powers to 'manage gender'. This is an im-portant distinction, because it means that the status of women who came through the deprivation era unscathed in fact improved. If the Board's political purpose, which was endorsed by the Licensed Victuallers' Association, was the forced adoption of professional, merit-based stan-dards of business by the hotel industry, then female publicans were included in this process of professionalisation. The women who con-tinued to run up to half of the vastly diminished number of Victorian hotels after the Board finished its work were, by definition, formally endorsed as the 'better class' of keeper of the 'better class' of hotel. Moreover, the Board's emphasis on accommodation facilities and 'house trade' in determining the credentials of a licensed premises tended to reinforce the domestic nature of good public housekeeping. While this stance may have been undermined by the introduction of the six o'clock swill in 1916, the official position on hotelkeeping continued to stress its domestic associations. This perpetuated the colonial tendency to *feminise* the notion of merit in the hotel industry. Thus women were not, in prin-ciple or practice, edged out of the licensing system.

The Supreme Court Justices in Minogue's case claimed that married women should not be allowed to take command of the public house. Some politicians claimed that female publicans were to be pitied as desti-tute but deserving widows and mothers. What female publicans could claim after the era of licence reduction was that they were respectable, professional businesswomen who owed their existence to credit rather than charity.

The Licensed Victuallers' Association

BY THE 1930S, WHEN THE work of the Licences Reduction Board was effectively complete, the Licensed Victuallers' Association of Victoria (LVA) regularly praised female hotelkeepers for their 'fine personal qualities' and 'high ideals of citizenship'.[1] The LVA, the predecessor of today's Australian Hotels Association, pronounced that women like Mrs Lillian Alice Boyhan, proprietress of the Graham Family Hotel, Port Melbourne, 'set a standard by which the industry aspires to be judged'.[2] Fine sentiments indeed, but the LVA had not always been so convinced of the value of its female members.

In the wake of the Minogue decision in 1884, the LVA filed a report in its weekly trade journal, the *Licensed Victuallers' Advocate*. The *Advocate* chose to hedge its bets: 'While we do not acquiesce in the soundness of the law as laid down, we believe it is, as a rule, inexpedient to allow married women to carry on public-houses in their own names'.[3] The article generously granted that widows and daughters of deceased publicans should be allowed to run hotels 'suited to their capabilities'. Taking the opportunity to expand on the scope of the Minogue case, the editor also chose to express his opinion on *single* female licensees: 'the fewer unmarried women we have as landladies the better'. He went on: 'There are no doubt many capital ladymanagers who persistently continue single, in spite of all offers. But really they must be made to listen to reason—and eligible proposals from fitting suitors. Then the license problem will be satisfactorily solved.' Thus in the view of the official mouthpiece for promoting the interests of the hotel trade, 'the licence problem' was reduced to the recalcitrance of its irrational female members.

In the fifty years that separated Mrs Minogue and Mrs Bonyan, the LVA patently had a change of heart. From suspicious to ambivalent to gushing, the LVA waned and waxed in its support for female publicans, but it could never ignore the presence of women amongst the traders it claimed to represent. As it happened, the LVA's somewhat reluctant embrace of female publicans in the crucial years between 1885 and 1916 became a chief political tool in its own quest for social respectability and professional status.

Two weeks after the *Licensed Victuallers' Advocate* had endorsed the Supreme Court's decision in the Minogue case, the same editor dramatically changed his tune. The editor now expressed his concern that the court's ruling would cause hardship to 'many very worthy women'. Far from railing against the inappropriateness of female licensees in the industry, he praised the self-sufficiency and dedication of such 'worthy women':

> We are acquainted with some whose husbands have not been heard of for years; others hold protection orders against their worst halves; some have husbands residing in distant parts of the colony or outside its boundaries; others are mated to lunatics . . . All these are hard-working, managing women . . . they suffer not for their faults, but for their misfortunes.

The appropriately beneficent editor took his new-found respect for female licensees even further, calling on parliament to remedy the unfortunate situation created by the recent interpretation of the law. He lamented that unless parliament rectified the anomaly 'we shall see a large number of clever deserving women debarred from ever resuming the business they have been trained to conduct'.[4]

However, the president of the LVA, Mr Meader, accepted the reality of the situation created by the court's decision. 'So, bashful husbands', he counselled in the *Advocate*, 'step forward please, and assume the position of respectable and respected Licensed Victuallers'. Meader's use of the language of space is telling here, as it is imagery that he employs again when trying, somewhat feebly, to voice his sympathy for the recent positioning of women in the industry: 'It is hard lines on the Ladies, certainly, to be so unceremoniously thrust into the background at the shortest of short notice, but they are so fertile of resource that I am persuaded they will speedily find means to cope with the difficulty'.[5]

Despite his obsequiousness, Meader cannot disguise his true opinion of where women belong in the social geography of hotelkeeping. There

75

was a foreground and a background to be negotiated, and Meader, as the highest representative of the trade's industry association, was content to see women finally relegated to the less visible (and thus less politically tenuous) position of helpmeet. Evidently, he believed that a 'respectable and respected' trade would be more ably constituted by greater numbers of those 'bashful husbands' and fewer of those wives 'so fertile of resource'.

In the end, though, Meader somewhat begrudgingly vowed to petition parliament for a resolution to 'the defect' in the Act. As the plot thickens later in this tale, it appears likely that the LVA's about-face owed a great deal to the unambiguous support of the powerful brewing industry for Catherine Minogue and her resourceful sisters.

A short history of the LVA: The quest for respectability

As an organisation, the Licensed Victuallers' Association had always been sensitive to opprobrium, shaping its identity according to a sense of the clear and present danger without. Unlike the majority of employers' associations, which emerged as a response to organised labour in the late nineteenth century, the publicans of Melbourne formed an association to advance and protect their trade interests as early as 1840, when 'the Trade' itself consisted of a mere two dozen hotels.[6] Buoyed by the success of the English licensed victuallers in exercising 'great public and parliamentary influence', their peers in Victoria hoped that through organisation and unanimity they might 'refute the gross misrepresentations of which, for so many years, they have been the victims'. At the same time, the trade association would help combat the 'legal and fiscal injustice they have so long endured ... subjected to the most vicious class legislation'.

Despite factional rumblings, in the last quarter of the nineteenth century the LVA was an influential lobby group. Like other prominent civic and commercial organisations of the time, it established many services for its members, including an employment agency, a recreation reserve (in Clifton Hill), a benevolent asylum, free legal counsel, representation at licensing hearings and reimbursement of legal costs for members charged with infringements of the Licensing Act. One of its first broad political successes was in petitioning the parliament for a grant of land for an asylum for 'decayed members of the trade and schools for the education of the destitute and orphan children of members'. The LVA made the request on the grounds of 'licensed victuallers being contributors to a very large extent of the revenue of the country'. The petition was granted by the Minister for Public Works 'on the distinct understanding that the privileges were not to be restricted or limited by party or sectarian feeling, but be as open as the trade itself'.[7]

The LVA maintained a strict code of ethics for its members. By advocating standards of 'first class accommodation' and 'quality service', the LVA attempted to prove that the hotel trade was as reputable as any other arm of commerce: indeed, 'Respectability was their guiding principle'.[8] By September 1884, when the LVA hosted its first annual dinner, its president was able to claim that the hotel industry was constituted by 'a respectable body of men, who did not want their reputations tarnished by the presence in the Trade of a few black sheep'.[9] For many years the LVA fought its own internal campaign against 'low houses' run by 'low characters'.

In its determination to prove and improve the respectability of the trade, the LVA was appealing to the same class bias—'the very nature of things'—as the *Age* readers and upright Justices of the Supreme Court. Responsible action, rational thinking and common-sense values provided the stage from which the LVA could launch its entry into the petty-bourgeois world of late-nineteenth-century capitalism.

However, the relentless quest for acceptance by the commercial and political establishment was to be the source of constitutional division. By the turn of the century, the LVA was accused of elitism by rank-and-file publicans, of primarily representing the freehold proprietors rather than the small-time suburban and country publicans who made up the bulk of the trade. Most hotelkeepers were not wealthy entrepreneurs, but rather struggling small business-people who typically worked long hours, did their own bookkeeping and, with assistance from family members, attended the bar, cooked meals and washed linen. In 1906, less than one-third of hoteliers earned more than £156 per annum and therefore paid income tax.[10]

Typically, the LVA's office bearers and committee members were drawn from the 'top twenty' Melbourne hotels—such as Scott's and the Menzies—and their wealth, power and profile were often used as an entrée into parliamentary careers. For example, in 1877, the president of the LVA, Godfrey Carter, was elected to the Legislative Assembly as the member for St Kilda. This pattern conforms to the model of businessmen-politicians in the last quarter of the nineteenth century.[11] Increasingly, the LVA saw that its future lay not in feeling persecuted and resentful, but in taking its (self-proclaimed) rightful place among the honourable powerbrokers and policy-makers of the colony.

As a socially conservative organisation, by the late nineteenth century the LVA implicitly endorsed many of the liquor control issues of the day, such as the enforcement of Sunday closing; its duty was to safeguard the reputations and livelihoods of wealthy businessmen. The LVA was not 'reformist' on broader social issues, declining to take a progressive stance on wage regulation or suffrage. Essentially, it lobbied to preserve the status quo and sought allies within the establishment. From the 1880s, it held lavish balls at the Melbourne Town Hall and genteel picnics in Queenscliff, to which politicians and other public dignitaries were invited. Its president also received an automatic invitation to civic events, the ultimate accolade of Victorian respectability.

In the quest to achieve social legitimacy and political leverage, the industry also stressed its links to the growing ideology of professionalism. The LVA pursued social exclusiveness by emphasising the fine, upstanding qualities of its members—honesty, industry, thrift and sobriety—and contrasted them with those participants in the trade who did not qualify for membership by virtue of their vices—insobriety, impropriety, lawlessness and filth. Although family dynasties continued to occupy the highest echelons of the hotel industry, the LVA, in the process of identifying itself with the politics and values of professionalism, distanced itself from its traditional association with small-scale family enterprises and their ethic of patronage. The majority of late-nineteenth-century liquor traders, its spokesmen argued, were very different from 'the persons who established hotels throughout the colonies [who] were, as a rule, drawn from a very objectionable class'.[12]

As a class of businessmen-politicians, the LVA in the late nineteenth century ultimately aligned itself with the ideals, values and ethics of industrial capitalism: social mobility, individualism, respectability and civic responsibility. To this end, the LVA was often prepared to sacrifice the more 'objectionable' members of its trade.

Female publicans and the LVA: Strumpets or trump cards?

How did female publicans fit into the profile of an organisation that had set its sights on acceptance and legitimacy within the bourgeois capitalist framework of establishment politics and commerce? The answer is not clear-cut. Rather, the LVA's attitude towards female hotelkeepers reflects its own shifting allegiances and agendas from its early stage of establishing its political credentials in the 1860s and 1870s to the latter phase of redefining its power base in the 1920s. The LVA's ambivalent relationship to its female members is intimately tied to the public profile that it wished to project, given that, as its chairman articulated in 1906, 'the duty of any association representing the trade, its traditions and aspirations is to firmly set its face against any action that may in the slightest degree induce contemptuous criticism'.[13] Ever mindful of bad press, the LVA stance on female publicans acts as a barometer of wider social attitudes.

In the 1870s, when the LVA was keen to cement its social position among the moral elite, it considered that female publicans might be a magnet for criticism. Although there was no official policy regarding female members, in January 1877 the committee instructed the secretary to return a one-guinea subscription fee received from 'a lady hotelkeeper'. It was deemed that the applicant was ineligible for membership 'on various grounds' based on an estimation of 'the character of the lady in question'.[14] No further justification is extended. In the same year, when the LVA published a list of its members, 43 out of 707 names inscribed on the role were identifiably female. This participation rate of 6 per cent is substantially lower than the 22 per cent of hotels that were licensed to women in 1876, suggesting that female publicans did not feel welcome as members, or were not convinced that their interests would be served by membership.

In the early volumes of LVA publications (1860s–1870s), little recognition is given to the contribution or participation of women as hotelkeepers in their own right. Indeed, the portrait of female activities complies with conventional notions of women's involvement with public organisations: the 'Women's Auxiliary' model of dutiful service. In 1864, the *Licensed Victuallers' Almanack* reported:

> An intelligent lady, wife of a Member of the Melbourne Committee, makes the following suggestions on the means of raising funds for the Asylum and Schools, namely that the wives, daughters and sisters of Licensed Victuallers should subscribe one pound each, form Metropolitan and Local Committees of Ladies, hold Bazaars, circulate Collecting Cards, and wind up by a Grand Ball. We know that this lady would cheerfully take her share in carrying out her suggestions.[15]

The same journal reports that one hundred gentlemen attended the Collingwood branch dinner on 24 June 1863, and 'The toast of "The Ladies" concluded an exceedingly pleasant evening'.[16]

While the LVA made the customary courtly acknowledgment of a feminine presence within the social quorum, it was not above making jokes at women's expense. In trade journals, women are typically portrayed as frivolous, if young and pretty, or nagging, if old and married. Socially accepted notions of 'woman's place' were also invoked in the trade press: 'An exchange makes the following suggestive statement:—"A young lady has taken the degree of B.A. at the Melbourne University. She hopes that her next degree will be that of M.A.M.A. Very proper, too."'[17] It is worth speculating (in the absence of any direct testimony) that it is this sort of patronising representation of the motivations and character of women which discouraged female publicans from seeking membership of the LVA, particularly given that so many of them had sought hotelkeeping for a living because they had been judicially separated from or deserted by morally shabby or dangerous men, leaving them with large families to support. The genre of humour that depicts the husband as meal ticket and wife as shrew may not have washed with this cohort.

Between the late 1880s and first decades of the twentieth century, the LVA increasingly recognised the contribution of women to the hotel industry. This can be seen in the numerous obituaries that bring female publicans into the LVA's fold. On the death in 1919 of Mrs Mary Ann Carolan, who ran several country hotels and finished her career with a twenty-year stint as the proprietress of the George Hotel, Fitzroy, the publican was remembered as 'a very old pioneer in the hotel trade . . . old members of the trade knew her well and can bear testimony to her many acts of charity and kindliness of heart'.[18] Similarly, Miss Leahy, of the Commercial Hotel, Ballan, was honoured for her feminine qualities of grace and charm, as well as her hotelkeeping skills: 'Miss Leahy will be greatly missed at the Commercial, where she was a favourite with the public, owing to her excellent management of the house, and her obliging manners'.[19] More telling than the posthumous adulation of female LVA members, perhaps, is the fact that the its journals start to refer to their readers in gender-inclusive terms. Members are no longer addressed as 'brothers' and women are routinely represented in the 'Trade Personality' profiles, personal gossip column and Licensing Court reports.

The LVA's equivocal reaction to the Minogue case can be seen in the context of this shifting era in its relationship to female publicans. On the one hand, the LVA confined its female members' value to socially acceptable, middle-class roles for women: their 'obliging manners' and 'industriousness'. At the same time, there was a growing awareness that the very qualities that made female publicans 'good women' could also be exploited for the benefit of the trade as a whole. If the male-dominated LVA felt women threatened its territory, it began to appreciate the value of using the growing female presence to advantage.

For example, an 1884 obituary for Mrs Sarah Uggles, of the Dover Hotel, Carlton, lamented the landlady's passing as a loss to the industry itself:

> [She] conducted her house in such a manner as to gain for her the warm esteem of any man who had the real welfare of the Licensed Victuallers at heart. She was good, she was honest, she was truthful, she has gone. I would we had many more like her.[20]

The theme of female publicans being a credit to the trade becomes a constant refrain, eventually, by the 1920s, drowning out the condescending quips about the deficiencies of womanhood.

By representing female publicans as kind-hearted, sweet-natured, maternally disposed, honest and industrious, the LVA had found a useful shield against the battle-axe of temperance's conviction that there was no such thing as a 'respectable publican'. As Sydney's Reverend Vanderkisk thundered from the pulpit in 1877: 'Where *can* be the respectability of a hateful and disastrous and unnecessary trade in poisons?'[21] With increasingly clear conviction, the LVA answered: in the unimpeachably feminine characteristics of the women who kept hotels. By 1935, Mrs Lillian Alice Boyhan's obituary witnesses the clear departure from that anonymous 'lady hotelkeeper' whose membership fee was returned for want of character. Mrs Boyhan, second daughter of Mrs A. Murphy, 'that widely esteemed licensee', died at age thirty-four while the proprietress of the Graham Family Hotel, Port Melbourne: 'She was noted for her fine personal qualities and was regarded as a hotelkeeper who, by zeal and high ideals of citizenship, set a standard by which the industry aspires to be judged'.[22] Further entering into a dialogue with the temperance claim that the liquor trade preyed on the impoverished bodies and souls of society's weakest members, Mrs Boyhan's obituary concluded, 'By her death, the poor of Port Melbourne have lost a compassionate and generous friend'.

Female publicans' broader involvement in community affairs was also trumpeted as a sign of the trade's civic responsibility: Mrs Coleman of the Stockade Hotel, Carlton, was congratulated for her contribution to various auxiliary movements, including being vice-president of the Anthonians, a fund-raising group for St Anthony's Home, Kew. The

Vigilante praised Mrs Coleman as a 'capable manageress ... noted for success in organising'.[23] Thus women were no longer merely recognised for their dutiful support of the activities of their publican husbands. They were now identified and promoted as agents of social improvement and uplift.

The LVA's anti-temperance strategy of elevating the position of its female members distinguished it from liquor trade actions in other states. In South Australia, that state's Licensed Victuallers' Association sacrificed its female publicans, along with barmaids, when legislation to restrict women's licence-holding capacities was introduced in 1908. By 1930, the LVA was prepared to make headlines of 'Women as Licensees—Position in Victoria':

> Rarely a sitting of the Licensing Court passes in Melbourne at which licences are not granted to women ... [there is] no parallel to Victoria's system of liquor control ... [women] impart a refining influence to licensed premises and are jealous for the reputation of their calling. Moreover, they are frequently insistent that their husbands or sons, as the case may be, display an intelligent interest in domestic questions of trade.[24]

Victorian industry leaders thus made the tactical decision to emphasise the positive effect that women—constructed as models of restraint, refinement and domestic control—could have over the known excesses of the trade in liquor. Some Victorian temperance campaigners conceded in 1925 that 'In the field of politics we have been but amateurs, while the Liquor Trade, who long ago declared "our trade our politics", have so far easily defeated us'.[25] Playing 'the good woman' as a trump card, rather than abandoning her as a fatal flaw, was a risky but ultimately expedient political flourish.

But the LVA's stance did not carry rhetorical weight alone. As a valuable political asset, female publicans gained a public visibility commensurate with their actual numerical representation in the industry. No longer were female licensees the trade's honourable but silent partners; increasingly, their own aspirations surpassed the traditional association with Ladies Committees, fund-raising events and annual balls where women's ornamental value was emphasised in reports of 'beautiful costumes adorning a galaxy of feminine loveliness'.[26] The issue of female licensees' under-representation in the LVA was raised as early as 1884, when the *Advocate*'s 'Trade Gossip' columnist reported that the number of South Australian 'landladies' holding membership of the SALVA was increasing, though they 'do not participate in the working business of the body'. This event had prompted a Victorian male member to question whether women could be committee members of the LVA. 'Why not, indeed!', the columnist writes. He confirmed that there was nothing in the rules to prevent such an occurrence: 'and we are not certain in our own mind that the presence of a few ladies with minds of their own at the committee meeting might not be productive of some useful hints being given to the somewhat apathetic members, who take things a trifle too easily'.[27] The first separate Ladies Committee, established in 1900, was largely responsible for arranging social events, although 'they were also active in canvassing for new members and seeking out subscriptions of lapsed members'.[28]

In 1910, a rival association to the LVA, the Hotelkeepers' Union of Victoria, was established to represent the particular interests of licensees. The HUV felt that the LVA—with all its pomp and ceremony—had come to exclusively represent the economic needs and social aspirations of wealthy hotel landlords at the expense of workaday tenants. The HUV's membership base soon outstripped the influential but narrowly constituted LVA. Although the HUV amalgamated with the LVA in the early 1920s, the grass-roots revolt voiced by the HUV fundamentally changed the agenda and conformation of the twentieth-century version of the association. Committee members were more likely to be elected from the ranks of licensees, rather than landlords, and significantly, women were targeted as new members, 'an issue which had always created problems for the old LVA'.[29]

After the impact of the amalgamation with the HUV, which was indeed more successful in recruiting female members than the old-guard LVA, female licensees began to use their 'success in organising' to become office bearers alongside their male colleagues in suburban branches of the association. In June 1920, Mrs L. McLean was elected as secretary of the Fitzroy chapter. By 1930, at a 'Historic Gathering of State Hotelkeepers' sponsored by the LVA to discuss aspects of the trade, including tourism, taxation and hotel engineering, the list of delegates published in the *Vigilante* was remarkable for its strong representation of women.[30]

If the 1880s can be characterised as a decade in which the LVA strove to reconcile its ambivalent attitude to women in the industry, the 1930s was a time when female publicans had won the public relations war. At the 1933 festivities to mark the Silver Jubilee of the LVA, 'the activity and zeal of woman licensees was not overlooked'.[31] In August 1934, a luncheon at the Menzies was held by the LVA to thank the Ladies Committee for their efforts in organising the annual LVA Ball. In front of a crowd of 1000 guests, Mr P. H. Collins commented that 'the ladies' admirable service was proof of their intense interest in the association . . . they would be ready and eager at all times to participate in trade efforts'.[32] A year later, the eager ladies were in a sufficiently powerful position to poke fun at male members. When the Ladies Committee convened to plan the 1935 ball, they set up a sub-committee of five men even though 'these were mere men and were handicapped by ignorance of matters on which the ladies were experts. (Laughter).'[33] The times had changed, and so had the culture of the hotel trade's internal organisation (see Plate 11).

By 1940, female publicans were speaking publicly on matters of a political nature. In September 1940, the Melbourne *Herald* ran an article

11. 'LVA Ladies' at their annual ball, Bendigo Town Hall, Victoria, 1948. Gloria Fry (then Cooney) is fifth from the right.

entitled 'Women Hotel Licensees Defend Spinsters' Rights' in which 'Melbourne women licensees' commented on a New South Wales High Court ruling that an unmarried woman was not eligible for a licence under the Liquor Act.[34] Miss E. Hutton, licensee of the Duke of Kent Hotel, lashed out at the decision:

> Of course a spinster should be allowed to hold a hotel licence. Being single shouldn't have anything to do with it, as long as the woman is old enough and sensible enough. Actually, the best licensees are women. A woman can handle men much better and with much more tact than a man can. And, as licensee, you need tact—plenty of it.

In a fascinating twist on the New South Wales High Court's position, the article revealed that Miss Hutton was in fact married but was known in the hotel trade by her maiden name. Mrs E. E. Mitchell, of the Swanston Family Hotel, asked: 'If they are business women, why shouldn't spinsters hold licences?' Mrs Maie Hickey, of the Hotel Houston, was more circumspect: 'It is a question that needs some going into. A lot would depend on the person.' Mrs Hickey's response suggests that female licensees were now prepared to be outspoken about the rights of their sex, something which did not happen in Minogue's case sixty years earlier. However, they also voiced the same code of reason that the LVA claimed for the industry generally: professionalism, individual character, good sense and the reformative powers of responsible women.

It was not until the second half of the twentieth century that female publicans began to go one step further with these claims and use their hotelkeeping backgrounds to launch political careers of their own. Margaret Card, Mayor of Ballan Shire in 2001, is one such woman whose public life began as a local publican. She was also a Labor candidate for the seat of Ballarat in the 1998 federal election. Dawn Fraser was elected as the Labor member for Balmain in the New South Wales parliament in 1988, after careers as an Olympic swimmer and publican.

Thus female publicans in Victoria, whether by keeping their heads down, riding the wave of the cult of respectability or speaking the conventional language of commerce, managed to maintain their position within the hotel trade through turbulent times. Ultimately, when women's ability to be politically active became more socially acceptable, this resilience enabled female publicans to increase their profile and status in the trade's chief representative body itself, and indeed, cast their 'organising' net more widely. This position of political strength derived in large part from the public support female hotelkeepers received from their male peers. The Licensed Victuallers' Association did not make an ally of female publicans in the late nineteenth century, defending their legitimacy as licence holders, because it fundamentally supported 'women's rights'. Rather, in the battle for political territory between the forces of reform and those of conservatism, the LVA realised that traditional concepts of virtuous womanhood could be used to combat wider fears of moral disorder and economic uncertainty. Its decision to patronise female publicans was, however, inspired by a force within the liquor industry that was far more powerful than the LVA.

The Brewers

WHEN PARLIAMENT WAS FIRST considering the ramifications of the Minogue case in late 1884, Premier James Service made public the fact that he had been personally lobbied by a group of women who threatened him with a trip to the Privy Council should his government not support the cause of married female publicans. In the absence of a record of this meeting, we can only assume that female publicans issued this warning themselves—organised, angry and acting independently of the LVA. But it appears that the hastily drawn up Amending Act, which preserved married women's licences beyond 31 December 1884, was not exclusively inspired by a mob of maverick women.

On 26 November 1884, the *Argus* reported a meeting of the executive of the LVA held the day before. According to this account, the executive agreed to make representations to the government to shield those married women disabled by the Minogue decision.[1] Two days later, the same paper published a letter to the editor by 'One Who Knows'— probably a woman, for men routinely signed their names to such correspondence. The letter-writer objected to the reporting of the LVA meeting, stating that her intention was to 'give honour where honour is due'. The credit for the bill didn't belong to the LVA executive, stated the one who knew: 'The facts are these. Mr G. D. Carter, seeing the danger impending over a large number of deserving persons, and that the association showed no signs of any intention to avert it, called a meeting of the leading brewers at his office.' The letter-writer concluded, 'those who appreciate generous and potent aid timeously rendered' desire the truth known.[2]

Godfrey Downes Carter, a director of Carlton and United Brewery and outspoken member of the Liberty and Property Defence League, was a man with considerable clout. He had also been the Conservative MLA for St Kilda from 1877 to 1883, was the Mayor of Melbourne from 1884 to 1885, and went on to become the member for West Melbourne from 1885 to 1894. The brewers assembled by Carter resolved to send a deputation to the Premier to ask for a short bill to be drawn up to protect married women licensees. No doubt, this band of prominent Melbourne brewers exerted more pressure on the government than a few refractory women threatening a trip to London.

The vested interests of any state government in maintaining a healthy hotel trade had long been the thorn in the side of temperance campaigners. International temperance publications regularly compiled vast statistical calculations of the 'drink bill', designed to prove that the direct and indirect loss to the economy as a result of intemperance far outweighed the revenue raised through liquor taxes.[3] While successive Victorian parliaments were prepared to tinker around the margins of the industry (barmaids being the notable sacrifice to temperance lobbying) and to speak the language of 'temperance economics', at the end of the day no government could risk alienating the power brokers of the liquor trade. As brewers stood at the pinnacle of the liquor lobby, their opposition to or support for any proposed legislative move was crucial to its success. This takes no great Machiavellian intellect to deduce. But it is worth speculating why brewers chose the question of married women's licences to play their political hand, at a time when public debates were raging over other important industry issues such as local option and opening hours. To speak the language of capitalism, what was in it for them?

The 1905 Select Committee into Tied Houses: Reading between the lines

In Britain, to which the Victorian parliament was constantly looking for political precedent, brewers were members of the propertied classes. With greater financial resources than the political parties, the English and Irish brewing industry constituted a formidable pressure group that allied itself with Conservative candidates and mobilised working-class votes through public houses. Among the shareholders of British brewing empires were many prominent members of society: in 1904, 25 per cent of the House of Lords and 20 per cent of the Commons declared their interest in breweries. In New Zealand, too, a disproportionate number of

nineteenth-century brewers were mayors and councillors, and the brewing industry regularly funded political parties.[4]

The economic and social landscape of brewing was significantly
less salubrious in Australia. Early colonial brewers were ostracised by
members of the respectable trades and professions, largely due to the
inferior nature of the product. It took many decades of trial and mostly
error before the scientific and technical difficulties of climate, transport,
storage and contamination in rugged Australian conditions were overcome. Moreover, the poor quality of colonial beer was highlighted by the
fact that it was sold at hotels at a discount price 'in an endeavour to avoid
total loss to the brewer'.[5] This led to claims that brewers encouraged
drunkenness. With a cheap and nasty product, known to be occasionally
fatal to the consumer, Australian brewing was off to an inauspicious start.

But the industry's bad reputation did not quash the entrepreneurial
spirit of prospective brewers or quench the thirst for local product. By
1889, there were 307 breweries operating in the colonies. In 1874, there
were almost 150 breweries in Victoria, thirty-one of which were located
in Melbourne. In the 1860s, Bendigo alone had twenty-five breweries, by
far the most of any Australian country town.[6] The 1880s witnessed the
peak of independent, family-owned brewing companies. In Australia, industrial pre-eminence was achieved through the amalgamation of these
small-fry companies. Swallowed up by the larger firms—Carlton and
United Breweries began its feeding frenzy in 1907 with the take-over of
six local breweries—the leaders of the increasingly capital-intensive
industry took their place among wealthy and influential industrialists of
the late nineteenth and early twentieth century.

Though their economic clout may have gone unchallenged, Victorian
brewers were never completely free from their earlier reputation for
encouraging vice and disease among the drinking population. While the
beer may have improved in quality, and indeed became the preferred
beverage of the new nation, brewers remained the focus of blame for
moral and social affliction. As in other countries, temperance reformers
attacked brewers as the 'heartless profiteers from others' misfortunes'.[7]
Unable to turn the tide of brewing production, opponents began to focus
on questionable industry practices. The most widely criticised feature
of the vast brewing empires was the 'tied-house system', which some
temperance advocates referred to as the 'octopus grip' of big brewery
interests on hotel property.[8]

The practice of tying houses had a well-established heritage in the
United States, where saloons were almost exclusively indentured to

brewers by the turn of the twentieth century, and in Britain where 75 per cent of public houses were tied by 1900. Ireland was the exception, as the brewing giant Guinness made it a policy not to buy public houses or bankroll hoteliers.[9] Although breweries employed a variety of methods of tying, the principle remained the same: breweries offered financial backing to tenanted licensees in exchange for exclusivity deals to sell their product. In 1905, under pressure to stem the monopolistic tendencies of the industry, the Victorian government convened a Select Committee to report on the system of tied houses that had become so integral to the liquor trade. The report of the Select Committee provides vital clues as to the close relationship between brewers and female publicans.

The tied-house system was entrenched in Australia by the 1820s, and reached its zenith in the 1880s boom. Andrew McCracken, director of the brewing company that bore his family name, estimated to the Select Committee that 50–60 per cent of Melbourne's city and suburban hotels were tied in 1905. In Bendigo and Ballarat, where the Select Committee also took evidence, it appears that almost all public houses were tied in some way. Under the most common application of the system in Victoria, a brewery would lend money to someone who wished to take over the lease of a hotel. The loan could amount to 50 per cent of the price for 'ingoings', which included lease, licence, chattels and goodwill, in exchange for a commitment from the licensee that only the draught beer of that brewery would be sold. (Bottled beer, which made up a tiny proportion of overall beer sales, could generally be purchased from other breweries.) The large breweries, such as McCrackens, Carlton and Castlemaine, would also take over the lease of the hotel in their own name, and the indentured licensee would then pay rent to the brewery, not the owner. Breweries also owned the freehold of many hotels and made the exclusive purchase of their product a requirement of tenancy. Some breweries had a complex array of legal documents that a prospective client was bound to sign, including power-of-attorney and licence transfer blanks, while other companies, most notably the Bendigo firm of Cohn Bros Brewers, proudly attested to the fact that they required nothing more of their lessees than the verbal promise to buy their beer.[10]

Most witnesses before the Select Committee of 1905 painted a strikingly similar portrait of the type of publican who approached the breweries for assistance: 'A man with a small amount of capital, and unable to borrow money from anyone'.[11] Thomas Parker, manager of Carlton Brewery, concluded that 'the brewer is practically a banker as well as a brewer'.[12] As banks were often reluctant to lend money to hoteliers, due to the high incidence of licence transfer, bankruptcy and fire, the brewers had stepped in as financiers to serve their own commercial purposes and the interests of the industry generally. For women 'with commercial ambitions', otherwise disadvantaged by systems of international finance, the existence of an alternative form of banking had long proved expedient.[13]

By the turn of the century, critics of the liquor trade were starting to pinpoint the tied-house system as one of the chief causes of depravity in the industry. Opponents claimed that there was a far greater number of licence transfers in tied houses; that the quality of beer sold in tied houses was inferior to that sold in free houses; and that licensees in tied houses were forced to engage in unlawful practices such as out-of-hours trading in order to turn enough profit to pay both their lease and the interest charged by the brewers to whom they were tied. Temperance campaigners also alleged that tied houses were more likely to be the 'lower class of houses', 'improperly conducted', frequented by a 'bad class of trade' and situated in 'poorer localities'. The abolition of the tied-house system through an act of parliament, it was claimed, would curtail a good deal of the nefarious social activities and corrupt business practices that fostered widespread drunkenness and vice.[14]

When representatives of the large breweries were asked by the Select Committee what the effect of a bill to abolish the tied-house system would be, they generally agreed that many decent, hard-working, respectable publicans would be put out of business. Moreover, they claimed that many such folk would never be afforded the opportunity to enter the trade in the first place. Brewers argued that the tied-house system was the key element in ensuring democratic entry to the trade, which would otherwise be the sole domain of that 'better class of men' who ran the wealthier free houses. Robert Lemon particularly pressed home the message that a good hotelkeeper's skills did not equate with access to financial assets and that respectability was commonly found in the 'class of men' who could least afford to engage in business and thereby 'better themselves'. He testified that 'provided a man attends his business and conducts it wisely and properly, I do not know of any business which yields a fairer return for well-directed effort than our own'. Abolishing the tie, he argued, would disadvantage the efforts of the respectable, decent and socially aspiring 'class of men'. Even Edwin Graves, the metropolitan Licensing Inspector and opponent of the tied-house system, had to concede that 'the publicans of Melbourne, take them as a class, are a very respectable body of men'.[15]

Despite the uniformly masculine references to hotelkeepers, it is clear that the Select Committee was in fact fishing for a connection between 'low' houses and female licensees. There was evidently a suspicion that many of the tied houses were run by women, and that this fact may have in some way accounted for the high rate of licence transfer, the poor character of the clientele and the ill-conducted nature of the businesses. James Newman, managing director of Castlemaine Brewery, was the first witness to let slip that the 'class of men' who ran tied houses often included women. Asked to defend the claim that tied houses made profits for the breweries at the often ruinous expense of the publican, Newman responded that he had seen tied houses make some people very wealthy, particularly those who wouldn't have had the opportunity to 'go in' otherwise:

> I have known cases, particularly where widows have been left with children, where they have gone into a hotel and made money, and brought up their children well ... I know of numberless cases [in the country] where small houses are properly conducted and the people are making a good living, where they could not do it by selling pins and needles and cabbages and lollies.[16]

Other respondents soon echoed Newman's glib reference to the alternatives available to such women.

Magnus Cohn, when asked why there were so many licence transfers in tied houses, stated that there were in fact very few transfers in his company's hotels. As an example of the sort of tenant Cohn Bros supported, he cited a recent transfer from a tenant who had held the licence for eighteen years: 'she lost her husband about eight years ago; she brought up a big family and is now able to retire. They had nothing when they went into the place.'[17] Thomas Pritchard, an independent Bendigo brewer, argued that the tied-house system was beneficial to the industry generally because it afforded the brewer some discretion in choosing a tenant:

> I have been able to bring in persons that I knew well, who were on their uppers, as the saying is. I have sympathized with them, and put them in the way of making their living ... I have a number of widows who are incapable of making a living anywhere else.[18]

Having said this, Pritchard was then asked the first direct question about women in the trade. The ubiquitous David Gaunson asked the brewer whether the number of men or women was greater in his hotels; Pritchard responded that the number of male and female licensees was 'about equal' and that the women were mostly widows. The subtext of the Select Committee's enquiry was now out in the open.

Never one to beat around the bush, Gaunson then proceeded to throw the next witness an explicitly value-laden question. Of Bendigo brewer John Illingworth he asked, 'Do men or women make the best tenants?' Illingworth equivocated: 'It is a difficult problem. I prefer a man who knows his business.'[19] But despite Illingworth's dodge, the issue of women in the industry was now well and truly on the table. The chairman asked the next witness, the pro-abolition Sub-Inspector of Police and Licensing in Bendigo, Alexander Gray, to estimate how many single men or women were running hotels in the district. Gray testified that, while there would not be more than five unmarried men, 'There are lots of widows in the Barkly division; out of 34 licensees there are 23 women'. However, Gray commented that it was difficult to say how many of these women were single because 'There are lots who are called "Mrs" that there is a doubt about'. Evidently, in the hothouse conditions of the temperance-influenced day—or perhaps to clear up any moral suspicions that both patrons and pulpit might have about single women selling alcohol—unmarried female publicans chose to obscure their marital identities. Some might have been living in de facto relationships. There was no need to disguise their gender completely, however, and Inspector Gray could readily cite figures as to the number of female licensees presently working in Bendigo: 44 out of 71 in Darling ward, 32 out of 57 in Golden Square and 23 out of 42 in Eaglehawk. From these figures, we can conclude that women ran 59 per cent of Bendigo's hotels in 1905.

When the Select Committee angled for a connection between these women, tied houses and the more ill-kept hotels of the district, Inspector Gray could not give a simple response, for he was evidently sympathetic to the conditions of many publicans' lives:

> A good deal [of how a house is run] depends on the circumstances. It might be a woman without a family. There are many cases within my knowledge where they do not employ anybody. One woman living in one hotel and she is housemaid, barmaid, cook and everything else.

Gray was clear on one point: no woman had been refused a renewal of a licence on grounds of character. Almost despite himself, given his desire to see the end of the tied-house system, Gray conceded that tenants in 'low' or 'poor' houses could be decent people doing good trade.[20] If female licensees were going to be the weak link that brought down the tied-house system, it was not going to be Inspector Gray who implicated them.

Although the Select Committee's report recommended that the tied-house system be abolished in the interests of a more respectable, better-managed hotel industry, no mention was made of women in its final reckoning. The connection between female licensees (particularly young and single ones), poorly conducted premises and tied houses was never firmly, or even remotely, established and the Select Committee did not see fit to include any reference at all to female publicans in its summation. Only a very long bow could be drawn between their resolution (which seems to have been decided on the basis of the brewers versus the rest) and the pervasive presence of female licensees in tied houses.

As a rule, tied publicans may have enjoyed less autonomy than free-hold licensees. However, women obviously benefited from their indenture in several ways. First, tied houses were generally small and thus required smaller capital ingoings. Second, women were less likely to have the assets required to 'go in' to the trade without financial assistance which, despite the advances in women's property rights in the late nineteenth and early twentieth centuries, was still difficult to secure. Finally, breweries offered other 'services' such as weekly or monthly tenancies and company lawyers to assist with paperwork. Such measures were criticised by opponents of the tie as preying on and protracting the vulnerability of impoverished and under-skilled publicans. Yet these business aids probably did assist those proficient if impecunious women who wanted an entry into the trade, whether for short-term survival or long-term profit. Despite the recommendations of the Select Committee, no bill was ever introduced into parliament to abolish the tied-house system. And when the new Licensing Act was debated in 1906, references to female licensees tended to follow the 'worthy widow' motif that had been so persuasively employed by the brewers a year earlier.

Knights of industry: Brewers to the rescue

It is not hard to see why female publicans needed brewers for their continued access to the hotel industry. But why did the brewers go in to bat for female publicans, at a time when every move of the trade was shadowed by temperance criticism? The report of the Select Committee on Tied Houses makes it clear that married women held a substantial number of the licences for tied houses. Therefore it was in the economic interests of the brewing companies to support their tenants. Should married women have been disqualified from licence holding, this would have dealt a major blow to the investments of those who had backed such

women to enter the trade. With a married woman's licence being automatically extinguished, there would be little chance of a brewer recoup-
ing any of the capital loan or interest.

Furthermore, the property value of a hotel building was very much
determined by its status as a *licensed* premises. In 1906, when compensation for licence deprivation was being debated in parliament, it was
estimated that the property value of a hotel decreased by 60 per cent
without a licence.[21] A brewer landlord suddenly without a tenant would
have certainly been looking to re-licence the premises, and patently,
married women fortified the pool of prospective transferees for licences.
Brewers only stood to lose from legislation that severely restricted female
licence holding.

But immediate economic self-interest was not the only reason for
brewers to support the rights of married women. In the heightened moral
climate of temperance agitation, brewers realised that ideals of virtuous
femininity could in fact improve the reputation of the liquor trade. Ever
political in the defence of their industry, brewers increasingly looked to
'the good woman' principle to secure their ground in the rhetoric of
respectability and responsibility. Let us be clear on one thing: late-
nineteenth-century brewers—wealthy, powerful and socially conservative—were by no means feminist sympathisers. Indeed, through its
official mouthpiece, the *Australian Brewers' Journal*, the brewing industry launched a vicious and highly sexist attack on temperance women. In
a campaign of public lampooning, 'The old ladies of the WCTU . . . the
bespectacled prim persons' were satirised as mean-spirited, humourless,
dull, irrational and pitiable crones.[22] Suffice to say that the brewing industry was inclined to verbally kick any enemy to its cause, and Woman was
a favourite political football.

In accord with the LVA's decision to promote its female constituents
as a credit to the trade, the brewers similarly voiced the utmost respect
for female publicans. Obituaries published in the *Australian Brewers'
Journal* express their customary lament at the passing of a 'well-known
landlady . . . connected with the trade for many years', but reports of
living female publicans were equally effusive. In a 1906 article detailing
the renovations recently carried out to the Queen's Arms Hotel, Swanston
Street, the journal reported that the hotel had once been licensed to Mr
Hawkins, who had sold the business to Mr Ben Champion 'whose widow,
Mrs E. Champion (Mr Hawkins' niece), has carried on the business to the
present day in a manner that has earned the profound respect of the
whole community, which respect is also shared by her family of good

citizens'.[23] The article continued to tap this rich vein of homage to the exemplary reputation of the female licensee:

> As a record place of business, having been conducted by members of one family for just half-a-century, the Queen's Arms has, we think, but one rival in Victoria—the Sir John Franklin Hotel, Collingwood, for about as many years in the Davison family. Mrs Davison, like Mrs Champion, is still with us, and both ladies amply give the lie to the aspersions cast at members of the trade by teetotal agitators.

With a final rhetorical flourish, the article concludes: 'When the new up-to-date and palatial building throws open its doors to the public, it will be the fervent hope of all of us that the present estimable licensee may long be spared to continue its management'. Mrs Elizabeth Champion did indeed meet the felicitous hopes of the liquor trade's chief stakeholders: she held the licence for the Queen's Arms Hotel for twenty years, passing it to her son William in 1916. Mrs Elizabeth Davison retired from the Sir John Franklin Hotel in 1905, after forty-three years as licensee.

Brewers knew that female publicans made good tenants for their houses: they worked hard, often had families to raise and had less commercial autonomy than male licensees, whose access to other lines of credit was not so precarious. It was also convenient, no doubt, that female publicans were substantially under-represented in the LVA and therefore lacked the organisational strength to challenge the terms of their indenture. The potency of the alliance between brewers and female publicans can be deduced from the fact that, as the practice of house-tying reached its pinnacle in the period from the 1880s to the 1920s, so too the numerical supremacy of female licensees in the hotel industry was firmly established. By twisting the arm of government in 1884, the brewers guaranteed a future supply of legally certified but economically impotent tenants.

In the battle to claim the moral high ground of civic and industry responsibility, female publicans became unwitting (though no doubt grateful) pawns. To influential representatives of the liquor trade, the presence of women raised the moral and ethical tone of hotelkeeping while offering proof that the hotel industry was run along lines of openness and decency. Female publicans were cast as industrious married women or widows and as members of a business class, both of which conveyed respectability in the late nineteenth and early twentieth century. They elicited a positive response from the male power-brokers of the day because they upheld the class interests of the petty bourgeois (self help, social mobility, independence) while at the same time allowing a chivalrous sense of manly duty and decorum towards honest, upright women and their dependent children. In the end, the trade defenders' victory served to secure the fortunes of female licensees, particularly married ones who had the most claims to feminine prudence and rectitude.

But fundamentally, such definitions of the 'natural' gender order rendered women the passive beneficiaries of male largesse. Though the discourse about 'destitute but deserving' womanhood ultimately protected married female publicans' legal rights, it also denied the full range of professional and aspirational reasons why many women chose hotel-keeping as a career. Thus the legal agency of female publicans, established in 1821, was not matched by political agency until at least a century later when hotel women began to demand an autonomous voice in industry affairs. Received notions of virtuous femininity and appropriate roles for women shaped the public image of female hotelkeepers. But, ultimately, once women got their 'in', they were able to shape the social institution over which they were given the legal and moral authority to preside.

PART III

'A First Class Family Hotel . . . Furnished Like a Home'

Hotel Space, a Woman's Place

Mapping Elizabeth Wright

ELIZABETH WRIGHT APPEARS TO HAVE been a good businesswoman. In 1866, as a widow with a three-year-old son, Mrs Wright took over the publican's licence for the Frankston Hotel in the Melbourne bayside town of Frankston. She ran a successful public house for nine years until, on 14 August 1875, she was murdered in the hotel's dining room by her business partner, Henry Howard. Wright's barman, Mr Harman, was also stabbed to death in the incident. Wright died of her wounds on the dining room floor, in front of the hearth; Harman died outside the door to the public bar. Multiple testimonies in the coronial inquest, which would ultimately lead to Howard's murder conviction and hanging at the Old Melbourne Gaol, bring such spatial details to the fore. It might have been the forensic particulars that interested the court, but for the historian, the coronial blueprint of Elizabeth Wright's murder provides a unique glimpse into the domestic arrangements of nineteenth-century hotel life, giving us a rare opportunity to see social practice peeping out from behind value-laden assumptions about the gendered nature of public space.[1]

It is not clear when Elizabeth Wright and Henry Howard formalised their business arrangements, but liquor licensing records show that the previous publican, Henry Simpson, had transferred the licence to the Frankston Hotel to the widow Wright in 1866. Simpson later transferred the licence for the hotel on the opposite side of the street, also known as the Frankston Hotel, to Henry Howard. Howard's wife was the licensee at a hotel in Mornington, where she lived with their children, but Howard resided at his Frankston establishment. Somehow, within these hazy arrangements, the records reveal that, instead of trading as competitors, Wright and Howard formed a business partnership and, by the time of the 1875 murders, they co-owned the two Frankston Hotels.

The coronial testimony of Mrs Harman, sometime hotel cook and widow of the barman, discloses that Wright and Howard were preparing to sell their establishments. Howard had drawn up an agreement that would buy Wright out of their partnership for a paltry £100. He presented this document to Wright in the dining room of her hotel, in the presence of Mrs Harman. Wright flatly rejected the offer. According to Mrs Harman's testimony, Howard was incensed by Wright's recalcitrance and warned 'It's the best thing you can do, little woman'. When Wright held fast, Howard promised 'It would be war to the knife'. On the night of her murder, Wright, her by now 12-year-old son George, Mr and Mrs Harman and their son, and Howard, were eating together in the dining room when Mrs Harman commented that she had been unable to find the meat knife to prepare the chops for the evening meal. Mr Harman suggested he would sleep at the hotel that night, as he had all week because of Howard's threats to his uncooperative business partner. After dinner, Elizabeth remained in the dining room; Mrs Harman and her son went home; young George retired to his bedroom, located off the dining room; and Harman returned to the bar.

The barman was serving a customer when he heard screams and ran back into the dining room. The customer also rounded the bar and, on entering the dining room, he found Wright lying on the floor at the feet of Howard, with the missing knife beside her, George crying, and Harman holding his chest. Harman managed to stagger out of the dining room, past the bar and out the front door in pursuit of Howard, where he died on the threshold of the licensed premises. Before his arrest, Howard boasted to the adjoining storekeepers that 'I've come of a race who take no insult from any man ... even if I should come to the gallows'. Any man, in this case, was a woman.

The spatial implications of the murder comprise a substantial amount of the sworn testimony in the ensuing coronial inquiry, injecting a note of Cluedo-esque melodrama to the affair: Mr Howard in the dining room with the chops knife. Thanks to the Coroner, Elizabeth Wright's murder lets us see how the Australian public house, as a physical and social location, encouraged the participation of women as hotelkeepers. Although several works have studied the architectural features of Australian hotel interiors, there has been no attempt to understand the way in which the creation of space—both materially and metaphorically—affects people's sense of entitlement, belonging and group identity. As the Frankston Hotel's licensee, Elizabeth Wright patently saw herself as more than just an institutional helpmeet, a nominal insider. By defending the worth of her business and her right to live and work at her licensed premises, she positioned herself as the genuine centre of gravity in the house.

While female publicans may have been marginal to the political structures that regulated and judged their characters and livelihoods, women like Elizabeth Wright were nonetheless drafted into the social landscape of the hotel. As we have seen, domesticity was a key category in the creation and organisation of the Australian hotel, as the language of late-nineteenth-century advertisements commonly reveals: 'a first-class family hotel ... furnished like a home'.[2] The public house also accommodated women in its function as a broad-based service provider to regional and working-class communities, largely male. If female publicans were both notionally and practically associated with the hotel's domestic profile, how did women themselves use that social category to expand the physical scope and creative possibilities of their own lives? How did women determine the meaning of hotel space? And how did women make the pub—with its peculiarly elastic blend of public and private space—their own? In terms of personal identity, family life, friendship circles and community networks, how can we imagine the hotel as a 'female domain'?

As the facilitators of every manner of exchange which centred on the nineteenth-century hotel—providing newspapers, organising transport, hosting clerics and doctors, sponsoring sporting events, lending money, distributing mail, housing civic meetings—female publicans were socially active to a remarkable degree. Their experience both reinforces and contests the trenchant association between the public sphere and social power. On the one hand, women who kept a public house definitely achieved a greater degree of cultural visibility, social esteem and financial independence than their sisters who engaged in non-commercial house-keeping in private homes. Occupied in the public realm of the market-place, female publicans not only had access to socially valued knowledge and resources, but also managed and controlled them. And they were financially recompensed for their services. On the other hand, their success and status rested largely on the fact that, as a public institution, the hotel relied on the values, skills and knowledges that were associated with the domestic sphere and maternal role. The function of the public house was precisely to provide the physical, spiritual and even moral virtues of a home life to those outside the family circle.

A publican was expected to be a provider, a listener, a confidante, an adviser, a moderator, a negotiator, an ally, a witness and a guardian. As such, the role of the publican owed as much to unique codes of community as the universal mercantile values associated with 'men's business'. The relationship between public house host and guest was at once personal and intimate, yet mediated by a financial transaction and thus free from the responsibilities and duties of familial or marital relationships. Besides providing a quasi-home to paying customers, the hotel was also the permanent domicile of the licensee and her family. By managing the public space, the hotelkeeper was also tending to her own domestic affairs. Thus the 'publicity' of the female publican was not derived from her organised and potentially subversive attempt to escape from the ideological prison of the private sphere. Nor was her public influence predicated on higher education, political activities and professional networks. The female publican was powerful because she was able to command respect, authority and legitimacy in a vast array of social relationships, commercial transactions and human exchanges, all located within her own home.

The Coroner in Elizabeth Wright's inquest was evidently more concerned with the geography of events than with making either celebratory remarks about her mothering or moralistic character judgements about the nature of Wright and Howard's 'partnership'. Although witnesses told the court that Howard and Wright were 'never known . . . to sleep in the same bed' and that Wright was 'given to drink' but was 'steadier this month than she had been previously', there is nothing in the Coroner's discussion or verdict which suggests that Elizabeth Wright was transgressing any social or sexual boundaries by running a hotel and engaging in business dealings with a male associate.

By mapping the murder of Elizabeth Wright, the Coroner's singular emphasis on forensic particulars thus elicits the sort of uncommon detail that can help flesh out notions of both public *and* private space within the social landscape of the Australian hotel. The bar, for example, figures as a significant focus of activities: the place from which the protective Harman is summoned, and around which witnesses must travel to enter the personal tragedy unfolding. The dining room is also important as the site of the last communal supper and the final struggle of the woman whose business sense—her refusal to be done out of the profits of her enterprise—would prove to be fatal. But before we are tempted to mark out conventional gender territories in this scenario, assigning the service counter the role of symbolic border between masculine space (the public bar out front) and feminine space (the living quarters out back), it is important to know something about the physical and social environment of the nineteenth-century hotel which offered women the chance to become domestic entrepreneurs.

'Open House'

PUBLIC HOUSES WERE VERILY a contradiction in terms. By law, Australian hotels were entirely public institutions, all areas being defined as 'public' for the purposes of the various Licensing Acts.[1] In practice, the spatial economy was a deceptive blend of social/public and personal/private space, access to which was determined by one's relationship to the institution. The publican's family, staff, lodgers, overnight guests, regular drinkers and casual drinkers all had a different status so far as entrance to the hotel's various 'public' and 'private' rooms was concerned. As places of public drinking, hotels were subject to high levels of statutory regulation; but as family dwellings, they were also sheltered by the law of the home: private property, individual responsibility and personal discretion. As a commercial enterprise, a hotel's success relied on its ability to provide a comfortable and convivial home-away-from-home to local or migratory populations. Similarly, the publican was both a businessperson and a neighbour; a service provider and a friend. As an institution, the public house was neither solely domestic nor entirely commercial: it was an 'intermediate institution'.[2] While many scholars have interpreted the appeal of the peculiar status of the public house/saloon for the predominantly male drinking clientele, the implications of this spatial indistinction for women have been less readily apparent. The blurring of spatial and social definitions in the pub helps us to understand why hotelkeeping was an attractive vocation for many women, otherwise limited, as they often were, by the ideologies and architectures of 'separate spheres'.

The earliest Australian hotels were generally not purpose-built commercial structures. Rather, they were the private residences of people who obtained a licence to sell liquor out of their own homes. This practice is in keeping with the traditional 'semi-public, semi-private' basis of commercial hospitality in Britain and the United States.[3] However, Australian public houses differed from their British and American counterparts in one fundamental respect. Until the 1960s, all places of public drinking were legally required to provide accommodation to travellers.[4] In Australia's early pub conditions, where the only things which distinguished a public house from a private home were 'a bar, a cellar and a sign', overnight guests typically ate with the licensee's family and slept in one of their bedrooms.[5]

By the 1830s, the distinction between the publican's dwelling and accommodation for guests had become more formalised, with licensing legislation dictating that hotels provide at least two sitting rooms and two bedrooms in addition to the residential rooms occupied by the family of the publican. In the Melbourne port suburb of Williamstown, the first house was also the district's first legal hotel; the Ship Inn hung out its sign in 1838. Women were quick to capitalise on the domesticated nature of the liquor trade. Sarah Baxter received a licence to sell liquor from her home in Sydney in 1798. She had arrived in Australia as a 14-year-old servant girl in 1792; six years later she had an illegitimate son, had built her own home, and was supporting herself and her child as a publican. Twenty-six women held the original licence to a hotel in metropolitan Melbourne, suggesting that Sarah Baxter's story was not exceptional.[6]

Hotel names, particularly in country areas, were testimony to the close connection between domesticity and public drinking: The Old House at Home, Our House Hotel, Retreat Inn, Harvest Home and numerous Travellers Rests, Half-Way Houses and Family Hotels. Country hotels were often situated on substantial properties that sustained domestic communities in their own right. At the Wattle Hill Hotel in seaside Apollo Bay, the hotel building consisted of a bar, lounge, kitchen, scullery, dining room and seven bedrooms, while the entire property supported beef and dairy cattle, a cheese factory and shop, vegetable garden and sale yards, an apple and pear orchard, a 'well kept and colourful flower garden', and work for seven staff. The grounds had designated areas for horse racing, a tennis club and rifle range. The Wattle Hill even employed a blacksmith on the property to make shoes for the farm's and mail coach's horses as well as making and maintaining tools and equipment for local settlers. Ruby McMinn, maid and waitress at the Wattle

Hill Hotel in 1913, remembers the establishment as a 'happy, industrious environment'.[7] Throughout the nineteenth century, hotels like the Wattle Hill provided a hostelry to travellers and local populations; literally, a house half-way between home and the next destination. For the perpetually rootless—transient single men moving to find work—such establishments *were* home.

Early hotels in Melbourne similarly associated their hospitality with the familiarity and comforts of domestic life, with names like Help Me Through the World Hotel, Nevertire Hotel, Angel Inn, Fail Me Never Hotel, Travellers Home, Happy Home Hotel and Strangers Home Hotel. Such names suggest the restorative powers of the home-away-from-home to the weary and alienated city-goer. Urban hotels were more likely to be purpose-built than their country cousins, but even in urban centres, pubs retained their own kitchen gardens, bread ovens and stock well into the nineteenth century. The British Queen Hotel in inner-city Fitzroy, built and run by Mrs Elisha Pearce from 1854 to 1869, was a 'single storey blue stone structure famous for its strawberry garden and fruit trees which extended to Ray Street while Pearce was the licensee'.[8] Similarly, The Bush Inn, Prahran, was renowned for its lyrical domesticity. The Bush Inn, established in 1854 by Mrs Storse, was celebrated as a 'shingled wooden house, wrapped in honeysuckle, and a cottage-garden of fox-gloves, hollyhocks, rosemary, thyme and lavender'. Mrs Storse's daughter, Evelina, was 'fairer even than her garden'; a road in Prahran bears her name.[9] The essentially domestic character of Australian pubs was retained until at least the mid-nineteenth century, and later in rural areas.[10]

While Happy Homes and Travellers Rests were overtaken by Commercials, Royals, Railways and Unions by the end of the nineteenth century, reflecting the dual processes of urbanisation and industrialisation, the domestic legacy of early hotel conditions was firmly entrenched in pub and civic culture. Until the 1880s, municipal voters' rolls designated hotels as 'houses' and hotelkeeping was classified as a 'domestic' occupation for taxation purposes until 1924. Colloquially, it was commonplace to refer to a hotel as a 'house' well into the twentieth century. Even today, as a century ago, the provision of accommodation is known as 'house trade'. While travellers in the automobile age may have preferred the modern provision of motels, boarders and staff continued to fill the bedrooms and dining rooms of many urban and rural hotels. Licensing regulations requiring the publican to live on the premises—a stipulation that existed on paper if not always in practice until the late 1960s—also ensured that hotels remained a functional domicile and extended the pre-industrial notion of a communal/commercial household well into the twentieth century. In legal terminology, hotel residents—including the publican and her family—were called 'inmates'.

The continuation of the residential function of Australian hotels beyond the nineteenth century stands in contrast to the situation in Britain. Where alehouses had traditionally mixed private living quarters with public drinking, by the beginning of the nineteenth century purpose-built drinking places were predominant. By the second half of the nineteenth century, one could not mistake a public house for any other building.[11] According to one historian, British pubs were 'architecturally and socially altered' to reflect the aspirations and aesthetics of bourgeois urbanity.[12] Respectability lay in the very distinction between public and private space. In Victoria, as the reign of the Licences Reduction Board was to underline, it was precisely the personalised, domestic character of the hotel that safeguarded its reputation as more than a mere dram-shop (see Plate 12).

In the latter half of the nineteenth century, Australian hotels continued to evolve as complex social institutions, as the buildings acquired more rooms to suit a variety of communal purposes. While the pre-1850s hotels were 'often like larger domestic buildings', the developing role of the pub as a centre for civic, community and political life meant that 'hotel bars and lounges [became] key spaces for defining social boundaries'.[13] Although there was an enormous variation in the size and fabrication of pubs—from tiny wayside wooden shanties to towering bluestone residential hotels—all shared the common purpose of supplying accommodation, shelter, food and drink, entertainment and social contact to the localities they serviced. Access to the location in which these services were provided was, however, dependent upon race, class and gender distinctions though such ground rules were by no means uniform.

As the hub of community life—particularly in country towns and working-class suburbs—hotels purveyed spaces for a broad range of leisure and civic pursuits: ballrooms, dancehalls, billiards and bagatelle rooms, even theatres, hair salons and bath-houses. Often, in addition to the core plan of public bar, parlour, dining room, kitchen, bedrooms and bathrooms, a hotel would have a built-on annexe in which these myriad public functions would be carried out. The largest and best-appointed hotels in the mid- to late nineteenth century became the centre of business, judicial, local government and mining transactions, while the more established hotels had concert rooms which attracted world-class singers, actors and lecturers.[14]

12. Interiors. Tallangatta Hotel, Victoria, 1954: bar (a), dining room (b), kitchen (c), saloon bar (d), bedroom (e).

Apart from public meeting space, hotels also opened their dining rooms (if small) and ballrooms (if grand) to a host of private functions: wedding receptions, baptisms, funerals. With hotels acting as both mortuary and labour ward, it is true to say that 'Life and death mingled at the inn'.[15] By law, nineteenth-century licensed premises could be used for morgues and inquests; by custom, hotels often ensured that a mid-wife was available to deliver the local citizenry. (This may or may not have been the hotelkeeper herself.) As the popularity of the Australian hotel reached its zenith by the turn of the century, women were riding the wave of that success. If many hotels were 'flashy and showy'—as one historian has described the vases of flowers, soft furnishings, curtains, art works and other decorative accoutrements adorning pubs of this era—this is no doubt a result of the increasing commercialisation of the industry. But it also reflects the influence of the escalating number of female licensees who called a hotel home.[16]

Hotels not only had the task of meeting the physical needs of settlers and settlement, but also of carving out the social distinctions of colonial culture through access to public space. By the late nineteenth and early twentieth centuries, the semi-public role of hotelkeeping had overtaken its semi-private role; that is, the hotel's primary social function was as a venue for leisure pursuits in a time of rapid urbanisation and industrialisation rather than as a hostelry in frontier conditions. Yet women's participation as the stage managers of that socialisation process continued apace, facilitated by the hotel's traditional domestic associations. As an intermediate institution—fundamentally attached to the commercial order yet offering essentially domestic services within a home environment—the hotel provided women with a space in which they could engage in business but not threaten core masculine occupations. Female publicans were 'public characters' to the extent that they organised social networks, participated in civic affairs, signed contracts and leases, managed financial transactions and employed staff, yet they performed all these financially remunerated tasks from the 'privacy' of their own homes.

Interior ambiguities: From snug to swill

If the hotel defied the notion of separateness institutionally, so too its own internal spatial arrangements worked against the clear delineation of public and private terrain. In the typical Australian hotel, residential facilities and bedrooms were generally situated upstairs, while rooms for communal use were located at ground level. Alternatively, in a single-storey establishment, drinking areas could be found nearest to the street, while bedrooms were positioned to the rear of the premises. But as the events surrounding Elizabeth Wright's murder illustrate, the borders of hotel spaces were permeable enough to allow an intricate and diverse range of social engagements within them. For example, the dining room of the Frankston Hotel was the interior space in which Henry Howard chose to present Elizabeth Wright with the contract to buy her out of their economic partnership, thus mixing business with domestic affairs. It was also the scene of Elizabeth's last dinner, where the publican's family ate together with her employees' family. Had there been any lodgers that fateful night, they too would have dined in that space; again, the indivisible territories of home and economic life. When Elizabeth was tending to her 'private' affairs in front of the fire that night, she was still within shouting distance of her clientele out front. And when young George Wright went to bed on the eve of his mother's murder, his room was within earshot of the chatter and laughter of the public bar. Within the spatial economy of the pub, commercial, social and domestic transactions were remarkably fluid.

The interior design of hotel space was largely responsible for such ambiguous territorial borders. Pubs drew their quintessential character from the 'breaking-up of the plan into small, distinct areas to give an effect of intimacy and enclosure and richness of texture'.[17] On the one hand, the collection of small, separate rooms under one roof afforded a sense of communal participation in the occasion of social drinking and companionship. On the other hand, the distinctions drawn between rooms acted as a device to stratify the group. Most pubs, British and Australian, had at least two, if not three, separate areas where alcohol was consumed. The bar offered the cheapest drinks and the simplest furnishings and was largely the terrain of working men who desired quick, casual drinking. The saloon was better furnished and charged slightly higher prices for the privilege; business and professional men made this their refuge. Finally, the lounge or parlour was the most lavishly appointed and 'snugly furnished'—if not most commodious—room in the house. This room might be used for council or lodge meetings, engagements where seclusion was prudent, and commonly by women, drinking in the company of their husbands or female friends.[18]

While the physical boundaries of these separate spaces might have been clearly marked by closed or open doors, external or internal entrances and signs warning 'Guests Only', the terminology used to describe the room is far from lucid. Some scholars have noted that 'the use of the same term for different parts of the pub in different generations is a common and confusing aspect of pub history'.[19] While the 'bar' usually refers exclusively to the public bar, other rooms are variously referred to as the 'bar parlour', 'saloon bar', 'saloon parlour', 'ladies parlour', 'lounge', 'lounge bar', 'lounge parlour' or 'ladies lounge'. Some hotels differentiated their 'top bar' from the 'bottom bar' or 'front bar' from 'back bar', depending on its position on the floor plan. It is difficult for us, therefore, to ascertain who might be drinking where simply from a room's name.

Furthermore, hotel space was nominally divided between private and public areas. It is by no means clear, however, which of the above drinking spaces were private or public. While the principal drinking location was almost always known as the 'public bar', the secondary bars were sometimes designated as the 'private bar', 'private parlour' or 'private lounge'. Some hotels even had a 'private dining room' as distinct from the common 'dining room' or 'ladies dining room' which could be found in some large city hotels. The rooms marked off for use by the licensee and his or her family further confuse the designation. These were often consigned as the 'publican's private parlour' or simply as the family's 'private rooms'. Lodgers and boarders, however, may have been free to inhabit the publican's private rooms, depending on the size of the hotels and the personal inclination of the publican. Quite clearly, drinking customers were denied access to such rooms, though they might freely congregate in the same hotel's 'private parlour'. The public private parlour, so to speak.

A New South Wales court case of 1906 illustrates that such seemingly arbitrary codes of spatial allocation were as much a mystery to contemporary observers as they are to the modern historian. The case was a licensing infringement hearing for serving alcohol after hours. Two men, who the court heard were 'neither boarders or inmates', were in the 'private parlour' after closing time when a Licensing Inspector entered. The licensee, William Hopgood, testified that the room was 'what is called a private parlour, the room is open to any gentleman to go in, it is a private room the door is often locked my daughter uses it when ladies call on her'. The men claimed they were there to discuss business with the publican, at his behest, and were not drinking. They testified that when they had arrived at the hotel and asked for the licensee, Mrs Hopgood had directed them to the parlour. The presiding judge expressed consternation, but the case was dismissed.[20]

If nineteenth-century social rules regarding one's rightful place in the hotel were highly contextualised and determined by the personal discretion of the publican, fundamental legal and material changes in the early twentieth century saw the Australian pub become, at once, more democratic and less accessible. Significant structural transformations began to be made to Victorian hotels after the emergency wartime provisions for early closing were made permanent in 1919. New South Wales and South Australia also instituted six o'clock closing during this era. Hotels were 'disembowelled' as walls were knocked down to accommodate the high-capacity drinking needs of the public bar's six o'clock swill (see Plate 13).[21] The distinct snugs and parlours which catered to a variety of intimate social exchanges were sacrificed to the 'egalitarian' needs of after-work drinkers. It was during this time that 'the Australian pub swung away from being a building in which the bars were physically only a small part of the whole' to a place where drinking was spatially and culturally privileged over other more 'homely' aspects of social life.[22] Tables and chairs were removed; billiard tables, dart boards and lounge furniture sacrificed for sheer empty space that could be filled

13. Dressed to swill. Gowerville Hotel, Preston, Victoria, c.1964.

by the daily crush of bodies. 'Perpendicular drinking' was the key to healthy turnover.

The remodelling of the structure and internal arrangements of the Australian pub, designed to cope with the evening onslaught of swillers, transformed the public house from a 'social centre for leisurely drinking and recreation' to a bastion of hard-drinking men.[23] The hotel bar during the era of six o'clock closing has been described as 'shabby and sleazy', having 'a cold, lavatory-like atmosphere'.[24] With six o'clock closing preserved in legislation for over fifty years of the twentieth century, Australian public drinking became pervasively associated with an overtly masculine style of social engagement: hard, fast, loud, competitive and gender-exclusive. The space in which this drinking culture was housed was similarly harsh, uncomfortable and devoid of ornament or refinement. Over the half-century of six o'clock closing, the front-of-house activities of the Australian pub secured its notoriety as an exclusively male domain. The tradition of female hotelkeeping continued, measured by women's high rates of participation as licensees, but the culture of the hotel was no longer imbued with the ideology of domesticity. In terms of public perception, the hotel came to be seen as a place which was, in fact, hostile to the traditional feminine world of hearth and home.

The architectural transformations that accompanied six o'clock closing ensured that perpendicular drinking was to become the cultural norm of the twentieth century. After the interior renovations which saw the demise of the intricately connected yet distinct drinking parlours, any extra rooms were indelibly marked as poor satellites of the primary, privileged drinking space. The temperance reform impulse, which advocated early closing in order to protect families, can be partially credited for creating drinking practices that were antithetical to civility, moderation and heterosociability.[25] It was not until the 1950s that Victoria, at least fifty years after the British experience of hotel gentrification, began to enact its own version of pub improvement, in the face of declining patronage, a tarnished trade reputation and a public push to extend drinking hours. In May 1955, the *Age*—an erstwhile ally of temperance —called the six o'clock swill 'a blot on the life of the State'.[26] Later that year, *Argus* journalist Cynthia Strachan encouraged women to campaign for ten o'clock closing in order to improve home life by joining their husbands for a 'pleasant social event' at the local.[27] The walls that had been ripped down in the 1920s to make way for expansive public bars were not rebuilt, but by the 1960s hotels began to 'modernise' their interiors to reflect the change in social expectations.

Hotels owned by the major breweries were especially likely to be renovated. *What's Brewing*, the in-house magazine of Carlton and United Breweries, ran a photographic series entitled 'Our Hotels' in the early 1960s, in which the images and accompanying text were designed to emphasise the more 'civilised' aspects of the extensive improvements carried out to these hotels. At the suburban Hotel Powell, we can see the Saloon Bar, 'with its indirect lighting and padded bar front' and the 'main Public Lounge with its attractive service bar'. Photos of The Quarry Hotel, in the heart of working-class Brunswick, reveal vases overflowing with flowers, wallpaper in one public bar, and a carpeted lounge with skylights, tables and chairs. The Orrong Hotel, in up-market Armadale, boasts a 'commodious lounge' and 'tastefully furnished' bedrooms (see Plate 14). At the White Hart Hotel in the regional town of Horsham, we are invited to admire 'the Saloon Bar with its carpeted floor [which] makes a restful rendezvous' while 'the spacious main bar [is] a far cry from the country bar of legend'.[28] While the rhetorical emphasis in these renovations is largely on 'modernity' rather than 'homeliness', there is no

14. *Modern comfort in 'the commodious lounge' at the Orrong Hotel, Armadale, Victoria, 1964.*

doubt that the interior embellishments are designed to make up for the perceived lack of decorum and delicacy in the post-swill drinking conditions. Carpets, upholstered furniture, flowers, mood lighting, art works and table linen were all intended to put back that 'richness of texture' that had previously been associated with small, intimate and enclosed spaces. And without doubt, they were intended to imply—if not advertise —'a woman's touch'.

Yet the conditions of the six o'clock swill—the sardine squeeze of men, supposedly stripped of social or class pretensions by their communal thirst and competitive joviality—came to symbolise Australian egalitarianism in the minds of cultural commentators of the 1960s to 1980s. For example, Craig McGregor, in his 1966 *Profile of Australia*, conflates pub drinking, mateship and national identity in his description of the lucky country: 'In Australia it is an occasion for raucous bonhomie, yarn-spinning, laughter, swilling down schooners, middies and ponies and, occasionally, pumping drinks into the girlfriend or wife—it is all part of that explosive good humour and companionship which Australians equate with the good life'.[29] Fifty years after the introduction of six o'clock closing, McGregor endows women with all the agency of a car at a petrol station—filled up and driven home. Many feminist historians and social commentators have decried the cultural insult of expecting women to sit 'alone in the hot, sparsely furnished and extraordinarily named Ladies Lounge' or, even worse, in the car out the front of the hotel.[30] But does this picture of social impotence reflect all women's experience of hotel life over that infamous half-century of exile from the public bar?

The Hotel as Family Home:
An Inside Story

HOW DID THE AUSTRALIAN PUB, with its peculiar status as a place of public drinking, a provider of public accommodation *and* a private dwelling place, operate as a family home? How did the hotel look from the perspective of its female residents? Did the masculine dominance of drinking activities in the public bar—particularly after the introduction of six o'clock closing—permeate every aspect of the hotel, leaving no place for women to call their own? Did women who lived in hotels feel segregated, invisible and otherwise marginalised from the spaces and activities that were regarded as socially valuable? Such questions have never before been posed by historians, fixated by women's 'confinement' within the insidious walls of the Ladies Lounge. The life stories of female publicans and women who grew up in hotel families can provide vital clues to understanding how the composition of space affected women's sense of entitlement and belonging in the pub.[1]

Nineteenth-century records suggest that the borders between private and public activities were shadowy. The testimonies of women who lived in Australian hotels in the twentieth century make it apparent that the lack of overt differentiation could be both a liberating and frustrating feature of domestic life for the hotel's inhabitants. Many women make the point that the cost of sociability was a lack of privacy. 'It was anybody's house', says the fictional publican, Fran, in Myra Morris's 1938 novel, *Wind on the Water*: 'The noises of the hotel would creep in. Feet trampling in the bar, voices sounding down the passage.'[2] Anne Parr, who was born in the outer suburban Braybrook Hotel in 1915 and grew up in her parents' various rural and city pubs, remembers the freedom of living in an 'open house':

> I always really enjoyed growing up in hotels because of the company; other people moving about all the time. There were always a few boarders, overnight people, and my family and their friends coming and going. When you're in a hotel, people are dropping in all the time for a cup of tea or a drink or a talk. Usually you've got a great big kitchen table and there's always somebody sitting at it. So, it was never lonely.[3]

Anne's daughter, Janet, who grew up in the hotel that Anne herself owned and managed from 1946 to 1963, similarly recalls the companionship she experienced as a child but later came to resent as a teenager: 'I did enjoy the company . . . always having lots of people around . . . as I got older, I think I wanted to feel a bit more privacy, but there wasn't any. It was all public.'[4]

It is interesting that publicans' daughters so keenly felt the restrictions on their personal control of space in the hotel, given that their mothers often cite the physical and emotional claustrophobia of 'living privately' as their reason for pursuing hotelkeeping. If nineteenth-century female licensees were often compelled to run hotels for their economic survival, it is apparent that many of their twentieth-century counterparts actively chose the hotel life despite having husbands with secure employment. Eileen Clatworthy's mother, Ellen Gray, used hotelkeeping as a means to educate her six children after the sudden death of her husband in the influenza outbreak of 1919. By contrast, Eileen explains the start to her own career of sixty-odd years as a publican:

> My husband Ken's mother bought us a house and we paid a mortgage on it once a week. Ken kept working in the insurance business and I couldn't stand it. I had two children. I missed people. You know, I was too lonely. I was so used to people. So I said we'd take a hotel. We sold our house just as the war started. Ken would have given me the world, I suppose. He was in love with me. He got used to it.[5]

Anne Parr also opted for the public life after the birth of her first child in 1946. She had been living with her mother-in-law during the war years, and had bought a house in the middle-class enclave of Camberwell with her husband, but chose to take up her sister's offer to run their family's hotel in Brunswick:

I was married to John when I took the licence to the Victoria but he didn't have any part. He didn't like it. He had his own engineering business. I think it was mainly the company that I liked about the hotel life. There was always something going on. There was always a little bit of excitement. And I liked the business angle. I liked keeping the books, working out menus, buying all the produce. It was fun. It was much better than stopping at home, doing housework.[6]

Although the activities Anne outlines are essentially domestic in nature —buying food, planning meals, managing a household economy—her response suggests that it was the opportunity to carry out these routines in a commercial, professional capacity, physically liberated from a nuclear family, which was the attraction of hotelkeeping (see Plate 15). This is particularly apparent because Anne admits to not liking bar work; the public bar was predominantly the terrain of her sister Jennie, a co-licensee, while Anne attended to the 'house'.

One of the chief appeals of *public* housekeeping for women was the ability to carry out their familial responsibilities within a broader social

15. *Commercial domesticity. Kitchen, Tallangatta Hotel, Tallangatta, Victoria, 1954.*

environment of staff and lodgers. Women were not isolated in their role as mothers, but rather were able to share the nurturance of their children with other adults while maintaining working lives. Gloria Fry, who raised six children in her two Bendigo hotels during the 1930s to 1950s reflects that:

> I found it a lot easier than some of these working mothers who have to go away from their homes and then come back after long hours. Whereas I had the children around me all the time. Some of the staff were like extended family. They were very, very good. But the children were never formally in their care.[7]

According to Anne Parr, 'It didn't really make any difference having my work and home in one place but the big difference was having someone to look after the child'. Anne employed a designated nanny.

On the other hand, Lillian O'Connell, who was a publican in Victoria and Western Australia from the 1940s to 1970s, enjoyed having house staff at her hotels because it meant being able to take time away to be with her daughter:

> We had a good staff, a lot of female staff, and that left me free. I was able to walk to the convent where Margaret went to school. I'd take Margaret in the mornings, sometimes pick her up at lunchtimes and we'd go for a drive to the beach and have lunch. It was really nice. I didn't have anything to do with the bar things, just the house, and Margaret.[8]

Within the historical spectrum of female hotelkeeping, Lillian's position was relatively luxurious. Certainly, many nineteenth-century publicans, particularly in remote districts, were financially compelled to do all the work—house and bar trade—on their own, or with the assistance of their older children. Indeed, this was Lillian's situation in the early years of her career as an unmarried country publican. Nonetheless, in larger, more successful hotels, it was possible for child care and housework to be fulfilled within a less physically confined, more communal setting, at the same time as an income was being earned to support these domestic tasks.[9]

A wide circle of householders could also be beneficial to the children of publicans. Mayse Young, whose own career as an outback publican is recounted in her facetiously titled 1991 autobiography, *No Place For a Woman*, remembers growing up in her family's Pine Creek hotel in the early 1930s:

> I felt grown-up, helping with the responsibilities of the hotel. There was a sense of satisfaction in it: starching and ironing, out on the veranda overlooking the garden . . . We would gossip with each other while we worked, and quite often the local girls and women would call in and talk to us while we finished off a task.[10]

This female camaraderie is an aspect of the hotel life that is also clearly drawn in Lyn Van Hek's 1997 novel, *The Ballad of Siddy Church*. In this largely autobiographical novel, Van Hek describes the female-dominated world of her grandmother's country public house, where she grew up during the 1950s. The novel's protagonist, Eadie Wilt, explains:

> I was a child with many aunties. The hotel was teeming with them. A hotel run by aunties. The cooks, the yardwomen, the cleaning women. I grew up with the poetry of aunties. On summer mornings, they would turn on the hoses and water down the tiles on the hotel's façade. All those women laughing and getting their feet wet.[11]

Van Hek's reminiscences might be lyrically portrayed but they reflect the experience of many other women who grew up in their mothers' hotels.

Edna Jory recalls the centrality of the women who populated her childhood world in the Universal Hotel, Fitzroy, where she lived with her publican parents between 1915 and 1923:

> We had a cook. The cook's name was Mrs Trugertha. I've never forgotten her name. She was a kind old soul. We had the big kitchen there with the big stove. I used to love to go down there and just sit in the kitchen, while she was getting the meals. I used to love to talk to her.[12]

Apart from house staff, Edna also had a nanny, Mrs Nietzsche, a friend of her mother's who had lost her doctor husband and was invited to join the family circle. The hotel's 'inmates' also included Edna's Aunt Polly and her family, Ruby the housemaid, and several long-term residents, who were often given jobs to do around the place in exchange for board. 'There were always a lot of people around,' laughs Edna.

Having a nanny, whether formally appointed or casually culled from the general staff, was a common experience in the lives of pub children. It is also an indication of the class position that many publicans achieved. Given that their publican mothers worked such long, demanding hours, their daughters often recall having formed deep bonds of affection and trust with their nannies. Nancy Reis remembers that it was always Jessie Wilkins, the housekeeper, who was 'there to open the back door when we came home from school'.[13] Anne Parr employed a distant relative, who was trained as a kindergarten teacher, to care for her daughter, Janet. But Janet remembers being most attached to one of the housemaids, Elsie:

> Elsie did our washing; she cleaned our rooms. I trotted around with her when she did those things. I loved it dearly; I loved this woman dearly. She was like another mother, she really was. There were a lot of women in my world. A lot of surrogate mothers.[14]

Staff, as well as various family members and boarders, lived 'on-premises' at hotels well into the twentieth century, making for the sort of pre-industrial household that was the economic and communal backbone of most colonial families.

Margaret O'Connell extends the theme of surrogate motherhood in her description of the female-dominated world of her hotel upbringing: 'We had a lot of European women working for us—what we called "New Australians" in those days. Mum called them "the girls", but really they were women. They were all very nice to me so I felt quite safe and wanted.'[15] Margaret also makes the point that her 'group of women' existed quite separately from the realm of the public bar, which she was forbidden set foot in while customers were about (see Plate 16). Nor did she feel comfortable entering other hotels where, as a woman, she felt she didn't belong. The feminised, domestic space in her hotel was particular

16. *Women's business. Elms Family Hotel, Spring Street, Melbourne, 1970s. Margaret and Lillian O'Connell (a), and O'Connell cousins (b).*

to her own extended family unit and their territory was, in a figurative if not material sense, a private one:

> Even though we were hotel people, the women wouldn't go in [to other hotels]. Within your own home, it was like a harem, in the sense of being like a cloistered area. Your family and your friends got invited in there. There was this hostile ring around it with the customers. They were charming people. There was nothing wrong with them, obviously, but there was that separateness. And then another hotel would be just another hostile place, unless you actually knew the publican there, when you'd get invited into the inner sanctum.

Lynn Van Hek's novel also explores the theme of the 'inner sanctum' of female activity in the pub. But her version comes with a feminist twist:

> Log fires crackled in the rooms, the aunties played darts and billiards. Grandma Siddy was polishing glasses and talking to the policeman [about her Aboriginal patrons] . . . 'If I had my way, I wouldn't let any men in here at all', she said. She smiled, 'But since by law I have to, I'm letting them all in, makes no difference to me'.[16]

The presence of strong women in her protagonist's memory is so great that 'All Eadie would remember was the big old hotel with no daddies and many aunties'.[17]

While the 'inner sanctum' of surrogate mothers could be nurturing and sustaining for some publicans' daughters, others keenly felt the absence of their hard-working parents. Edna Jory recounts that her mother was often too preoccupied by work to attend to her needs, sending her to house staff instead: 'Mum was too busy. She was in the pub all the time. It wasn't such a good place for kids to grow up because they couldn't give you the same attention as if Mum would have been home, in her private home, like a house.'[18] Nancy Reis similarly reflects a sense of loss in her recollection of the busy working lives that her parents lead. Like many pub families of the six o'clock swill era, the Naughton children rarely ate with their parents, who would be involved with closing routines at dinner time:

> When I look back, I feel that my mother was very involved in the business and it cut down the closeness. Yet when they lived privately and I went to live with them after I was married, she was marvellous. She did her housekeeping and I had my two children and

she was wonderfully good to me but when we were in the hotel, well, she'd be working and as a little girl, you wouldn't see her, wouldn't come home to your mother. I'd come home to Jessie.[19]

Many publicans sent their children to boarding school to remove them from the chaotic lifestyle of the hotel (and to protect their daughters from the risk of moral contamination associated with public drinking), a decision which some women say compounded their sense of disaffection. Other women lament that having all their household needs catered to by hotel staff meant that they never acquired basic skills like cooking and laundering. Pam Sleigh-Elam went through two years of an elite finishing school after she matriculated from Presbyterian Ladies' College because growing up in a hotel meant 'it was not easy to learn how to be domesticated'.[20] While publican mothers express the personal, material and practical advantages they achieved by living in and running hotels, their daughters could, in turn, feel alienated from a wider society that, in the 1950s and 1960s, condoned less fluidity and mobility in women's life experiences and expectations. Nancy and Pam both cite the disruption to their own childhood family life as a reason for prioritising motherhood over career. Other women, however, maintain that growing up in hotels gave them a set of social skills and attitudes—including tolerance, generosity and broad-mindedness—which well equipped them for the exigencies of life.

The recollections of women running hotels or growing up in them from the 1920s to the 1970s tend not to refer to the masculine orientation of space but rather to focus on female and family relationships. Their reflections on the shortcomings of the hotel environment stress the disruption to 'normal' family life due to the all-consuming nature of hotelkeeping. The overall impression created is not one of low self-esteem and physical inertia, conditions that are often presumed to plague female identity when women are 'forced' to live on the margins of male-dominated sites of cultural activity. This book cannot fully explore the issue of female subjectivity from the perspective of women as drinking patrons, but we should note that female publicans and their daughters have consistently included such women in their depiction of the hotel community. Women who took their leisure in the Ladies Lounge often combined social drinking with domestic chores such as preparing food and mending clothes. Female customers brought their children to the hotel (publicans' daughters often minded them) and knew they could rely on the publican to feed or clothe impoverished children in need.

Female publicans point to the strong community focus that the Ladies Lounge provided for local working-class women. Such disclosures suggest that women used the separate space of the Ladies Lounge to define their own public culture, putting paid to the notion that women were 'invisible' in the twentieth-century hotel.

A sceptical reader might claim that the women interviewed here are merely 'making the best of it' in telling their life stories, but it is nonetheless significant that women who have experienced an intimate relationship with the hotel and its inhabitants have largely elected to portray the pub as a place of shared humanity and positive female identification. While there is always room for nostalgia and sentimentality in a self-selected sample of interviewees, these women's perspectives still form a legitimate source for interpretation. Oral history is valuable because it suggests a way of viewing the hotel which refutes the widespread premise that the hotel is a place of *inevitable* discomfort and alienation for women. The gendering of space did occur in hotels, but the insiders' story suggests that this process did not necessarily mean that masculine sociability had to be privileged over the rights of female association. By and large, the physical and ideological blurring between public and private space in the hotel—and most importantly, the lack of an oppositional relationship between the two—allowed room for both men *and* women to develop a positive personal and social connection to the institution.

Pub-licity

IF WOMEN REAPED PRIVATE rewards for their role as public house-keepers, the continuing contribution of female licensees to the hotel industry was no secret. In 1930, a *Vigilante* reporter recognised that 'Women licensees in Victoria are successful not only in management, but also as units of trade organisations', suggesting that, in the post-suffrage, inter-war years, female publicans not only pursued their own individual business interests but also sought more co-operative means to express their local authority.[1] Lucius Boomer, in his 1929 book on hotel management, offered an interpretation of such attainments:

> There are many reasons why women should be unusually successful in hotel operations . . . because there is no business so closely related to what is termed 'the woman's sphere'. A hotel is a magnificent domestic establishment—a home away from home for those who travel. Women have always been the homemakers of the world.[2]

Unlike other small businesses run by colonial women, which became fewer as the boundaries imposed by marriage and family ties became more restrictive in the latter half of the nineteenth century, hotelkeeping became an increasingly female-dominated terrain.

This situation stands in contrast to another popular public avenue for 'women's work': shopkeeping. Despite the respectability of shopkeeping as an occupation, in the late nineteenth and early twentieth centuries women became increasingly confined to the role of helpmeet in small family businesses and corner shops, while 'the shopper could expect to see a man behind the counter to serve her'.[3] In an unexpected role inversion, the predominantly male clientele of the hotel became accustomed to the public face of a woman running the enterprise while a man serviced the largely female cohort of shoppers. The spatial arrangements within hotels—both social and physical—were as much implicated in this situation as legal and political factors.

While marital and family networks were by no means irrelevant to hotelkeeping, the territorial boundaries in which these gendered relationships were played out were unconventional. Hotel spaces were 'ambiguous territories' where, on the one hand, guests were invited to share (female) domestic locations such as dining and sitting rooms while, on the other hand, the primary reason why most people came to the hotel was to engage in a masculine pastime, public drinking. It is precisely the ill-defined nature of the space which resulted in the cultural correlation between ale-selling and harlotry in medieval England.[4]

But in Australia, where the notional association between liquor selling and prostitution never gained a popular foothold, female publicans found a point of leverage in the ambiguity of hotel space. They managed to achieve not only financial recompense but also great social esteem for their efforts at public housekeeping. As businesswomen, female licensees attained a prominent public profile, one that not only condoned but also celebrated their enterprise, skills and hard work. To credit the success of female hotelkeepers is ultimately to contest the portrait by influential feminist historian Miriam Dixson of the pathetic state of 'Australian women's overall public dignity, standing, profile, self-belief and self-concept'.[5] Female publicans managed to walk the fine line between acceptable versions of femininity, and the role of independent businesswomen and community leaders.

Tolerably good success stories

Female publicans were honoured with public recognition of their accomplishments as far back as the early colonial period. In 1827, the *Sydney Gazette* paid tribute to the extraordinary achievements of ex-convict, Mary Reiby. Wife of the trader and merchant Thomas Reiby, and 'the better half of his business', Reiby was responsible for the retail and liquor sales of their empire. She continued to run her public house after Thomas's death and became an extensive property owner and developer. After she had built a prominent private dwelling for her retirement, the *Sydney Gazette* noted:

What between the erection of splendid edifices and the ramification
of children and grandchildren, no respectable colonist has done
more than Mrs Reiby to 'Advance Australia'.[6]

Praise for Reiby's public productivity is intertwined with acknowledge-
ment of her reproductive success, indicating that female publicans were
not seen to be transgressing the bounds of acceptable womanly activity.
Indeed the first birth announcement printed in Sydney's daily press in
1803 was in honour of Mrs Elizabeth Driver, licensee.[7]

The social prominence of female hotelkeepers is similarly attested to
in the many published obituaries of these women. For example, Mrs
Marion McKinney, publican at hotels in Shepparton, Hay and Melbourne,
was remembered in her 1884 obituary as 'a most business-like, capable
manager, and of very agreeable demeanour, her smiling countenance and
pleasant converse ensuring customers becoming friends'. Similarly, Mrs
Marianne Jessel of the St Osyth Hotel, Port Melbourne, was held up as
'one of the many sensible, knowledgeable ladies who do credit to the
Trade'. Mrs Elizabeth 'Granie' [sic] Svenson was honoured upon her
death in 1934 with a lengthy tribute in the *Vigilante* entitled 'Fine Career
Ends'. It reported that Svenson, who died at the age of ninety-three, had
lived in and held the licence for the Royal Mail Hotel, Aberfeldy, since
1875—a 58-year reign (with forty-two years as a widow) in which 'she
had a career filled with adventure and kindly deeds'. 'With true pioneer
spirit', Svenson raised eleven children in her hotel, which possessed a
dining hall with a single long table and a fireplace fit to accommodate
eight-foot logs. She was also remembered as 'an indomitable spirit' and
'fearless horsewoman' who took supplies to isolated prospectors. The
writer concludes, 'Where a harder nature would have gained her a comfortable bank account, her kindly nature and generosity gained her a
place in the affections of all who knew her'.[8]

This sort of public recognition was not just sentimental, nor confined to internal trade publications. Female publicans, particularly in
country towns, played a key role in local politics and were central to
many community and recreation activities, either as the facilitators of
meeting space or the disseminators of information. Women did not just
manage hotel bars and house trade, but also directed the networks and
exchanges which were positioned in and around the pub. In the rapidly
developing and settling Australian colonies, hotels were at the forefront
of imperial expansion, generally preceding banks, churches and other
public buildings. In February 1865, the *Argus* commended Mrs Janet
Bowman, licensee of the Gippsland Hotel, Beaconsfield, for her efforts to

colonise the district: 'The public are indebted to her for the opening up of the new track to the Jordan'.[9]

The first meetings of newly constituted shire councils were often held in pubs during the time that council chambers were being built, while it was a statutory obligation that hoteliers use the cold-rooms of their premises as morgues and for coronial autopsies. The 'private' parlours in country hotels were routinely used as temporary consulting offices for visiting doctors, dentists and opticians. The first hotelkeepers in a town played the multiple roles of storekeeper, banker, postmaster and bush-lawyer while organising transport and church services. There is barely a local, shire or town history written in Australia which does not mention the key role of publicans, both male and female, in the establishment and growth of rural settlements in the nineteenth century, not only as traders but also in terms of their contribution to church, sporting and civic affairs. Publicans were 'pioneers', and as such they no doubt assisted in the European colonisation of indigenous lands in other ways that celebratory histories fail to mention. If nothing else, they profited from the sale of alcohol to Aborigines despite the illegality of such transactions.

A lasting symbol of the appreciation and high regard that contemporary settlers had for country publicans and their work, regardless of their gender, can be found in the town of Marysville, so named after the licensee of a wayside inn that served diggers heading to the alpine goldfields.[10] Similarly, Mother Johnson's Flat, on the diggings in the Cobungra between Bright and Omeo, was named after the landlady of a local shanty while Pretty Sally, a hill south of Kilmore, also owed its title to a popular publican.[11]

In an interesting inversion of this theme, Mrs Morrell, a publican on the Dargo High Plains in 1868, called herself Mother Freezeout, so named after the local mountain. The poor widow was 'old and solitary and always cheerful, and apparently happy . . . many a lone traveller had not only to thank her for shelter, but for his life'.[12] In 1849, publican Mary McKinlay petitioned the government against establishing a town around a fellow settler's property. She claimed the plan would ruin her hotel business. Her petition was successful, and the town of Casterton in western Victoria was laid out around McKinlay's hotel.[13] Evidently, female publicans identified strongly and possessively with the communities they served and the landscapes they inhabited. While naming rights were no doubt a source of personal pride, they were also good for business.

When boomtime Melbourne blew its own trumpet in the 1888 com-pendium, *Victoria and Its Metropolis: Past and Present*, seven female publicans were honoured with published biographies in the section on 'prominent members of the hotel trade'.[14] The fact that only a handful of women are mentioned in the entire book of some thousand pages points to the low public standing of women in general in this era and suggests the extent to which female hotelkeepers were able to rise above such civic anonymity. That entrants paid a fee to have their activities recorded for posterity is further testament that some female publicans were not backward about coming forward with their achievements in order to boost their public profile.

Female hotelkeepers regularly publicised their establishments, alongside their male peers, in the local press. An advertisement for Dale's Law Courts Hotel in the *North Melbourne Advertiser* of 1874 represents the typical language and style of such self-promotion: 'Mrs Marion Dale has much pleasure in announcing that she has opened the above house, and intends to conduct it as a first-class Family Hotel'.[15] Women such as Mrs Dale saw no shame or indignity in openly declaring the personal pride and civic virtue inherent in running their own licensed premises. Female licensees also advertised their establishments on a national scale. In 1903, Mrs William Gannon, licensee of Petty's Hotel in Sydney, cast her publicity net widely by placing an advertisement in the *Australasian* magazine (see Plate 17):

> This well-known Family Hotel is Unsurpassed by that of any other
> in Sydney for Comfort, Privacy, Convenience, and Healthy Situation.
> The Sanitary Arrangements are of the Most Perfect Description.
> The Hotel is Under the Direct Management and Supervision of Mrs
> William Gannon, Proprietress, Church Hill, Sydney.[16]

Mrs Gannon clearly believed that her own reputation, coupled with the hotel's superior plumbing, were the chief drawcards of her establishment.

Female publicans' social confidence could become manifest in other self-congratulatory ways. Mrs Mary Ann Dale was the licensee of the Court House Hotel, Jamieson, in the foothills of the alps, for sixty-two years and was proud to be known as the unofficial historian of the district.[17] Financial success could also see female publicans become local philanthropists. In September 1870, Mrs Martha Lewis advertised her recent prosperity, informing 'her numerous patrons and friends that she has just completed extensive additions and improvements to the Old

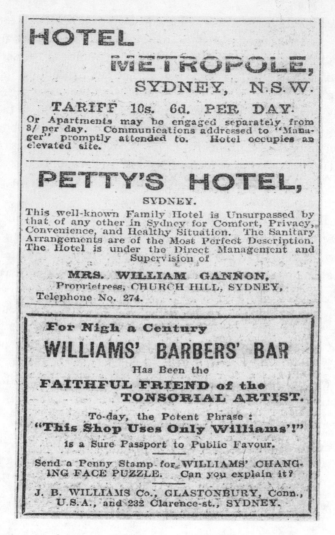

17. *Advertisement for Mrs William Gannon's Petty's Hotel, Sydney, 1903.*

England Hotel'. In December 1872, the *Argus* announced news of 'the new Heidelberg Hall, built at much expense by Mrs Lewis of the Old England Hotel. A concert . . . will initiate the proceedings and the whole receipts will be given towards the new Catholic schools of Heidelberg.'[18]

Like their male counterparts, female publicans sponsored local sporting teams and were among the largest donors to charities. Publicans' reputation as unstinting benefactors to local causes was no doubt one way in which they were able to overcome accusations of profiteering or social irresponsibility. Many children of publicans also make it clear that their parents were generous, caring people who felt an obligation to assist those in need. Edna Jory recounts multiple deeds of kindness on the part of her parents, including taking customers' children to the circus and donating biscuits to the local kindergarten. Pam Sleigh-Elam's mother held an annual jumble sale at the rear of the hotel, the proceeds of which went to 'buying a bed' at the Royal Children's Hospital.[19]

While some philanthropic turns were openly known, many more daily acts of compassion were performed without fanfare. Nancy Reis and Edna Jory both recall their publican mothers 'taking clothes off our own backs to give away' to less fortunate children. Anne Parr reflects on the complex role of the hotelkeeper in the group dynamics of the Ladies Lounge. Intimately aware of customers' family situations, the publicans' superior financial situation and sense of community obligation often saw them act as a patron rather than simply a neighbour.

> They [the customers] were quite friendly with me. They'd invite me to their parties. They used to bring their babies in to show me, give me a nurse. One little girl—we pretty well fed that child until she was about four. Her mother used to go to work and her grandmother used to bring her in. Poor kid was always hungry. We used to go and get a meal for her very smartly.[20]

In *The Ballad of Siddy Church*, Lyn Van Hek details the pivotal role that Siddy, the publican, played in ministering to her rural constituents:

> Something was always happening. I came home from school at three, Gran and [Auntie] Mantel would be standing in the saloon bar giving advice to a bruised wife or financial assistance from a knotted handkerchief . . . This was floating money . . . Money that was alive and doing. Gran's floating money could blitz people's problems, change their circumstances for a week or two. It paid for operations and escapes, sleep-outs for extra kids, chicken coops for widow's chickens. Giving life-saving advice was Mantel and Siddy's exclusive domain.[21]

Although publicans' charitable acts may in part be attributed to ameliorating social stigma and securing a good reputation for the trade, it is nonetheless important to recognise the historical significance of hotelkeepers in the maintenance of community health and welfare.

A sign of the times?

Female publicans' prominent social standing in Victoria was in part assured by the complex legal framework enshrining the principle that 'the general control of the house must be in the hands of the keeper'.[22] The independence and autonomy inherent in this rule was embodied in a physical, as well as philosophical, sense: by law, the licensee's name had to appear in large lettering above the most conspicuous door of the public house. Indeed, before the advent of purpose-built hotels, signage was often the only way to tell the difference, from the outside, between a private house and a public house.[23] Traditionally, the hanging out of the inn sign was an 'indication of privilege', as the innkeeper 'proclaimed a separate identity' from other householders.[24] It was the publicity of the hotelkeeper's name which symbolically transformed the largely private, domestic space into public, commercial space; the privilege of doing so was not overlooked by Australian women.

It was the prominent and compulsory display of the licensee's name, rather than any decorative, witty or grandiose sign, which alerted the drinking public to the fact that they were entering a particular person's house. This is an important distinction. In his study of early modern European shop signs, one historian has argued that 'signs and names conveyed more than simply information . . . Naming a house was a way of taking possession of it: it was a statement of power . . . a symbol of status . . . The signs they chose were physical reminders of their claim to authority'.[25] Signs were used to 'create and renew relationships of domination and subordination' whereby certain people could affirm their identity as prominent citizens through an external show of power. This analysis is useful, for it suggests that, even if a particular hotel was small, modestly decorated or even shabby in appearance, its keeper was able to claim authority over the space and assert the power of their position as licensee through the display of their name (see Plates 18–20).

For a female publican, this feature was a telling reminder of her identity and status as a property-owner and figure of public significance. Colloquially, hotels were often referred to by the name of the house and its keeper: Dunphy's Stork Hotel, Dillon's Royal Oak. The example of Dale's Law Courts Hotel, cited above, illustrates that this trend was equally followed for the establishments of female publicans. A woman's name over the door served to reinforce her locational, functional and cultural centrality to the establishment. At a time when few women were professionals who could command jurisdictional power over public affairs

18. *Ruth Beck's North Star Hotel, Canadian Lead, NSW, c.1870–75.*

19. *Margaret Keenan's Diggers' Arms Hotel, Gulgong, NSW, c.1870–75.*

20. *Annie Tuohy's Queen's Bridge Hotel, Bendigo, c.1960.*

and relationships outside their immediate family circle, the female publican's ability to place her name over her door was indeed significant.

Women also laid claim to their public house by changing its name when they took over the licence, in keeping with the common practice of re-naming a hotel to signify a new managerial beginning, a new social development or current fashion. For example the Coach and Horses Hotel might become the Railway Hotel, the Glasgow Arms became the Yorkshire Arms and the Quarryman's Arms resurfaced as the Engineers Arms. Female licensees generally renamed their hotels according to these conventional principles of time, place and identity.

One name change is arresting. In 1866, a Mrs Wilton took over the licence for the Old Gold Diggers Hotel, situated in working-class Collingwood, from the previous licensee, Kate O'Brien. Perhaps resenting the mercenary implications of the hotel's former name, or perhaps wishing to emphasise the calibre of her own nature, she changed it to The Good Woman Hotel. Perhaps she even intended to cock a snook at the traditional inn-quip of naming a pub The Good Woman, The Silent Woman or The Quiet Woman as 'a joke against the females whose loquacity . . . is considered to be satirised by this representation'.[26] It is unlikely, given a publican's need to maintain the respect of her clientele, that Mrs Wilton was making a joke at the expense of her own sex. If the ability to name a public place or institution signifies proprietorial power and creates relationships of domination and subordination, then female publicans felt perfectly entitled to claim such sovereignty over their domain.

Straddling the (gender) bar

Interpretations of hotel culture that impose a rigid gender template over notions of public space can tend to obscure the centrality of feminine control over the *whole* space in instances where the publican was a woman. For example, the counter from which alcohol is served has typically been represented as the focal point of gender relations within the Australian hotel.[27] Diane Kirkby refers to the hotel bar as 'a large impenetrable barrier', 'an insurmountable obstacle', dividing workers from customers and transforming guests into clientele. In her reading of the social implications of the service counter, Kirkby argues that 'bar staff were contained within a prescribed space behind a large impenetrable counter', and further, that the bar 'separated workspace from playing space, masculine space from feminine space, the customer from the servant'.[28] While Kirkby's book focuses on barmaids and related class issues, and thus rightly questions the basis of labour relations within the pub, the negative language she uses to describe the cultural impact of the bar tends to paint all gender relations within the pub in the same pessimistic hue. To define the bar as a barrier—and then to 'contain' feminine space behind it—is to impute a fatalistic immobility to all women present in the hotel environment.

The barmaid—as employee—may have been required to stand behind the counter, but the female publican—as employer—exercised more autonomy over her movements. For the licensee, the bar could provide a powerful dominion. Its central position, often opening into several different drinking spaces, made it a useful base for crowd control because the publican could overlook the entire area.[29] However, a significant distinction can here be made between the English and Australian experience. In England, the central service bar did not become a standard feature of public houses until the 1890s. In Australia the advantages of the bar counter were fully realised by the 1830s. The chief value of the bar lay 'in the increased speed of service and ability to keep a watchful eye over the customers'.[30] Kirkby points out that optimal surveillance was 'no doubt a necessity in a primarily convict population'.[31]

However, the early introduction of the bar counter may have also been a particular blessing to female publicans, encouraging their participation as independent proprietors of hotels. If the counter made surveillance easier, how much more critical must this have been to the solitary woman whose job it was to patrol and control the terrain? Physically distanced from her potentially rough and rowdy clientele, the publican could move freely and inconspicuously between public bar, lounge bar and dining room, depending on where her jurisdiction was most needed. This technique was as useful for watching over untrustworthy staff as reining in recalcitrant drinkers.

But at the same time as the bar counter provided a garrison, it was also a base that solicited social contact: a 'camaraderie of the counter'.[32] Because of their control over the whole hotel space, female publicans were central to the inviting sense of friendly intercourse without being objectified—sexually 'framed' by the bar counter—as barmaids could be.[33] The bar also acted as a signifier of hotel power relations, demarcating and protecting the personal space required to maintain sexual propriety and thus ensure general authority. Enthroned behind the bar, like a magistrate behind a court bench, the female licensee was 'off-limits', physically and symbolically at arm's length from the general public whom it was her job to control. Rather than limit the movements of the publican, the bar put customers in their place.

Long-serving publican Lynne Cox explains her deliberate manipulation of the bar as barrier:

> If ever I'm out there in the public bar, talking to a customer, and I get the sense he wants something more from me—or thinks I'm offering it—I just go back behind the bar, into my private safe haven, which tells him I'm off limits. It says I'm in control. You don't have to be rude. It's all very subtle.[34]

The bar might provide a physical barrier but for the female licensee, who has sovereignty over the whole of the public house, its symbolic meanings and practical applications are much more expansive.

When we begin to conceive of hotels not only as women's workplaces but also as their homes and businesses, a provocative story of agency and entitlement begins to emerge. The fact that the barmaid's boss was often a woman questions the dynamic of labour relationships in the discussion of obstacles to power or access to social and economic capital. That the customer's access to a drink was so often the prerogative of a woman demands a reconsideration of notions of dependence and servitude. Female publicans could be—at the same time—workers and mothers, wives and businesswomen, widows and entrepreneurs, spinsters and social beings, employers and servants. Borders to social and self-definition were constantly being traversed. Public and private personas, like the built environment which shaped them, skirted the edges of conventional delineation.

This potential for 'personal growth' appears to have been recognised (in surprisingly modern language) by contemporary observers of the hotel trade. A 1929 article on female publicans noted that the woman who thinks she can run a hotel because she has previously kept servants was unlikely to prosper: 'This is the type of person who is useless unless she finds herself and is able to determine what she has to offer the business, rather than what it has to offer her'.[35] This remark suggests that women who 'found themselves' through public housekeeping were able to avoid the narrowly defined prescriptions of dependent wife and homemaker and, in doing so, create a social and personal identity based on activity, not inheritance.

'The seamy side of things'

If women reaped both the public and private rewards of hotel life, they also took on the dangers inherent in the endeavour. Female publicans are quick to point out that their intimate involvement with public drinking exposed them to the 'seamy side of things': alcoholism, violence, suicide, family breakdown, mental illness and other manifestations of personal and social trauma.[36] While some women developed the resources to cope with the perpetual parade of human aggression, frailty and misery, others were evidently less suited to the job. Licensing records reveal the notably short tenure that some female publicans held on their hotels. The Prince of Wales Hotel in Collingwood must have attracted a particularly troublesome clientele: it had seven female licensees in the years between 1902 and 1908, the longest holding out for eight months.[37] In 1935, Marguerite Sullivan, who was the licensee at the Terminus Hotel in the port suburb of Williamstown for a mere five months, applied to the Licensing Court for dispensation to transfer her licence in less than the statutory period of one year. Marguerite pleaded that 'domestic trouble had occurred'. In these circumstances, 'and in view of her nervous condition', she had been advised by her doctor to 'retire from business'.[38] The licence was successfully transferred to Gertrude Donegan.

Pub-lic life could invite dangerous as well as demoralising behaviour. Numerous reports in trade and daily newspapers attest that arson was a common form of retribution against a publican who refused to sell liquor to an already intoxicated patron or who rigorously adhered to opening hours. In 1919, the *Vigilante* reported an arson attack on the Golden Horseshoe Hotel, Kamballi, Western Australia. The licensee, Mrs Alice Morton, was injured when dynamite exploded inside the window of her bedroom; the bomb shattered furniture and 'gashed her a good deal'.[39] People rarely lost their lives in such attacks, but damage to the predominantly timber hotel buildings could be extensive. There is no evidence to suggest that female publicans were any more vulnerable to such attacks than their male peers, and there is certainly some indication that pub women could give as good as they received.

In 1870, Mrs Jenkins, of the Jachariah Jenkins Beer House in outer metropolitan Templestowe, was charged with 'incendiarism' after attempting to burn down her competition on the opposite side of the street, the Louis Le Compte Hotel. Bedelia Parkington of the British Hotel, Queen Street, Melbourne, was convicted of arson for attempting to burn down her own pub in 1866; she was sentenced to three years' imprisonment. It would appear that business was not going well for Bedelia and, as for many desperate publicans before and after her, an 'accidental' fire was an attempt to dissolve her debts. The fire did not destroy the British Hotel, which would later be licensed to the doyenne of Melbourne publicans, Annie Opitz.[40]

Despite being in charge of a thriving social institution, female hotelkeepers in far-flung districts had to contend with loneliness and isolation, and particularly, in early colonial times, the absence of other female company. This experience lies at the heart of the tragic story of Elizabeth Scott, the first woman to be executed in Victoria. In 1853, Elizabeth migrated from England with her family. Soon after, her impoverished parents arranged her marriage to Robert Scott, a 'reputedly wealthy miner'. The bride was thirteen years old; Scott was three times her age. Ten years later, Elizabeth had two children (three more had died in infancy) and was living at 'the bush inn established by the couple' on the river bank between Mansfield and Jamieson. Elizabeth ran the remote Scott's Inn as Scott was a notorious inebriate. When Scott was shot in the head while lying in bed in a drunken stupor, Elizabeth was charged with his murder. David Gedge, her 19-year-old lover and the hotel's ostler (horseman), and Julian Cross, an Asian general hand, were also charged and tried at the Beechworth courthouse. Despite public appeals for clemency for the young mother, Elizabeth was hanged at the Old Melbourne Gaol on 11 November 1863.[41]

As businesswomen, female licensees had not only to struggle against personal misfortune but also to contend with the inevitable pitfalls of life in the marketplace. Tidy fortunes could be made, but life savings could just as readily be lost at the hands of unscrupulous hotel brokers. Mrs Elizabeth Burt paid £125 for the goodwill and furnishings of the Kilkenny Hotel, Melbourne, in May 1877, but she was left with 'nothing but her clothes' one month later when she discovered that her licence had been illegally brokered. Mrs Burt, who had a history of 'intemperate habits', was reported to have once more taken to the drink 'upon discovering the truth of her ruinous speculation' and 'suddenly fell dead on Thursday last whilst at dinner'.[42] Commercial gullibility may have had dire ramifications, but again the sources give no indication that women were any more susceptible to dodgy industry practices than their male counterparts. The fact that male licensees also felt the sting of deceitful hotel agents is borne out by the persistent campaigns by the Licensed Victuallers' Association to have the brokerage industry regulated.

Indeed, in the same year as Mrs Burt was hoodwinked, the *Licensed Victuallers' Advocate* published a story about a female publican who was locked in dispute with a hotel broker. The story was apparently written to counter the assumption that publicans lacked education and were therefore easy targets for dishonest brokers. The woman, who is not named, procured a licence transfer for a hotel, a property which she had previously discussed with the broker. After the transfer was approved, he charged her £5 commission, though she had never formally engaged him. She sent him a long, terse letter in which she railed 'your mind cannot be quite so devoid of retentiveness as to forget altogether, in so short a time, the nature of that conversation'. He replied that a lady could not have written her letter 'as he was sure she did not possess the ability to incite such an epistle'. The *Advocate*, reporting the exchange, noted: 'Mrs —— is naturally indignant at such an insult being offered her so openly, and vows that she is not only competent to write Mr Broker down, but will also knock him down if he summons up the courage necessary to

make a personal application for the "fiver"'.[43] Nor, evidently, was Mrs
—— shy about bringing her altercation and smarting ego to the attention of the newspaper's editors.

As the holders of a liquor licence—a highly regulated and closely
monitored piece of property—female publicans were accustomed to
defending their activities in a public forum. All licensees were required
to renew their licences annually, and anyone applying for a new or transferred licence had to advertise their intention in a newspaper. Although
some women earned glowing reputations for running highly respectable
establishments, others attracted disrepute for their less illustrious activities. Numerous women sustained convictions for breaches of the Licensing Act, and such stains were routinely used as evidence of lack of 'good
character' when applying for new or renewed licences. In 1933, Mabel
Jeffs applied for dispensation to transfer her licence for the Town Hall
Hotel, Collingwood, after nine months, due to ill health. The licence was
taken by her sister, Mary Weibye, who remained in charge for three
years, during which time she sustained many convictions for licensing
infringements. On applying for a licence renewal for a fourth year, Mary
justified her wrongful acts on the grounds that the hotel was 'rather difficult to manage, and these were difficult times'. Ultimately, she pleaded
in her defence, 'I have always been a trier'.[44] Her licence was renewed.

Annie Nicholson's 1935 application for the licence of the Tower
Hotel in central Melbourne, was opposed by the Licensing Inspector on
the grounds that her mother and aunt, both of whom would live and
work at the hotel, had previously sustained convictions during their
respective careers as licensees. Although the chairman of the Licensing
Board noted that 'the real difficulty . . . was the family tradition', Annie's
application was approved.[45] Thus although female hotelkeepers could be
rapped over the knuckles, they were not often unjustly chastised or
punished for their wrongdoings. Nor do women appear to have attracted
any more attention from the Licensing Inspectors than male publicans.

One indication that women did not feel victimised by authorities is
that they regularly took their grievances to court, often litigating against
other female publicans if needs be. When Miss Mary Meagher applied
for a new licence to build the Morning Star Hotel in the outer metropolitan district of Doncaster in 1872, she found Mary Ogilvie, licensee of
the Long Hill Hotel, had lodged an objection. The proposed licensed
premises were to be built 'a few yards from the Toll gate at which Miss
Meagher helps her father collect the tolls'. Evidently, Mary Ogilvie was
anxious that her own business would be affected by the competition.

The licensing court did not share her concerns; the licence was granted and the Long Hill's proprietress was fined for 'prevarication'.[46]

In September 1930, Mrs Annie Alexander of the Sylvania Hotel sued Mrs Catherine Sims of the Manchester Arms Hotel in the County Court. Mrs Sims lodged a counter-claim. Mrs Alexander argued that Mrs Sims had made false representations regarding the weekly takings of the Manchester Arms for the purpose of a contract of sale. The court found that there had been no fraudulent misrepresentation. (The counter-claim was also dismissed.)[47] Litigious female publicans thus attracted publicity through their financially vested interests in seeing commercial justice done. This observation lends complexity to the notion that women in the late nineteenth and early twentieth centuries largely achieved public recognition through their efforts at pursuing social justice and reform.

Women who were engaged at the entrepreneurial end of the hotel industry were therefore subject to the hazards of moral scrutiny, financial vulnerability and threats to personal safety. But can such dangers be attributed to their occupation of public space? Is the world of politics, commerce and industry more perilous than the supposedly sheltered retreat of one's private home? To which 'sphere' do we assign Elizabeth Wright's murder: was it the result of personal grievances or cut-throat business competition? Was Henry Howard's crime one of prideful passion or commercial greed? Was Howard simply a vengeful and dangerous man, and Wright a headstrong and determined woman? Clearly all of these scenarios may be 'true', but equally, maybe these are the wrong questions to be asking. Perhaps a more interesting if untravelled road is to consider whether a woman who lived in a hotel could achieve both public dignity and private self-esteem.

By examining the importance of hotels as women's homes and businesses—as places where their management of the household continued to have a public charter—it is possible to conceive of the Australian pub as a site of 'domestic liberty'.[48] In the pub, housework and child care were performed in a communal context, often supported by staff or extended family, while the more skilfully one practised the domestic arts by creating a congenial home-away-from-home, the greater the economic reward and social prestige. Upstairs, or out the back, the private life of marital and familial relations, child-rearing and other acts of domesticity unfolded in the cyclical rhythms of sickness and health, better or worse. Downstairs, or up the front, the public world of commerce, employment, social interaction and leisure generated its daily hum, with a halt to business on Sundays. With a staircase or passage to bridge these multiple levels of responsibility and reward, locating the two realms of human activity within the same built environment could spare female hotelkeepers the fragmentation, loneliness and alienation in which separation too readily becomes segregation.

Cast in this light, the bar counter, which physically distanced female publicans from their clientele, can be interpreted not as a restraint, but as a threshold. Rather than a deterrent to social engagement, it was a marker of the transitional space in which women's engagement in both an economic and family life could see them transcend the limited expectations of a conventionally constructed 'woman's place'. With the division between the 'separate spheres' of work and home less formulaic, female publicans could become historical boundary-crossers.

Elizabeth Wright was not a rebel. Nor was she a martyr. Like many nineteenth-century women, she was a single mother working to support herself and her family. Like many women before and after her, her home was a hotel. She was the victim of a vicious crime, but she was also the agent of a powerful institution. Although certain aspects of twentieth-century drinking culture unquestionably created gendered relationships to pub-lic space, hotels have traditionally been places that could fulfil women's economic needs, psychological desires and social aspirations. To understand the hotel as social institution with a complex and often contradictory spatial economy is to take a less fatalistic approach to female identity in a male-centred national culture. Ultimately, portraying the hotel as a location that offered women the prospect of using their 'feminine' skills and energies to enhance their financial independence and public identity raises questions about personal and social power. Elizabeth Wright's death was tragic. Providing a context for her life, however, can add an intoxicating ingredient to any reconsideration of the sexual dynamic in history.

PART IV

'She Knows What She's About'

Controlling the
Public House

Making an Impression

'A STRIKING FEATURE of hotel control is the longevity and robust health of many members of the industry, notably women.'[1] So declared an article entitled 'Women's Long Licenseeships', published on Christmas Eve 1937 in the trade journal, the *Vigilante*. The article went on to profile female licensees with 'distinct claims to be regarded as pioneers in the industry'. One such woman was Mrs. A. E. Gellie of the Mt Elephant Bridge Hotel, Darlington (see Plate 21). Mrs Gellie was born at the hotel in 1860. Her father held the licence for only a few months before his premature death, when Mrs Gellie's mother became the proprietress. In 1888, she transferred the licence to her daughter. Mrs Gellie ran the Mt Elephant Bridge Hotel for the next forty-nine years. Darlington, halfway between Geelong and Hamilton, was a busy changing station for coaches and wagons and, according to the article, Mrs. Gellie never slept for more than five hours a night.

Control is a word that continually resurfaces in the language of hotelkeeping in the late nineteenth century and well into the twentieth. The term is used to denote the guidance of the industry generally (liquor control), the management of individual hotels (crowd control) and the responsibility of the licensee to safeguard their own reputation and authority (self-control). Vigilance, as the title of the hotel trade's journal attests, was a virtue born of legal and practical necessity. Those who passed the test were duly praised in a frontier, and later, national culture that valued independence, proficiency and resilience. That female hotelkeepers had the skills and endurance to provide domestic comforts and facilitate social conviviality in public houses—without challenging ortho-

21. *Elephant Bridge Hotel, Darlington, Victoria, 1937.*

dox notions of 'woman's place'—offered them a path to social and self-accomplishment. But their personal qualities also secured them a place in the lexicon of 'noble frontiersmen' who were celebrated by nineteenth-century writers, artists and nation-builders.[2] The ability of female publicans to 'make an impression' through their control of a prominent institution invites a fresh approach to notions of women's social power and cultural agency in Australia.

The story of Mrs Alice Jackson, who capitalised on the vogue for waterside recreation by opening Anglesea House in 1886, exemplifies the nineteenth-century tendency to acknowledge the role that female publicans played in fashioning the local landscape. Jackson's hotel became the holiday destination for affluent families from Geelong, Melbourne and surrounding districts, as the *Geelong Advertiser* noted: 'Anglesea House rapidly became the centre of activities in the bustling new "watering place" and, under the control of Mrs Jackson, its fame spread throughout the area'.[3] Mrs Jackson continued to garner accolades and clientele throughout the 1890s until, in February 1898, the Anglesea coastline was devastated by one of the area's infamous bushfires. The three-storey weatherboard hotel, with balcony views of the ocean, was gutted by fire, despite the efforts of 'the visitors staying at the hotel, including several ladies [who] worked with splendid energy beating back the flames'. Within days of the disaster, Alice Jackson had applied for a temporary licence to run her business out of a local residential home. She rebuilt Anglesea House and—despite another bushfire in 1906, which destroyed the stables and chook house—ran the business for twenty-two more years. She sold the hotel in 1920 for £3000. Alice Jackson's capacity to battle against the elements was both a personal survival strategy and a valuable business asset in an industry that rewarded personal command, endurance and the 'pioneering spirit'.

The terminology of control was often used to convey a publican's influence with regard to both their own business and their community more generally. When the widowed publican Ellen Gray died in 1952, her obituary in the *Nathalia Herald* affirmed her practical command over her business affairs and linked this diligence with other forms of public obligation:

> The late Mrs. Gray, who was affectionately known throughout the district and the Goulburn Valley as 'Ma', had conducted the Bridge Hotel, Nathalia, since 1914 . . . [a hotel] which she controlled until her death . . . Though her main occupation and enjoyment was the conduct of the hotel, Mrs. Gray, with her daughters, took an active part in the catering for many of the town functions, and were very active in the affairs of St. Mary's Catholic Church.[4]

Like Mrs Gellie of thee Mt Elephant Bridge Hotel, Ellen Gray's position of authority owed a good deal to her longevity in the trade. Her control was seen as a positive attribute; the writer makes no attempt to soften the edges of such a description to impart a feminine refinement based on passivity or vulnerability.

By the same token, the *Vigilante* reporter makes a point of the fact that Mrs Gellie took only five hours of sleep a night. Why did the reporter feel it was significant to comment on Mrs Gellie's lack of sleep? Was she a chronic insomniac? Did the coaches stop at the hotel throughout the night? Was there a need for constant surveillance? Or was her wakeful nature symbolic of a deeper restlessness of spirit and insatiable energy? Whether the reason for Mrs Gellie's nocturnal habits was prosaic or mythical, the detail acts as a catalyst for weaving a story, real or fabled, about female fortitude and dominance born of the hotel environment.

Coping with adversity and sudden changes of fortune was a skill required by female publicans. The capacity to carry on their occupation may have been at the mercy of legal, judicial and political approval, but on a more daily basis, the exigencies of death, calamity and survival were of greater concern. The qualities that female publicans brought to bear in governing difficult and sometimes dangerous situations were a common source of commentary for contemporary observers, as well as more recent practitioners of local and family history. Bridget Cruise, for example, was an Irish immigrant who settled in the Blackwood goldfields town of Red Hill and, with her husband, opened the Victoria Hotel in 1861. The business was successful and the couple became local landholders. Bridget continued in her occupation as a hotelkeeper in Red Hill, and later West Melbourne, through the deaths of seven children and two husbands as well as a disastrous fire at the Victoria. Reporting the fire, a local newspaper commented 'The poor woman seems fully alive to the necessity of immediate action on account of her young and helpless family'. Bridget mortgaged her other town allotments and rebuilt, opening the Family Hotel in 1878.[5]

New South Wales publican Hannah Byrne has been remembered as 'the woman who probably influenced the settlement of Gilgandra more than any other person, over roughly fifty years. A tough lady who survived three husbands and produced children by all three, Hannah was the daughter of a convict.'[6] Hannah received the district's first liquor licence (in 1867), named the town, opened the first bridge and organised the first school, despite having 'suffered more than her share of sorrow'. She lost three children as well as her trifecta of husbands.

This tendency to stress the resourcefulness and self-governance of female publicans was arguably the result of two factors: first, the emphasis on 'character' that lay at the heart of the licensing system, and second, the practical need to create order and establish authority as the head of a public house. A hotelkeeper could not afford to be (or be seen to be) hysterical, weak-kneed, prevaricating or sexually vulnerable. Their reputations relied on strength of character and self-control. This public image, in turn, fed into a gold rush pioneer legend, and later, a nationalist mythology that stressed autonomy and tenacity. While female licensees won political approval through the paradigm of female helplessness, their public identity within the social institution of the hotel was fundamentally associated with power.

Hotelkeeping was seen as a respectable way for women like Alice Jackson, Bridget Cruise, Hannah Byrne and Ellen Gray to transcend their humble circumstances (the convict stain, immigrant dislocation), overcome adversity (widowhood, bereavement, natural disaster) and achieve a degree of financial independence, social recognition and personal autonomy as property owners, small-scale entrepreneurs and community benefactors. Not all female publicans, of course, fit this model of capitalist achievement. Many hotelkeepers (male and female) held hotel licences for less than a year, particularly in inner urban locations. For others, the economic tie to brewers made true independence a chimera. Nonetheless, social mobility and class consolidation were prominent features of the hotel trade in Australia.

Historical agency—most simply defined as the ability to have an effect on people or events—is central to interpreting the personal motivations of the women for whom hotelkeeping was both a livelihood and a way of life. By introducing the subjective experiences of female publicans into broader debates about female social power, we may begin to appreciate how women influenced the conditions of the hotel as much as hotels shaped the conditions of many women's lives.

Women's Temperance, Class and Social Power

ON 5 JULY 1875, MR E. W. COLE, founder of Cole's Book Arcade in Bourke Street, Melbourne, took out a full-column advertisement in the *Herald*. It read: 'A Good Wife Wanted: Twenty Pounds Reward'. Cole might have been desperate, but this didn't stop him from being fussy. According to his ad, any prospective wife had to be 'A spinster of thirty-five or six years, good-tempered, intelligent, honest, truthful, sober, chaste, neat but not extravagantly or absurdly dressy, industrious, moderately educated, and a lover of a home'.[1] If not for the fact that Cole was a pre-eminent temperance advocate, any number of female publicans would have met his requirements.

It is impossible to discuss either the politics of drink or the public role of women in the late nineteenth and early twentieth centuries without reference to the temperance movement. During the course of the nineteenth century, the notion that intemperance was the cause (not the result) of social and economic distress grew in popularity, and became increasingly bound up with religious reform movements. From the 1840s to the 1870s, temperance 'crusades' in England, Ireland and the United States sought to redeem the souls of those wretched individuals who had fallen under the evil spell of 'the demon drink'. Indulgence in alcohol was perceived as a moral weakness to be overcome by spiritual and social uplift; the 'cultural self-improvement ethos' borrowed from Protestantism was applied to all denominations of temperance zeal.[2] These religious-based orders, predominantly populated by professional men with a strong foothold in the capitalist order, reflected the hegemonic values of the last quarter of the nineteenth century: thrift, sobriety, upward mobility, hard work and an individualist philosophy of self-help.[3] The Woman's Christian Temperance Union (WCTU), an international organisation founded in the United States in 1874, which famously developed into the most popular women's network of the late nineteenth and early twentieth centuries, added 'the defence of the family' and 'home values' to this list. By the dawn of the twentieth century, the emphasis on individual salvation had waned in temperance campaigns as reformers 'now looked for a legislative, rather than spiritual, solution to the problem of the drink traffic'.[4]

The women's temperance movement, with its international organisational structures, broad reform agenda and associations with suffrage, has received much historical attention. In particular, feminist historians have focused on the WCTU in order to establish critical links between female social power and political agency. Several influential works have demonstrated the historical alliance between temperance ideology and first-wave feminist agendas, pointing to the 'pro-woman politics' that lay at the heart of the temperance movement and its bid for female control over men's deleterious behaviour towards women.[5]

So how did Australian temperance women respond when faced with another model for female social power—the woman as publican? The WCTU was, in truth, conspicuously silent on the issue of women being granted liquor licences, even while it campaigned against the employment of barmaids in hotels. Why didn't the WCTU, in its drive for moral purification and social reform, target female hotelkeepers in much the same way that it pursued barmaids? Surely the fact that there were so many women running hotels could have provided a convenient Achilles heel in an otherwise omnipotent industry. Is it possible that female hotelkeepers and temperance women shared more territory than either group would care to admit in terms of their cultural values and class identity? Could presumed political foes in fact be tacit accomplices?

As the self-styled moral conscience of the liquor industry in this period, 'Temperance' closely shadowed its nemesis, 'the Trade'. Yet it is also true that liquor industry heavyweights in Victoria gained much of their own political leverage by mirroring the principles and values of social reformers—respectability, social mobility, civic virtue—in their own public standing. This is nowhere more apparent than in the construction of 'true womanhood'. That women as a sex were the bearers of culturally reformative and spiritually restorative virtues was a central notion in both temperance rhetoric and, as we have seen, female publicans' political survival. As the *American Prohibition Year Book* of 1915 expressed the sentiment which the Licensed Victuallers' Association itself adopted, 'Women have purified every position they enter'.[6]

Understanding the fears, values and goals of the international WCTU helps to make sense of the organisation's response to female members of the Australian liquor trade. Temperance became intimately aligned with broader gender issues as 'women pitted themselves against what they saw as institutions of male culture'.[7] A 1916 speech by Victorian WCTU member, Mrs Helen Barton, graphically alludes to the sexual dynamic that was at the heart of women's temperance: 'The liquor question was a woman's question, and therefore one of the highest national importance, for anything which lowered the social status of women, and tampered with the moral value of a country's womanhood, struck a direct blow at the vitals of the nation'.[8] In the 'protofeminist politics' of the WCTU, liquor was but one spoke in the wheel of a cultural reform movement which embraced social equality for women and expressed antagonism toward men and masculine values. The WCTU preached under the banner of home protection, believing that the world's salvation rested in the feminine values of domesticity, maternalism and sexual restraint—all ideals which were threatened by alcohol abuse.

A poem published in the Victorian WCTU journal, the *White Ribbon Signal*, illustrates the iconographic gap that was drawn between the nurturing female domestic model and the vice-ridden male public arena, as exemplified by the hotel:

> That would create together here
>   A dungeon and a star
> Two things that lie two worlds apart
>   The cradle and the bar.[9]

The evangelical WCTU believed that hopes for the world's deliverance rested with the feminine values of self-control, thrift and respect for family life.

Frustrated by their confinement to the middle-class private sphere, WCTU women used 'the power of the domestic ideal' not only to protest against the destructive effects of liquor on wives and children, but also to legitimise their place in wider public activities, organisations and campaigns. At the same time as the WCTU championed the power of the bourgeois home, it also exhorted women to improve their status by making significant incursion into the public realm, particularly through paid work and 'social service'. Thus women's temperance used the ideology of sexual difference both to define an essential 'woman's place' and to gain a moral and cultural foothold in a wider public arena. Within the complexity of this position lie clues to interpreting the relationship of women's temperance to female publicans.

The cradle of the bar? 'Universalist maternalism' meets the hotel matriarch

If it is untenable to discuss the politics of public drinking without recourse to temperance ideology, it would be distinctly possible to discuss temperance in Australia without ever mentioning the practice of female hotelkeeping. This is because temperance advocates did not single out female publicans for public criticism or wade into the political debates about women's rights to hold liquor licences. Indeed, the role of female publicans played no part in the WCTU's reform agenda. Barmaids, however, were central to the temperance movement's protracted crusade against the consequences of public drinking.

Temperance advocates campaigned against the employment of barmaids through a twofold strategy. On the one hand, they argued that the combination of barmaids' sexual allure and youth contributed to the general pall of sin and degradation that hung over the hotel industry. At the same time, they held that the depraved working conditions and nefarious environment of hotels put young women at risk of embarking on the 'downward road' to moral degradation. The barmaid was constructed as both artful lure and innocent victim, and criticised for not performing 'womanly work'. As the WCTU's Victorian president, Mrs McLean, lamented in 1902, 'They have not found their right vocation . . . We look upon them with pity and regret.'[10]

Female publicans, on the other hand, were not cast as objects of pity, requiring the benevolent intervention of righteous sisters. In 1885, the year of the new Licensing Act that preserved the right of married women to hold licences, a Victorian temperance publication, the *Alliance Record,* noted that where barmaids were 'liable to insult', female publicans held a legitimate place within the hotel: 'We know that an hotel business could not be conducted without women on account of the many domestic details to be arranged'.[11] Evidently, a distinction was made between the women who were installed behind the bar as employees and the women who commanded the bar as employers. Although Australian temperance campaigners worked towards the reduction of hotel licences and the restriction of opening hours, Prohibition was not on the mainstream political agenda, as it was in the United States. If some hotels were to remain, it seems that reformers did not entirely wish to rid them of feminine influence. Rather than using the centrality of female publicans to hotel business as an argument against the trade, the WCTU recognised that, as agents of domesticity, proprietresses were responsible for the very values which temperance wished to confer on society more generally. The female publican was almost universally constructed in the public imagination as a 'good woman' of her times.

One plausible reason why the Australian WCTU may not have included female licensees as part of its reform strategy relates to the internationalism of the WCTU. As a worldwide movement for social improvement, the WCTU was a 'relatively integrated society pursuing common policies and sharing a common organisational framework, ideology, and international leadership'.[12] Although it was not all one-way traffic between the American-dominated WCTU and a suppliant international following, it is clear that the revered American women who served as worldwide missionaries for the WCTU were largely responsible for setting the international agenda. Mary Leavitt, for example, began a worldwide campaign against barmaids in her eight-year tour of the globe, commencing in 1884 and culminating in the Victorian and South Australian bans on barmaids in the early twentieth century.[13] Other 'do-everything' social causes apart from the liquor question—opium consumption, social purity, peace and arbitration—also had their framework and ideologies set within an American context before receiving international application by local WCTU chapters.

If this is the case, there is every chance that female publicans were not on the Australian WCTU's hit list because such licensees were very far from an American consciousness. For as we have seen, by the 1880s, when female hotelkeeping was on a steady rise in Victoria, the practice of women selling liquor had all but vanished in the United States. American women's ability to run legitimate businesses and make an independent living through the retailing of alcohol had been relegated to the informal, illegal fringes of the liquor industry. Temperance campaigners, who concentrated their reforming energies on the legal frameworks that allowed the demon drink to flow through authorised channels, subsequently overlooked their activities. American temperance literature—for all its vast lists of numbers and statistics, poems, proverbs, prayers and essays —is silent on the issue of women selling liquor for a living. The cultural invisibility and structural marginality of these 'bootlegging mothers' no doubt makes this an understandable absence. In Australia, where female publicans were a salient feature of the industry, there may have been no formal campaign structures to deal with their presence.

But strategic and cultural differences within the WCTU's internationalist framework cannot alone account for the truce that was informally negotiated between temperance women and female publicans in Australia. Reading the temperance literature of the WCTU, it is striking how much of the substance of their social and cultural reform accords with the values and conduct that many female publicans themselves espoused. The ethic of maternalism—the virtuousness of motherhood—is central to this convergence.

The WCTU believed that women possessed special gifts and attributes, which could be used to better the world through their dedicated role as mothers and homemakers. As the *White Ribbon Signal* expressed this domestic archetype: 'The human race, as a whole, is governed by ideals. Among them, there is none finer than the idealised mother. She is a compound of patience, love, wisdom, and goodness, with a saving sense of humour.'[14] 'The idealised mother' gave rise to what one historian has dubbed 'political domesticity' or 'public motherhood'; that is, 'action, formal or informal, taken to affect the course or behaviour of government or the community' based on women's claim as mothers.[15] In the late nineteenth century, precisely the time when women in Victoria were taking to the helm of public houses in unprecedented numbers, the 'universalist maternalism' preached by the WCTU was the presiding ethos for understanding women's claim to exercise public power.

As a political philosophy, maternalism 'extolled the private virtues of domesticity' while 'legitimating women's public relationships to politics and the state, to community, workplace and marketplace'.[16] As we have seen, the way that female publicans were most commonly written into the public discourse of Victorian parliamentarians and trade defenders was as hard-working mothers striving to support themselves and their families through their honest involvement in the marketplace. If state policymakers were prepared to argue for the legal and moral legitimacy of female licensees on the grounds of their status as mothers, it was hardly in the interests of women's temperance advocates to refute that claim.

Yet female publicans' association with 'universalist maternalism' goes further than the protection of their own homes. If barmaids were allied with sexual dissoluteness in the public imagination, female hotel-keepers were more readily portrayed as mother figures. Often referred to by their customers as 'Mother', 'Ma' or 'Granny', or by marriage status

('Mrs C.', 'Mrs Kelly') women who ran hotels were not considered to attract male clientele through sexual allure. Nor were they seen as vulnerable to male advances. As the head of the house, the female licensee represented feminine authority rather than sexual licentiousness or exploitation. Even single women, who often had long careers and whose influence thus extended over generations of patrons, were able to take on the roles of confessor, comforter and carer, in much the same way as nuns provided spiritual guidance and pastoral care. They provided the fundamentally feminine services of hospitality, accommodation and victualling to their clientele. The WCTU would have called it 'womanly work'.

In Australia, female publicans played an important role as surrogate mothers and grandmothers to transient, unmarried and immigrant men, particularly in colonial circumstances where men significantly outnumbered women.[17] By contrast, one American historian has noted that the very few female saloonkeepers who did run businesses of their own in the United States were 'colorful characters' working under saloon names such as 'Peckerhead Kates', 'Indian Sadies' and 'Big Tit Irenes'.[18] The connotations of these names are obviously a far cry from the Ma's and Granny's of female hotelkeeping in Australia, where female publicans conformed to an appropriate model of femininity that was defined by women's 'natural' maternal orientation towards accommodating the interests and needs of others.

There is evidence to suggest that WCTU campaigners in Australia were aware of the essentially domestic role that public drinking houses played in the lives of many men, especially under frontier conditions. In some instances, the WCTU even sought to replicate the maternal services of female publicans—minus the provision of alcohol—as a means to pluck vulnerable men from the straits of drink. In the late nineteenth century, temperance bodies in Australia opened 'coffee palaces' to rival the public house as a venue for non-alcoholic social interaction. The WCTU took this idea one step further. WCTU guru Frances Willard counselled that 'Every sailor should have a mother in every port, someone to take an interest in him'.[19] Following this advice, in 1892 the Western Australian branch of the WCTU established the Sailors Rest—a place for sailors to wash and mend clothes, write letters and 'obtain practical and spiritual advice when needed'. This version of the home-away-from-home would provide them with 'an alternative to spending leave in the bars of local hotels'.[20] Similar alcohol-free public houses were set up in Melbourne, regional Victoria and in other states.[21] Such an approach to achieving temperance appeared to recognise that men went to pubs as much for home comforts as for drowning their sorrows; the need for a respectable form of public home-making was not denied.

Some temperance women may have implicitly endorsed the matriarchal ideal that was the foundation of female hotelkeeping, but the WCTU never explicitly advocated for the rights of female licensees. Nor is there any documentary evidence to suggest that female publicans participated in any of the broader social reform campaigns that the WCTU supported, such as citizenship rights and age-of-consent legislation. The WCTU and female publicans may have drawn their claim to social power from the same source, but they were never political bedfellows. The fact that female licensees were disproportionately Irish and Catholic was probably enough to quell any overt empathy between them and the largely Protestant teetotallers.

'The home as vocational outlet': Independent (but appropriate) careers for women

As a tenet of its 'protofeminist politics', the WCTU believed that, if women were allowed to decide for themselves, they would choose to pursue independent careers that were suitable to a woman's skills and demeanour. The organisation also believed that women should acquire professional qualifications and be financially remunerated for their efforts in the 'Domestic Arts and Sciences'. Although female publicans acquired no institutional training for their work (tertiary hospitality courses were not introduced until the 1970s), there is no doubt that they could command cultural respect and fiscal reward for being 'public mothers'. They embodied the idea that women could gain social status and financial independence without breaking the mould of orthodox nineteenth-century views about appropriate activities for women. Engaged in the public sphere without promoting 'unwomanly behaviour', female publicans thus fulfilled some of the WCTU's far-reaching goals: the achievement of social standing and economic collateral based on professional merit rather than acquired marital status.

The preoccupation with merit and service rather than inheritance has particular relevance in the Australian colonial context. In nineteenth-century Australia, prior to the 1890s depression, there existed a high degree of social mobility among a comparatively fluid pastoral and commercial class. Moreover, most colonial women in Australia, irrespective of their class, had to work in some form of productive labour due to severe shortages of domestic help and the exigencies of the family economy. The combination of these factors created a situation whereby it was relatively common for women to use work, not marriage, as a route to social improvement. This was particularly true for Irish immigrant women, for whom marriage often meant a move *down* the social scale due to the low status of Irish men.[22] Hotelkeeping, as the early examples of convicts Sarah Bird and Mary Reiby reveal, had long been a route to social improvement for some humble but hard-working women.

It was not just the potential for generating considerable wealth that distinguished publicans from other traders. It was also the prestige of being in charge of a powerful social institution. In the city, the urban free-hold elite of hotel families took pride in being accepted among the 'town fathers' and married their daughters into Society families. Another version of social mobility through hotelkeeping existed whereby the publican's daughter succeeded her father or mother as licensee, then married a pro-fessional man while continuing her trade; their children then married into Society. Publicans' social visibility was even more apparent in country towns, where the male hotelier ranked among the local establishment class of councillor, bank manager, doctor, school principal and landed gentry. Indeed, long-serving publicans were often town councillors.

In the late nineteenth century and first decades of the twentieth, female publicans could not expect to hold the same public positions as their male counterparts; no matter how much influence they exerted as community matriarchs, political disenfranchisement limited the civic op-portunities of otherwise active and influential women. Female publicans certainly contributed to local affairs, but their role was limited to financial sponsor and informal benefactor rather than elected representative. This could mean giving space in the hotel for regular meetings or annual balls, or donating food and liquor as prizes for racing carnivals, raffles and sports meets. Anastasia Thornley's act of generosity in using her Foster hotel as a makeshift hospital after devastating bushfires is typical of such patronage. In an era when women's participation in public affairs was confined to ladies auxiliaries and social committees, the female publican could not emulate the political and civic profile of her male industry peers.

Besides the social expectations of 'woman's place', there was another major impediment to female publicans joining the ranks of the municipal leaders: time. The *physical* mobility required to attend meetings, dinners and club affiliations was more difficult for female publicans to achieve. Where the male publicans who held various public offices had the luxury of a publican wife (or sister, mother or daughter) to hold the fort, female licensees were less likely to delegate authority. Before the advent of salaried managers in the second half of the twentieth century, hotel-keeping was a hands-on occupation, which required the constant pres-ence of a familiar and commanding figure in the house. For most of the nineteenth century, this meant having the publican on the floor from 6 am until 12 midnight. While male publicans could leave their helpmeet as a suitable proxy—a wife commanding respect by virtue of both her own skills and her husband's credentials—a sole female licensee could less readily afford to absent herself from the minute-by-minute business of running the hotel. Female publicans' social power was thus largely wielded from within the material confines of the hotel. This factor too suited an ideal of female agency that stressed the cultural value of domes-ticity and, in so doing, conformed to patriarchal forms of social control over women. Female publicans were not women 'of the street'.

Publicans, as an occupational group, have traditionally been politi-cally conservative and socially aspirant. In Australia, this tendency is par-ticularly apparent for Irish Catholic immigrants, for whom hotelkeeping was a common method of establishing a foothold in a predominantly Anglo-Protestant society. Publicans formed part of the 'Irish elite', along with doctors, lawyers and successful merchants, taking their place among these bastions of respectability.[23] While not all Irish publicans became wealthy members of the Irish establishment, hotelkeeping provided Irish families with a means to send their children to Catholic private schools and accumulate other middle-class credentials associated with education and professionalism. This pattern can be seen well into the twentieth century. Some historians have argued that the Irish in Australia aspired to keep up with English standards of morality and respectability in order to prove their superior virtue.[24] In the sexually charged arena of public drinking, keeping up appearances was even more important for Irish female hotelkeepers.

Irish women, who often married late in life in colonial Australia, commonly used hotelkeeping to better their personal circumstances. Licensing registers in Victoria attest to the large number of female licence holders with identifiably Irish names. Licence holding within families was also particularly common among the Irish. For example, the licence for the Golden Cross Hotel, King Street, Melbourne, was held by Gregory Doyle from 1873 to 1882, then by his wife Johanna Doyle from 1882 until 1884, when it was passed to Miss M. Doyle—almost certainly a daughter or unmarried sister—who continued to run the hotel for a further three years. Three Irish spinster sisters ran the Australian Hotel in Montague Street, South Melbourne, over a period of thirty-eight years. Bridget Crotty held the licence between 1874 and 1884, when it passed to Mary Crotty until 1898, and then to Margaret Crotty until 1912. Bridget Crotty, presumably the oldest sister, had previously held the licence for the Queen's Arms Hotel, Dorcas Street, South Melbourne, from 1868 to 1873. And while their relationship to each other is uncertain, no less than six O'Callaghan women ran ten different hotels in metropolitan and suburban Melbourne between 1864 and 1909: the unmarried Mary, Minnie, Margaret, Nann and Catherine and the married Ellen and Mary.[25] Irish hotelkeeping patterns and behaviours confirm the observation that in the nineteenth century, some women were able to achieve a relatively high degree of public power due to their vital role in the family units which provided the economic basis of society.[26]

If the Irish were the largest ethnic group to use hotelkeeping for both self-help and self-improvement, there are many examples of other immigrant women who similarly sought a liquor licence as their meal ticket. The list of female licensees who ran metropolitan and suburban hotels from the 1850s includes Eusibio Clota, Rose Greenberg, Catherine Maggia, Nellie Lim Kee, Hannah and Leah Cohen, Madame Isabella de Boehm, Madame Marie Reich, Antonia Meniza, Andrea Lagogiannis, Severina Pescia and Mrs S. Gras-y Fart. Annie Opitz and her husband Franz were German immigrants who became magnates of the late nineteenth century Melbourne hotel industry. With Franz as licence holder, they ran several city hotels between 1874 and 1884, when they took over the Globe Hotel in Swanston Street. The Globe boasted 'Accommodation for 70 persons, 3 storey, 4 billiard tables' and was said to be 'Much frequented by Theatrical people and travelling companies'. Annie herself held the Globe's licence between 1891 and 1893, then took the licence of the British Hotel, Queen Street (1893–95), Pastoral Hotel, Bourke Street (1895–97) and the Freemasons Tavern, Port Melbourne (1897–1902).[27] Besides building a small commercial empire, Annie also produced eight children between 1865 and 1879. Another renowned hotelkeeping family to establish themselves in Melbourne society was the Spanish Barbeta clan, who cemented their position by marrying into the Parer family, also prominent hotelkeepers. Intermarriage among publican families was a common form of social consolidation, creating hotelkeeping dynasties. Public housekeeping thus afforded women the opportunity to follow a career in which the path to independence and status was safely confined to the orthodox territory of the domestic and family economy.

Propriety and good conduct: Femininity and the female publican

If hotelkeeping could provide a route to social and economic ascendancy, with male heads taking up positions of political prominence, how did female publicans manifest their class identity? In colonial Australia, the 'class ideal' of female social mobility was defined more by how a woman behaved than by whether or not she worked, as was the English model. Colonial women defined social prestige not through their association with exclusive institutions (as would-be gentlemen did), but through their own standards of comportment. Their status hinged on the extent to which they conformed to definitions of 'genteel femininity'.[28] It has been said that this acute attention to behaviour in colonial Australia can be attributed to the fact that there were so few 'real' titled ladies.[29] Such observations provide a useful framework for understanding the class identity of female publicans generally and why their version of femininity did not clash with the WCTU's designs for female social power.

In her public performance, a female hotelkeeper did all she could to distance herself from vulgarity, pretension, and crudity—anything that could be construed as a lack of 'orderliness' in her person. If female publicans pursued vocational work that elevated them socially, their transcendence occurred through conventionally defined notions of 'womanly' work and manners. Far from aspiring to masculine models of behaviour, women who ran hotels only stood to gain from being lady-like. For women, the legal authority to hold a liquor licence was not necessarily enough in itself to ensure social status if a female publican's behaviour was construed as crass, lewd or otherwise disreputable. But the double-act of licence holding *and* outward shows of gentility could be an effective recipe for social power. As if to underline the point, female licensees in the nineteenth century rarely referred to themselves as publican, hotelkeeper or victualler. Their public title was 'proprietress'.

As part of an aspiring business class, female publicans upheld the very values of both middle-class femininity and bourgeois respectability: propriety and good conduct. There are, however, some indications that female licensees were not always 'angels of the hearth'. A local woman charged Mrs Mary Linnehan, licensee of the Royal Mail Hotel, Blackwood, from 1893 to 1898, with using vulgar language. The court heard that the coarse language of the plaintiff, a customer at her hotel, provoked Mrs Linnehan. The result: 'a shouting match of unsavoury type then taking place in the main street of Golden Point'. The magistrate ruled the case 'a draw' and dismissed the charges.[30] But such incidents were the exception that highlighted the rule. Indeed Licensing Inspectors rarely opposed the issue of a licence to a woman on grounds of 'character', and the testimony of licensing officials, police officials and parliamentarians illustrates that little fault could be found with the 'type' of women who ran hotels.

Whether all female publicans aspired to join the ranks of the mercantile gentry is debatable; for many, a loyal clientele and reliable income was enough recompense for the hard work of hotelkeeping. But it is clear that many did achieve a degree of social acceptability beyond their local constituencies by complying with the values of genteel femininity: 'good taste, good manners, refinement, education, morality, restraint and modesty'.[31] Apart from education, which was not often achieved until the second or third generation of hotelkeeping, the other markers of class status were proudly followed.

Female publicans particularly defended their social and sexual identities by conforming to modest and tasteful standards of dress. Edna Jory recalls the social prominence her parents achieved as publicans (see Plates 22–23). Charlie and Minnie Jory were regular guests at mayoral balls (Charlie was himself encouraged to run for mayor) and, according to Edna, 'My mother was the Belle of the Ball nearly every year.' Edna poignantly remembers how determined her mother was to introduce her daughters to polite society:

> Mum wanted me to be a lady, like her. I didn't want frocks. I used to
> get up the trees, do everything. I remember she was friendly with
> one of the politician's wives, Mrs Tunnecliffe. She invited Mum for
> afternoon tea at her place in Clifton Hill. So Mum got Nancy and I
> dressed up and over we go. Mrs Tunnecliffe opened the door and she
> said, 'Oh, Mrs Jory, have you got two daughters? I've only heard you
> speak of Nancy.'

After Charlie was incapacitated by a stroke, the Jory family lost their hotel and found themselves in dire financial straits. Edna recalls how hard it was for her mother to 'come down to that level'. Minnie's fall from social grace was characterised by living in a 'worker's cottage', her children leaving school to provide for the family, and isolation as 'just a housewife'.[32]

Other daughters of female publicans similarly attest that their mothers rarely socialised with the women who were customers at the hotel and lived in their immediate neighbourhood. When she was able to win any precious leisure time at all, the licensee or licensee's wife was

22. *Charles and Minnie Jory (marked on photo with x), with friends, patrons, other publicans and Masonic Lodge members in the dining room of the Universal Hotel, Fitzroy, c.1920.*

more likely to play cards or go to parties with the wives of professionals and other businessmen. These were the people with whom most publicans identified themselves as being 'on the same level'. Yet if they performed certain rites in the cult of gentility, it is important to note that publicans also rejected others. If the gentry cloaked themselves in an air of superiority, exclusivity and criticism of people 'not of their kind', publicans made a virtue of their tolerance, generosity of spirit and commonality with customers. Indeed, their trade relied on making friends of strangers. Even colonial etiquette manuals perceived that, 'in a young country like Australia' where 'rapid change of fortune' is commonplace, women were required to exert 'unruffled strength' and 'flexible dignity' in balancing a respectable female comportment with 'a spirit of independence' and 'knowing how to transact their own business'.[33]

23. *Edna Jory (left) with publicans Charles and Minnie Jory and sister. Universal Hotel, Fitzroy, c.1919.*

This recipe for success had special appeal in nineteenth-century Australia. The east coast communities of industrialising America, with their more stable capitalist commercial framework, could support rigid gender relations of breadwinning husbands and dependent wives; in contrast, family desertion and early widowhood were undeniable realities in colonial Australia, particularly after the gold rushes. This fact permitted more elastic boundaries in the dominant cultural understanding of the 'good woman'. Female independence was a survival strategy, rather than a threat to the more fluid social and sexual order. It was not that industrialising and soon-to-be-federating Australia was not capitalist or commercial in orientation, but women were more readily built in to the entrepreneurial model of success and self-improvement than their American sisters. The Victorian WCTU appears to have understood the peculiar, and potentially precarious, situation of its women; it actively promoted the ethic of self-reliance and independent careers for young women and cautioned against the idea of marriage as a meal ticket.[34] Temperance women and hotel women may not have formally embraced each other's ways of life, but they certainly shared more class affinity than reasons for antagonism.

Ultimately, female publicans in Victoria both represented themselves, and were viewed, as industrious, enterprising, resourceful women *and* as members of a business class—all of which conveyed respectability in the late nineteenth and early twentieth centuries. While female temperance advocates did care passionately about drink, they arguably took a neutral stance on female licensees because these women did not offend standards of feminine decency; on the contrary, their role and status in society were those that reformers sought to claim for middle-class women more generally. And while the temperance movement fell victim to the very modernity that saw women become legitimate consumers of alcohol in the jazz age, hotels continued to be run by strong, independent-minded, capable women.[35] Frances Willard famously proclaimed that women should 'do everything'; female publicans generally did.

'The Buxom Matron Behind the Bar'

UGLY, BAWDY, DISHONEST, blasphemous, deceptive, adulterous, pimping, immodest, sinful and unruly: these were all labels of disparagement that were attached to female ale sellers in late medieval and early modern England. Through poems, drinking songs and popular literature, female liquor sellers were continuously and consistently 'singled out for particular reproach'. Some scholars believe that misogyny lay at the heart of the cultural response to female ale sellers, arguing that the negative portrayal of such women worked as a safety valve to dispel anxiety about women's dominance in an important and valuable trade.[1] Others have similarly pointed to the fact that women's behaviour, when touched by the actual or notional influence of alcohol, has traditionally been defined as deviant or disorderly by society's moral defenders and voiced by its cultural gatekeepers—the literary elite.[2]

With such a legacy of negative cultural representation, women who sold liquor for a living in the Australian colonies could easily have attracted a bad name for themselves, regardless of their legal authority. Yet as we have now seen, Australia's female publicans were not cast as deviant or disorderly women by either government regulators, pragmatic trade politicians or society's moral guardians. Traditional presumptions about the motivation and character of women who traded in alcohol did not accompany the new settlers as part of their cultural baggage from Britain. Through a close reading of literary representations, drawn from the early goldfields balladeers and later the *Bulletin* school of nationalist writers, it is possible to see that the female publican did not act as a cautionary 'folk type' in the Australian lexicon of popular heroes and villains. Conversely, the image of the indomitable and fearless female publican was included in the mythical equation of drink with power, individual autonomy and egalitarianism which has been critical to Australian nationalism.

The contention that female publicans have been culturally celebrated for their strength of character and business acumen is particularly relevant in Australia, where some feminist historians have argued that the restrictive nature of sex-role stereotypes has diminished women's sense of self and place. Yet female licensees, while working in a location often associated with immorality and disorder, have not been represented as akin to prostitutes; nor has their social power and financial independence seen them pejoratively labelled as 'wilful and self-governing women', as was the case with English ale sellers.[3] On the whole, their exploits have shared the stage with other male culture heroes—and often for the same reasons. They have been painted as adventurous, enterprising, resourceful, resilient and fearless. Yet these qualities are always matched with an equally 'feminine' set of virtues: compassion, generosity, self-sacrifice, dignity and modest adornment. Female publicans have not achieved their elevated cultural status by acting like men. Far from it: they are shown to imbue 'masculine' traits with a decidedly womanly essence.

Most representations of female publicans in fiction, poetry, folk song and folk tale emphasise the female publican's strength of character, public dignity, independence, resourcefulness and resolve. There are no shrinking violets here. But neither do we find a cast of bawds, vixens or hags. What is even more remarkable is that there are *so many* representations of female publicans in the literature of the late nineteenth and early twentieth centuries, given that the case has frequently been made that there is no place for women in Australia's popular mythology or academic versions of it.[4] It might be true that scholarly renditions of 'the Australian legend' have largely excised women from the picture, but in short stories and poetry published in literary magazines such as the *Bulletin*, the *Lone Hand* and the *Australian Town and Country Journal*, and in collections of traditional folk songs and lore, there is no doubt that female publicans occupied a considerable portion of the male creative imagination. They were there on the ground, and on paper too, written into the mainstream literary landscape by the very authors who have been criticised for their 'separatist model of masculinity'.[5] While the masculine orientation of the *Bulletin* school's nationalist values cannot be denied, it is wrong to say that women *only* inhabit their consciousness as part of an oppositional world of domesticity. Women—in the shape of female publicans—could be 'noble frontiersmen' too. In Australia, female publicans enjoyed a rare degree of 'cultural potency'.

Big Poll the Grogseller: The goldfields legacy

The earliest representations of female liquor traders focused on the sly-groggers of the Victorian goldfields. With the sale of alcohol officially banned on the diggings, popular balladeers interpreted women's infringements of the licensing law in line with a political radicalism that advocated republicanism and free thought. In this context, female grog-sellers were portrayed as showing an admirable pluck and colonial courage. Charles Thatcher, a popular goldfields entertainer who believed in the egalitarian possibilities of the gold rushes, immortalised the image of the robust, independent female liquor trader in his song, 'Poll the Grogseller' (see Plate 24). According to folklorist Bill Wannan, Thatcher sang this

24. *'Concert room, Charlie Napier Hotel, Ballarat, June, '55, Thatcher's popular songs.'*

tune 'to appreciative audiences of gold-diggers at Bendigo's Shamrock Hotel in the 1850s'[6]:

> Big Poll the Grogseller gets up every day,
>   And her small rowdy tent sweeps out;
> She's turning in plenty of tin people say,
>   For she knows what she's about.
> Polly's good-looking, and Polly is young,
> And Polly's possessed of a smooth oily tongue . . .

When two sly-grog detectives 'roam about in disguise' and 'several retailers of grog are done brown', Polly is 'prepared when they enter her tent'. She offers them ginger beer:

> And she adds, 'Do you see any green in my eye?
> To your fine artful dodge and disguise I am fly';
>   For, if Polly you'd nail, you'd have, without fail,
> To get up in the morning early.[7]

Read in the context of a goldfields culture of anti-authoritarian sentiment, Polly's own 'artful dodge' is held up as truly commendable. Her activities might be illegal, but in a setting where the issue of licensing (for gold, not liquor) was to erupt in open rebellion at Eureka in 1854, Polly's dexterity in evading the law is not viewed as threatening to the social order. Conversely, there is an intimation that Polly's worldly experience —despite her youth there is no 'green in her eye' that could see her easily 'nailed'—lends her an enviable power. Her own brand of youthful rebelliousness conforms to a colonial narrative that stresses the inevitable movement towards independence and self-rule.

Big Poll became a figure of nineteenth-century nostalgia, as the lawlessness of the gold rushes gave way to an established bourgeois colonial life. When a more conventional commercial order replaced the cheek of frontier entrepreneurialism, wily sly-groggers became authorised licensed victuallers. In this context, the female publican came to represent both the new respectability and civility of the post-gold rush era of settlement (often symbolised in verse by her marriage) and a sentimental reminder of erstwhile freedoms. In this rendition of 'the golden years', liberty means the ability to indulge in honest, simple pleasures and to be treated with decency and consideration. Unlike the lawman, the boss or the hustler (a category which includes barmaids and prostitutes), the female liquor seller was on the miner's side.

This image of the landlady as surrogate helpmeet is exemplified in 'The Grog Tent We Got Tipsy In', a wistful folksong in which a Bendigo miner fondly remembers the days when he was part of an instant community of like-minded men, brought together by circumstance:

> It wasn't more than 12 by 8, no window had or door,
> The tables, seats—were all bush made, and fixed into the floor . . .
> The landlady was pretty, the chaps all flocked you know
> To that grog tent we got tipsy in on old Bendigo . . .
> I think I hear her kind Good Day each evening that we went
> To have a chat and smoke our pipes in that poor little tent;
> My word, mates but I've often seen (you know this ain't a sell)
> More cash spent in that little place than many a flash hotel.
> She married a young Cornishman, and left, to our great woe,
> That grog tent we got tipsy in on old Bendigo.[8]

Here the female alcohol seller is a figure of warmth and respect. Though her good looks are admired, she does not take advantage of her customers through sexual charm. Unlike representations of barmaids, such as 'The Flash Colonial Barmaid', which accent the 'showy satin dress' and 'cheap lace collars' as devices of fraud and artifice, the Bendigo shantykeeper offers a frank and open display of affection: 'her kind Good Day'.[9] She earns her patronage by providing men with a snug, convivial environment in which to 'chat and smoke our pipes'. In this tale, the female liquor seller is not associated with danger and deceit, but with the genuine possibilities and comforts of domesticity. The motif of the female publican as sympathetic companion contrasts with the common representation of the cold, unfeeling barmaid—an 'unnatural' woman who, unlike the proprietress, could never 'understand motherhood'.

Other colonial folksongs use the female liquor seller as a symbol of the advantages offered in the new country, far from the rigid class restraints of England. In 'Australia versus England', Charles Thatcher celebrates the independence and freedoms to be won on the diggings:

> No workhouse have we here, no Poor Law coves so cruel,
> No bullying overseer, no paltry water gruel,
> No masters to oppress a wretched starving devil,
> But here, I rather guess we're all upon a level.

Paradoxically, Thatcher then introduces a cast of characters who have managed to rise above their humble beginnings to achieve some degree of affluence and influence. The very first example on his list is a female liquor seller:

> Mother Smith last week gave up sly grog selling,
> Bought land at Bullock Creek and with consequence is swelling;
> And another one as grand, a man named Harry Potter,
> Bought an acre and a half of land and fancies he's a squatter.[10]

Unlike the Bendigo shantykeeper who transcends her situation through marriage, Mother Smith (most likely a widow) finds fulfilment through her own resourcefulness and autonomy. Her 'swelling' is a telling metaphor for her improved social status; through affluence she has been well fed. The gradual act of 'swelling' is also readily associated with pregnancy, a feminine act of creativity. Her personal and financial growth is thus not interpreted as threatening, but organic. Mother Smith retires on the proceeds of her liquor selling, which, in the spirit of colonial enterprise, is emblematic of the natural justice and freedom that could never have been won in England. Thatcher's commentary on class is thus given a particularly gendered inflection.

The physical dimensions of Mother Smith's social and self-improvement invoke a theme common in the portrayal of female alcohol sellers. Descriptions of physical appearance often accentuate the female hotelkeeper's generously proportioned figure. An *Argus* report on Healesville commented in 1866 that 'Healesville has one tolerably good inn, kept by a lady of vast dimensions and uncertain temper'. The publican at the Medway Hotel was famed for her 'seventeen stone of Irish womanhood'. The fictitious Kitty Doherty, grieving widow of a publican, also 'weighed siventeen shtone . . . Poor Kitty! Her heart was as big as her waist.' In a 1906 story, 'Publicans and Sinners', the publican's wife, Mrs Moss, is described as 'a big bold-faced woman . . . a mass of woman was Vi'let'.[11] Such descriptions, while verging on parody, reinforce the image of a female publican's strength by representing her body as a symbol of her weighty authority.

But the female publican's bodily presence is unsexualised, perhaps even defeminised. While unmarried female liquor sellers are sometimes described as 'pretty', the word most commonly used to suggest a sexual identity is 'buxom'. Here the connotation is one of a healthy, strapping, vigorous physicality to match an equally potent temperament; the implication is never tawdry. For example, the publican's wife in the 1889 story 'And He Didn't Get His Drink' is described as 'the buxom matron behind the bar'.[12] A full-bodied physique is here associated with matriarchal power, not sexual aggression. This image was reserved for the archetypal female social pariah—the barmaid—whose physicality is conversely described in diminutive terms, as in popular *Bulletin* writer E. J. Brady's 'Little Bo-Peep' (1924):

> Oh, Little Bo-Peep is young and slim:
> Her breasts are round and her ankles trim
> With saucy eyes, in a low-cut gown,
> She watches the roadway up and down.[13]

This barmaid's 'vigilance' is attributed to her rapacious nature, her grasping desire to entrap gullible male patrons. By contrast, cultural representations that stressed the physical and mental potency of the female publican or shantykeeper carried the message that such independent women were a vital part of a frontier society in which risks had to be taken in order to conquer an often hostile land. The fact that such legendary women did not need male protectors conveniently supported a frontier myth of self-reliance that disguised the social reality of wife desertion, family breakdown and female poverty.

A good indication of the way that female publicans fitted into a colonial mythology of intrepid settlers is the ubiquitous non-fictional description of such women as the 'first white woman' to reach a particular district. Mrs Martha Brand, wife of licensee William Brand, was said to be the first white woman to reach the Overland Corner, South Australia. She famously arrived 'as a bride' and three hundred Aboriginal women attended her reception.[14] Mrs Ben Singleton and Mrs Phillip Thornley, publicans' wives, were celebrated as the first white women to settle Patrick's Plains in the Hunter Valley.[15] The phrase is used to impart both a sense of personal achievement and wider civic importance. Its cultural value rests on a combination of racist and sexist prejudices: white women as the vehicles for bringing civility and refinement to an otherwise uncultivated and degraded social environment. In the eyes of contemporary observers, female publicans were central to the process of nation-building through their roles as settlers, traders and surrogate mothers.

Creating a legend: Radical nationalists and the home-away-from-home

From the 1880s professional writers and artists in Australia made a conscious attempt to create a distinctive national culture. Centring on the coterie of contributors to Sydney's *Bulletin* magazine, including E. J. Brady and Henry Lawson, a young generation of professional writers scoffed at Victorian-era morality with deliberate irreverence and derided received notions of respectability as out of step with 'the democratic Australian temper'. At the same time as they attacked outdated cultural values, the radical nationalists romanticised the period of imperial expansion, the bush and the 'noble frontiersman' as symbols of escape from urbanism. The qualities ascribed to the 'Coming Man'—'comradeship, self-confidence, generosity, restlessness and resourcefulness'—were defined against the debunked ideal of domesticity. Women, therefore, were rejected as part of the old social and cultural order.[16] To later writers and historians, Lawson's bushman became a national culture-hero.

Some feminist historians have challenged the subsequent conflation of male cultural practices with a 'national tradition'. Most notably, Marilyn Lake has argued that at the end of the nineteenth century, men and women contested 'the control of national culture' as female temperance campaigners engaged in 'a project of cultural reconstruction'. Meanwhile, male writers and critics took every opportunity to portray women as the spoilers of men's pleasures: a bunch of 'vain, snobbish, conservative, parson-worshipping killjoys'.[17] But what of the women who facilitated men's pleasures through the provision of an alternative domestic space—the public house? While it is clear that female publicans do not figure in Lake's appraisal of the female social power that by the 1920s, she claims, had significantly 'feminised' Australian society, did the *Bulletin* similarly cast female liquor sellers as irrelevant to the age of the Lone Hand?

The hotel itself is pivotal to the depiction of life on the road, travel to and from the diggings, political mobilisation and the boom-and-bust leisure rituals of pastoral workers. As such, it is celebrated as the cultural heart of life in the colonies, and later the nation. But the celebration is not all beer and skittles. The wayside shanty or bush inn is as much the scene of personal destruction as of social cohesion. The union buries its dead in a hotel of Henry Lawson's making, but innumerable hard-working yet undisciplined shearers, diggers and drovers are 'lambed down' in the imaginary pubs of Mulga, Piker's and Grumbler's Gully. In spite of the mixed emotions it conjures, the hotel has remained a central motif in Australian literature until the present day.

Publicans are depicted with the same ambivalence as the hotels they operate. Feared and revered for their power to determine who could share in their alcoholic communion, publicans are largely portrayed as a class enemy. Hotels were 'never for bushmen, never for the people of the land', complained one *Bulletin* correspondent in 1903; their purpose was not to provide food, comfort and rest to the weary worker but rather to fleece him of his money with bad grog.[18] Publicans were viewed as dishonest profiteers or drunken scoundrels, described variously as the 'lynx-eyed landlord', 'the watchful spider', 'skilled and wary elves', 'priests of Bacchus' and 'not a soft breed'. One writer noted that hotelkeeping was 'a sorry calling' and the hotelkeepers 'generally, are vicious and poor and mean' because tenant leaseholders were 'tied, bound to iniquity, compelled to rob, cheat and betray' in order to pay their exorbitant rents to rich landowners.[19]

If publicans, then, were generally represented as untrustworthy and irresponsible, it is remarkable to discover that *female* publicans enjoyed considerably more sympathetic treatment than their male counterparts. Female publicans were seen to suffer for the failings of their husbands, but through no fault of their own. This was particularly true when the landlord was portrayed as a drunkard, who relied on the *honest* toil of his wife to sustain the business. In 'An Incident at Stiffner's', Henry Lawson ridiculed 'the proud and independent position of landlord and sole proprietor'. The vaunted autonomy of hotelkeeping, scoffs Lawson, is revealed as a sham when the publican is a drunkard, dependent on his wife's labour: 'Stiffner was always drunk, and Stiffner's wife —a hard-featured Amazon—was boss. The children were brought up in a detached cottage, under the care of a "governess".'[20] While Lawson might be judgemental of the man who forced his wife away from her true calling as mother, another of his stories suggested that his condemnation did not extend to the woman herself.

In 'Jimmy Grimshaw's Wooing', the drunken, slovenly publican of The Half-Way House, Daniel Myers, died from one too many nobblers:

> So the widow buried him . . . and the sign altered to read, 'Margaret Myers, licensed, etc.' and continued to conduct the pub just as she had run it for over five years, with the joyful and blessed exception that there was no longer a human pig and pigsty attached, and that the atmosphere was calm.

The story continues to tell how Mrs Myers 'settled herself to enjoy life comfortably and happily' as the now officially installed publican. A hard life had not spoiled her 'good humour and nature', and she remained 'a pleasant-faced dumpling' despite being 'baked solid in the droughts of Out Back'. Many customers courted the widow Myers and 'reckoned [her] a good catch in the district'. But 'she was not to be caught':

> In answer to the suggestion that she ought to have a man to knock
> round and look after things, she retorted that she had had one, and
> was perfectly satisfied . . . About the end of each shearing the sign
> was touched up, with an extra coat of paint on the 'Margaret',
> whereat suitors looked hopeless.

Lawson was clearly in favour of his heroine's spirited independence and
good sense in avoiding irresolute stooges like her late husband: 'her fame
was carried far and wide, and she became a woman whose name was
mentioned with respect in rough shearing-sheds and huts, and round the
camp-fire'. Many years later, Mrs Myers finally found a man worthy of
her affections, 'a clean-shaved, clean-shirted, clean-neckerchiefed, clean-
moleskinned' widowed selector who took the licence and, together, the
temperate Mr and Mrs Grimshaw ran The Half-Way House Hotel with
dignity and discipline.[21] As much of Lawson's historical knowledge was
gleaned from folk reminiscences, it is fair to say that the respect that
rural communities felt for their female publicans was perpetuated for a
wider audience through such literary treatments.

While the traditional association between alcohol and power—and
particularly, self-empowerment—was implicitly present in the representation of female publicans (note the attention to Margaret Myers' right to
hang her name over the door), Lawson's story is the most clearly drawn
example of the tendency for these women's authority *not* to be interpreted
as disorderly or threatening to patriarchal relationships. More commonly,
a strong woman was seen to bolster the inherent weaknesses in her man.
Stiffner's wife may have been a 'hard-faced Amazon' but even this description gives her a heroic dimension, suggesting a warrior's courage and
prowess. Where female publicans were concerned, a hardy nature and
stern manner were commonly interpreted as 'indomitable' rather than
churlish. Her spirit was one of determination and perseverance rather
than the bad-tempered obstinacy that characterised literary depictions
of hotel patrons' wives. While there was often a hint of flamboyance, this
was delivered as star turn, rather than dismissed as feminine indulgence
or vanity.

Folklorist Bill Beatty, in his 1968 *Australian Folk Tales and Traditions*, evokes Lawson's legacy of respect for Mrs Myers when he claims
that 'Of all the stories which still are told around the camp fires of south-
west Queensland none is more colourful than that of the Eulo Queen'.
This publican's magisterial control of her frontier subjects at the Eulo
Hotel, 'where the Queen held court', was legendary. Beatty immortalises
this publican's famed beauty, bush skills and reputation for having the

'finest collection of opals in the world' thanks to her esteem among the town's miners in the 1890s. Though she lost her liquor licence for 'unscrupulous' trading practices, the Queen is said to have kept male dummies for she was determined 'that come what may she would never forsake her "domain"'.[22] The Eulo Queen died in 1925, in her nineties, and became a folk heroine. Many poets, balladeers, journalists and authors subsequently paid tribute to her as a 'great business woman and a fine lady'.[23]

There are very few exceptions to the archetype of the dignified, gallant female publican who relied on her mettle, not her marriage, to get by in the world. The counter-examples are telling, for in their own way they confirm the characteristics and values that are so readily associated with the 'good woman' who did credit to her trade. In 'On Guard', published in the *Bulletin* in 1892, the anonymous author tells the story of the day that Paddy Boyle left his Mulga Hotel in the care of his wife. While 'on duty', 'Mrs B.' began drinking rum with a teamster customer and the hotel's Aboriginal hand. After the group had 'thirty-eight consecutive drinks', we witness 'vermilion chaos in full undress'. The teamster and the 'black-boy' proceeded to wreck the hotel, chopping down the verandah posts and setting a keg of rum alight while:

> Mrs B. began to bombard the teamster with promiscuous bottles, and smashed the only other window, and knocked sieve-holes into everything but the man she aimed at. Then she jumped on the counter and yelled 'Fire!' and wept aloud for her native country, which was Ireland.

When Paddy Boyle returned, he found his wife asleep in a drunken stupor (after having 'danced jigs in the most joyous style'), and he set to fighting with the teamster. The whole bacchanalian scene is concluded 'In a confused kaleidoscope of curses, mud, gore, woman, scorched nigger, stampeding horses, man-eating dog, utter exhaustion, discovery of grog, famine, and a wild hunt after the remains of the half-grilled black-boy'.[24] Racism and sexism combine to create a tableau of complete moral disintegration. The indignity of a drunken woman forms the centrepiece of a warning of the dangers inherent when colonial white men lose control of their domain. This tragi-comedy underlines the fact that female publicans were only accorded respect when they conformed to orthodox notions of feminine decency and order. Literary landladies were decidedly teetotal.

One aspect of the 'natural' sexual order that is confirmed in literary presentations of pub culture is women's true calling as mothers. Where earlier goldfields accounts stressed the anti-authoritarian streak of female liquor sellers, many late-nineteenth-century accounts emphasised the maternal role of the female publican. Feminine strength was interpreted as being a particularly motherly ability to exercise authority yet remain patient, gentle and endearing. The proprietress of the Amherst Hotel, Avoca, in 1854 was regarded as a 'jolly faced matron'. Mrs Hubbard, who first ran the Ship Inn, Geelong, and then the Cricketers Arms, North Sandridge, in 1877, was nicknamed '"Mother Hubbard", owing to her good nature'.[25] There is also evidence that Australian soldiers in World War I transported their mother icon to distant frontiers. In a short story in the 1918 soldiers' magazine, *Aussie*, the female innkeeper in a Flemish village is called 'Mother' by her Australian patrons, for 'it wouldn't have been natural to call her anything else . . . somehow Mother's place seemed a bit like home'.[26]

An interesting twist on this theme is offered in David Falk's story 'At the Loyda Crossin'', serialised in *The Centennial Magazine* in 1889. Falk's central character is a publican's only daughter, 'a true daughter of the bush; like it intractable, wild and untamed'. The story depicts the misfortune of the girl's 'passionate nature . . . developed amid surroundings of the roughest and wildest type', a nature he attributes to her being raised by a father alone. Without a mother, the girl remains 'untrained in all modes of womanly restraint, her whole mental and moral organization was so untutored'.[27] Falk's morality tale is significant for it underscores the responsibility for 'moral organization' that was ordinarily ascribed to female publicans. Without a woman's influence, the licensee at Loyda Crossin' cannot hope to tame the rough-and-ready behaviour of his male-dominated landscape. Thus, although the radical nationalist school of writers did not condone an urbanised, gentrified model of domesticity, it did use the image of the female publican to represent a certain nobility of spirit to which bush dwellers could aspire through mastery of their environment and their own character flaws. The home-away-from-home (the romanticised bush/pub) is a place free from the daily control of a woman, yet indebted to her benevolent guidance (see Plate 25).

By the early twentieth century, another type of woman was emerging in the range of hotelkeeping classifications: the single businesswoman. By the 1920s, singleness was equated with youthful enthusiasm, desirability and social, sexual and economic freedom. So long as women did not remain out of the marriage market for too long—in which case they became a threat to the social and sexual order—young 'career women' were considered to exhibit an attractive independence.[28] While

25. 'Jersey Clarke . . . came to her as if she were a schoolmaster and he an erring boy due for a thrashing.' Illustration from Randolph Bedford's serial story, 'The Lady of the Pluckup', about a young woman who takes over the running of a remote country pub and soon has the mining town's all-male inhabitants eating out of her hand.

single women had long played a role in the hotel industry, it was not until after World War I and the emergence of the idea of the 'New Woman' that they became visible as a culture type. In 1918, the *Vigilante* reported on a visit to Melbourne by the Sydney hotel family, the Kellys. Mr Kelly, publican and vice-president of the New South Wales Licensed Victuallers' Association, had come for the Victorian Racing Club carnival, accompanied by his daughter, also a licensee. Miss Kelly, noted the trade journal, 'is a well-known figure in Sydney financial circles, and is a pluck and enterprising investor'.[29]

A year later, in a foil to the temperance claim that Australia was being corrupted by alcohol and its merchants, the same paper included women in its portrayal of the potency of the post-Gallipoli nation: 'Is Australia drifting to the bad? The honest answer to this question is a trumpet-tongued "No". Our manhood and womanhood are as virile and healthy, and as courageous and enterprising, as any nation ever created.'[30] While this assessment does not specifically address female publicans, it is significant that the trade was able to invoke women in overtly sexualised terms, marrying 'virility' with productivity, resourcefulness and endeavour. Nineteenth-century representations of female publicans certainly included the latter qualities in their portrayals but steadfastly dismissed any association with female sexuality. In a sense, the arrival of the New Woman allowed the image of female publicans to return from the cradle of middle-class respectability to Big Poll's spirited era, where youth and attractiveness comfortably collided with business acumen and survival skills. While the two examples cited above are taken from the hotel industry's own journal, their confidence in celebrating the 'self-governing' nature of women in the liquor trade can be attributed to the popularising of the female publican as an examplar of national confidence, resourcefulness and fortitude.

Publicans walked an ambivalent line: they aspired to be a socially mobile class of traders *and* to represent a cultural tradition rooted in working-class value systems. In late-nineteenth-century Australia, when male writers, commentators and critics were establishing a national identity based on the digger or frontiersman type with the virtues of self-reliance, independence and anti-authoritarianism, political fathers were creating their own visions of democratic freedom and stability based on principles of sexual and social order. Ironically, these dual processes were *both* sympathetic to the archetypal female publican. As an overtly maternal woman, 'the matron behind the bar' conformed to middle-class standards of femininity. As a cultural type, Big Poll the Grogseller affirmed working-class expressions of conviviality, communality and freedom from tyrannical constraint. Female publicans, therefore, escaped ridicule and castigation on both sides of the class divide. They occupied a distinct social and cultural category, representing neither the Wife nor the Whore nor the Wowser. Yet, as maternal characters making a living by regulating male excesses in public drinking places, they embodied elements of all of these stereotypes. Their power, it seems, was based on this very independence from conventional definitions: they knew what they were about.

'Dignity Is the Right Word'

AS PUBLIC HOUSEKEEPERS, female licensees enjoyed legal authority, institutional support, cultural kudos and the moral benefit of conforming to middle-class standards of appropriate femininity. The convergence of these levels of affirmation placed female hotelkeepers in a strong social position *vis-à-vis* other working-class women, and arguably some bourgeois women, of their times. But how did female publicans' relatively elevated public status impact on their own sense of personal empowerment? How were gender relations regulated within the particular codes of pub culture? Some writers have stressed the way in which male drinkers have used the pub as a site of patriarchal oppression, employing both subtle and obtuse means to keep women 'in their place'.[1] Their discussion, however, focuses on the relationship between male and female drinkers and has not touched on the issue of how a woman, as the hotel's keeper, was both required and able to keep *men* in their place. Female publicans had to navigate the masculine orientation of public drinking as much as the male-dominated public realm of business and bureaucracy. How on earth did they manage it?

The social experience of hotels presents an unconventional perspective on sexual politics in Australian history. Many accounts of men's and women's mutual occupation of public space stress their 'struggle for control' and 'opposing interests', with women coming off second-best.[2] But inside the pub, we find a story of female authority and male compliance. Unlike other working women, who had only their labour with which to bargain, female publicans had the ability to restrict men's access to a desirable commodity. Unlike prostitutes, who also traded in a currency that was valued by men, female publicans ran businesses that held legal and commercial legitimacy. As licensed liquor sellers, they bargained with an asset that was arguably more powerful than labour, money or sex.

According to customary hotel practice, customers who violated acceptable standards of behaviour—as set by the publican—could be 'barred' for their transgressions. As Margaret O'Connell describes her publican mother's role: 'Being a female publican is not a sexualised kind of work, like being a barmaid is. It's a position of power because Mum had the authority to say who stays and who leaves.' In a private home, women may have inherited the Victorian-era legacy as being sentinels of morality, but, as rates of domestic violence suggest, there were few barriers to a man's physical monopoly over 'his' castle. In a public house, by contrast, a woman's moral entitlement to govern behaviour was backed up by her legal authority as the licensee. While some suffragists campaigned for citizenship rights to further women's influence in shaping male conduct generally, female hotelkeepers used their legally prescribed proprietorial rights, and the personalised nature of the publican–customer relationship, to maintain order and control in their domain.

Predominantly, female publicans' narratives of their professional lives reveal a sense of empowerment and satisfaction that was facilitated by their role as hotelkeeper. In a sense, however, it is academic whether female publicans possessed quantifiably more or less power than other women, or in relation to men. The value of oral testimony (particularly in the absence of written forms of self-reflection) is in conveying women's subjective definition of their own power—how they felt about themselves and their lives. Whether there is 'truth' to these self-assessments is immaterial when exploring women's perceptions of self-worth and feelings of personal efficacy.[3] What is compelling is to determine how women assessed and articulated their own sense of order, meaning and importance within the hotel and its culture.

Lady-like, business-like and likeable: A balancing act

Many of the devices used by female publicans to exercise control over their largely male crowds could have been stripped directly from the pages of temperance protocol manuals. The rules of acceptable comportment set by female publicans were not only aimed at carving out a respectable reputation within a wider social context, but also at establishing relationships of authority within the hotel. To maintain order in the (public) house, a female hotelkeeper had to prove, through her own performance, that she was not herself a 'disorderly' woman.

In the late nineteenth century, the image of feminine restraint, taste and dignity was inextricably linked to women's sexual and class identity as a 'lady'.[4] For a female publican, establishing an identity based on moderation and self-possession was even more crucial given that she lived in the shadow of the conventional taint of 'woman plus alcohol equals promiscuity'. In the early twentieth century, as certain aspects of bourgeois femininity became less restrictive, female publicans continued to champion the idea of 'standards' in a way that made them seem peculiarly unmodern. Indeed, if female modernity was linked to youth culture, female publicans gleaned their authority from age. The longer a woman stayed in the job, as the *Vigilante*'s testament to the Mrs Gellies of the industry confirms, the more she could claim mastery over her domain.

What were the aspects of 'lady-like' behaviour that female publicans used to establish their command? Most strikingly, women who ruled from behind the bar ensured that they themselves remained dry. All of the publicans who began their hotelkeeping careers before World War II revealed in their interviews that not drinking in front of customers was crucial to maintaining control. Gloria Fry asserts that only an upright, sober woman, who is in control of herself, can establish a relationship of authority over customers: 'Authority is a matter of how you conduct yourself. Let's face it—I don't drink behind the bar. You're breaking down straight away if you do . . . I think it is definitely the thing a female publican shouldn't do.'[5] Mrs Fry uses the imagery of disintegration to underscore the importance of sobriety to a female publican's sway over the space. Where drinking is associated with potency in men, it implies weakness on the part of a woman; once cracks in the armour appear, the whole edifice may crumble (see Plate 26).

Pam Sleigh-Elam similarly describes her mother's dominion over their family's suburban hotel in terms of her physical and symbolic uprightness and vigilance:

> My mother never drank. In the main bar—it was a very long bar—she'd just stand up like a matriarch and look down the whole time. She'd talk to some of the customers that she knew because they liked to talk but she was just there to keep an eye on things. My mother was very good at what she did. She dotted her i's and crossed her t's, she really did.[6]

26. *Gloria Fry, aged eighty-eight, four months after her retirement from hotelkeeping, Bendigo, 2002.*

Pam contrasts her mother's schoolmarm 'iron hand' with her father's version of sociability with customers. While her mother could chat, her father was bound by masculine rituals to participate in the drinking culture of the pub:

> Dad was a gentle, kindly man who mixed with all levels and was very well respected and liked. He had his little school of friends in the saloon bar, mostly businessmen from our area . . . They all took

their turns in paying because that was the way it was. You couldn't walk away after one or two drinks. If your school was five, you did have to stay there for five drinks. It was a code in those days.

Female publicans, freed from the cultural restrictions of 'the shout', were thus able to assert their power without compromising their health, dignity or managerial competence. As Pam suggests, her father was popular but 'My mother had the authority because she was the boss. She did the hiring and firing.' Interestingly, although her father was the licensee, Pam suggests that it was through her mother's more aloof and restrained behaviour that customers and staff knew who was truly in charge.

With characteristic good humour, Eileen Clatworthy points out that she found it useful to have more than sobriety up her sleeve when it came to disciplining an unruly customer:

> People can play up when they're asked to leave, when they've had too much liquor or they're misbehaving. I can handle it without any trouble. I was never scared or frightened of anyone. If I felt they had too much, I'd just ask them to go. Also, I'd have a soda syphon on standby![7]

As Eileen's anecdote suggests, resourcefulness was one of the key skills of the successful publican—an expertise that required keeping one step ahead and at a measured distance from the crowd mentality of 'one in, all in'. Female control required independence from masculine codes of behaviour.

If drinking could impair a woman's prestige in the pub, so too there were other important ways in which the female publican consciously maintained her position of respect. One of these was the name by which the customers referred to her. As we have seen, calling a female publican Mother or Ma was a customary way of signalling maternal deference. While affectionate, the title was not merely sentimental. The designation implied moral strength and authority. Kath Byer's customers went so far as to call her the 'Reverend Mother', the very image of 'a gentle and loving autocrat', a 'moral tyrant in the home'.[8] Kath's house-name evokes a cheeky blend of schoolboy veneration and impertinence.

Not all female publicans agree on what a particular naming policy implied. Gloria Fry holds to the theory that a formal address ensures appropriate deference: 'My customers only called me by my name, Mrs Fry. That's something that I've always insisted on. You know that old expression "familiarity breeds contempt". I've always felt that if you're to keep your dignity, it's very important.' Thus Mrs Fry insisted on formality as an instrument of compliance. Eileen Clatworthy also associates the use of a formal address with respect, but unlike Mrs. Fry, she suggests that her customers chose this route rather than it being a matter of grave importance to her: 'The customers respected my position. They called me "Mother". Some of them. Others just called me Mrs Clat, Mrs Clatworthy. People could have called me anything. I wouldn't have worried.' Again, Lillian O'Connell interprets the ceremonial reserve of being referred to by her surname as a mark of esteem: 'The clientele were very respectful to me. They were so nice when they realised a woman was in charge . . . always treated me like a lady. For thirteen years I wasn't called Lillian; I was always Mrs O'C.'[9]

But if there were some standard tricks of the trade that ensured that a female publican was treated 'like a lady', it is also clear that individual temperament and personality were important factors in establishing a relationship of control over clientele. The version of feminine propriety adopted by female hotelkeepers owed more to the 'grand dame' than the 'demure damsel' motif. Speaking of her mother, Pam Sleigh-Elam laughs heartily at my question about maintaining authority over a crowd:

> How did she keep control? Well, you didn't know my mother! She was very good, very emphatic. She was a bit highly strung and they just would not have crossed her. She had an iron hand. My mother was a very, very good businesswoman. She knew exactly what was going on anywhere.

Pam also indicates that being a good publican meant having 'to be friendly with everyone. Not over-friendly, but friendly.' Lillian O'Connell similarly states that she 'wanted to be the boss but friendly'. Gloria Fry also comments that of her six children, the only one to be seriously interested in helping her out in the business was her daughter Elaine: 'She's got the personality for it. She's very amenable . . . easy to know. She loves talking politics, which is dangerous, but she does!' Kath Byer attests to the openness that is required to be capable of hotelkeeping: 'To be a good publican, I think you've got to be somebody who likes people. A lot go in and they should never go in. You've got to be very down-to-earth, of course. Broad-minded and very tolerant. That's how I run it.' The personal characteristics of tolerance, congeniality and sincerity resulted in the successful female publican lending an incontrovertible air of control to her hotel environment. Aware that the need to be charitable but not permissive required a particular disposition, female publicans attest that the hotel life was 'not for everyone'.

According to these women, then, female publicans upheld standards of decorum, decency and self-regard that owed their force to notions of respectable female behaviour. These standards had their origins in Victorian-era gentility but continued to be pertinent well into the twentieth century. Female publicans' professional dexterity, however, lay in balancing a show of dignified, lady-like distance with a personality that was upfront and gregarious. The reward for this juggling act was a trustworthy clientele, a sense of control, and the important interpersonal foundations for a profitable business enterprise. Female publicans did not rebel against conventional feminine mores but rather used them to their advantage within their own cultural context. What some interviewees are perhaps less ready to articulate is the toll that the constant public performance of feminine goodness could take on one's sense of personal space and self-expression. Novelist Debra Adelaide's recent fictional account of a female hotelkeeper's life suggests that women 'reared on Greer, Millett, de Beauvoir' find it more difficult to play the role of the ever-accessible surrogate wife and mother figure than women of a previous generation. 'It's not so much being a woman', she writes, '. . . but a particular type of woman . . . I don't understand the need to efface oneself in order to achieve acceptance.' Even Kath Byer alludes to the flip-side of maternal vigilance: 'I'm everybody's from the time I wake up till I go to bed'.

The other side of the bar: Amenable men and their steadfast keepers

One of the paradoxes of female publicans' control over their customers is that, contrary to the pervasive 'border conflict' model of gender relations, some men appear to have welcomed a matronly hand of restraint. Negotiating the use of hotel territory, women set house rules that men agreed to abide by in return for the publican's favour. Psychoanalytic theorists stress that all humans crave a 'symbolic caretaker', as 'we never usually outgrow our yearning to be guided by someone more powerful than ourselves'.[10] In hotels men generally accepted a woman as 'symbolic caretaker', willingly placing their alcohol-induced helplessness in her capable hands. Far from mounting a counter-attack on the exercise of female muscle, men respected the female hotelkeeper's right to use her proprietorial and matriarchal power to restrict the excesses of male behaviour. This theme is constantly reiterated by interviewees. Moreover, the maternal influence is particularly evident in the case of single or widowed hotelkeepers, where there is no 'father figure' present in the public house.

Kath Byer comments that a woman 'can get more respect in a hotel than on the street'. She believes that men look to women to set their boundaries. Where male customers will feel threatened if a male publican challenges their ability to handle another drink or back down from a stoush, Kath's six decades of experience as a publican have shown her that men feel safe, and even relieved, when a trusted woman takes control of their actions:

> They take more notice of me than they would of a man in authority. You've got to remember, you're not drinking and they are. They get confused. They want to be controlled. If they play up, they know they're given a rest [barred]. It's automatic, and they know that and they accept it.

Gloria Fry similarly believes that men respond positively to clear behavioural guidelines set by level-headed women:

> The people in a hotel behave the way you want them to behave. If you allow them to be vulgar in their speech, they will do so. But if you make a firm line, they will stick to it. And they obey it. They respect you. Sometimes you might not actually feel very calm, you might get a bit frustrated, but generally speaking it doesn't do to have a person with a fighting sort of a nature. Women are less inclined to fight with customers. It's not in their nature for a woman to be like that. Women are pacifists more or less.

These publicans' observations suggest that male patrons are willing to acquiesce to a woman's judgement where masculine pride will resist the attempts of another man to control their behaviour. This insight challenges the twin assumptions that sexual antagonism is a natural consequence of men and women inhabiting the same territory and that power relations of dominance and submission must always be established to male advantage.

One of the most common 'house rules' that female publicans established was that male drinkers did not swear in front of a woman. As Gloria Fry puts it: 'I always insisted on the language being above reproach'. In return for this gesture of respect, female hotel workers did not criticise or meddle in 'men's business', only giving advice when asked for it. Mayse Young clearly articulates this gendered ground rule in her autobiography:

> For all their rough exteriors, most of these men were gentlemen and always treated women with consideration and respect. If a swear word slipped out in conversation when we were within earshot, it

was followed by an apology. On the other hand, females also respected the bar as men's private sanctuary, and we knew that we
weren't supposed to listen in on their talk.[11]

When Lynne Cox was running a rough bush pub in the 1980s, she kept a
'swear jar' on the bar counter complete with a sign that read, 'You can
swear if you can afford it'. 'Well,' laughs Lynne, 'I made a fortune for the
Children's Hospital!'[12]

Most men do not appear to have resented the restriction of their
language in the presence of women, but rather incorporated it into their
own code of proper public behaviour. Anne Parr explains:

> The difference between a hotel being run by a man or a woman
> might be in the reactions of the customers. They were very respectful
> of women. The customers themselves helped to control it, the lan-
> guage and so forth. You see, one little group might start getting agi-
> tated or throwing in a swear word or something. A fellow about three
> feet away up the bar there would come down and say, 'You just cut
> that out'. So the customers themselves policed each other.

The example of 'bad language' illustrates the point that men and women
could inhabit separate moral territories even while they shared the same
physical space. Men were prepared to acquiesce to the behavioural guidelines that were seen as indisputably appropriate to the heterosocial landscape, while women reciprocated by not prying or offering unsolicited
judgement.

The picture that emerges is one of a territorial negotiation with the
aim of mutual satisfaction. Men could drink publicly if they minded
their manners; women could run their businesses smoothly if they kept
customers in line but also on side. Many interpretations of the gender
order view the rigid and ideological prescriptions of 'true femininity' as
a historical source of subordination for women.[13] But perhaps the strict
observance of codes of respectability could also give a woman the capacity to control the actions and movements of others, and thus achieve a
sense of control over her own life. Within their own communities—on
their own local stage—female publicans were indeed commanding
women. They could define a customer's eligibility for entry to a desired
location, exclude miscreants, deprive them of the object of their affection
or validate their entitlement to continued service. That female publicans
relied upon conventional attitudes towards feminine strength and influence does not undermine the effectiveness of their approach.

The fact that personal identity is often bound up in the physical place where control is exerted is evidenced by the tendency of female hotelkeepers to remain in their vocations long past retirement age, even when they had established financial security. Kath Byer, who plans to see out her days at the helm of her hotel, affirms that to make an impact on pub culture one has to be there 'long enough to really gather up'. Kath draws on imagery of the mother hen, watchfully tending her brood, to explain the motivation for staying on in a profitable business beyond the point where financial security is an issue. She evidently relishes the influence and importance of her role as symbolic and practical caretaker. It makes her feel strong. Eileen Clatworthy, who has now relinquished the licence to her hotel, but still lives on the premises and acts as an un-official *maître d'hotel* to customers, counts herself lucky to have achieved so much independence in her sixty-odd years as a publican. She defines her success in terms of not having to 'ask people for anything'. Johanna Clancy concurs that being a publican meant she was 'a free agent'. Lillian O'Connell reflects that she was able to achieve 'the sort of place I wanted to run' because 'it was in me to be able to cope and keep things running nicely'. Though a modest and unassuming woman, she articulates the knowledge that she has achieved a remarkable level of self-determination in her life. Lillian's daughter, Margaret, also notes the importance of hotel-keeping to her mother's emotional survival, particularly in widowhood: being 'in the public space . . . in the centre of the action' helped her to cope. Gloria Fry, who witnessed the tragic deaths of two husbands, simi-larly stresses her personal role in creating a hotel environment which reflected her own value system: 'A hotel is what you make of it. "Dignity" is the right word.' Norma Crowe further suggests that self-respect lies in having the freedom to call the shots: 'At least in a hotel you're your own boss, not being told what to do . . . I think more women would have done the things I've done if they had a chance.'[14]

In the early to mid-twentieth century, a time when the dependent wife and mother was enshrined by law and convention as the model for social harmony, some women found that being able to take up a position 'in the centre of the action' and be 'their own boss' was the key to avoid-ing the cultural invisibility and social isolation that can result in a life of passivity and frustration. Most theoretical analysis of the meaning of work in Western industrial society has stressed socially productive activity as being the chief means by which people lay claim to personal agency.[15] The experience of female publicans suggests that, while access to paid employment may be crucial to social status in a capitalist political economy, the ability to *control* one's work environment has a notable effect on feelings of self-empowerment and self-esteem.

The combination of legal legitimacy, a general level of political tolerance and strong cultural endorsements for the influential role of women in hotels, helped create an environment where women felt empowered in their personal lives and public relationships. Although female publicans conformed to orthodox notions of genteel femininity in order to establish their moral right to authority, they were able to use conventional gender codes (maternalism, sobriety, restraint) to achieve unconventional female experiences (financial independence, social recognition, personal autonomy). The hotel, as a cultural institution which lay outside the bounds of polite society yet was ever responsive to hegemonic standards of respectability, thus provided a place where women, too, could follow the rules but shift the goal posts. The female publican could be controlling without being 'manly'. She could make her own living without being rebellious. She could sell alcohol without being unseemly. She had social power without seeking social change.

And she could inhabit 'a man's world' because, by her own definition, she had made the hotel a woman's world too.

The More Things Change

I always felt in control. I guess it's a very territorial thing and I think women are probably more territorial in that instance. A hotel is very homely if you have lived there, or even if you're there all the time, so you make your presence felt.[1]

THIS IS HOW SAMANTHA GOWING describes her relationship to the hugely successful, fashionably refurbished hotel she ran from 1990 to 1998, the Gowings' Grace Darling in recently gentrified Collingwood. Samantha was twenty-four years old when she took over her father's mantle as a prominent Melbourne hotelier. As an attractive, energetic, educated young woman seeking an income and an outlet for her talents at the end of the twentieth century, she could have chosen any number of professions. She selected hotelkeeping not only because of her family connections but also because it gave her the opportunity to—in her own words—'have a public persona', gain 'notoriety', use her 'natural born' womanly inclination to be a 'provider' while at the same time be 'in the thick of things'. As a 'social person', Samantha found that the job suited her inherent abilities while giving her the chance to make a difference. As she explains: 'I definitely wanted to inject some femininity into the place ... an overall softness ... and a lot of women used to come and comment or thank us'.

But for Samantha, one of her greatest challenges was reconciling her role as an agent for change among a new generation of hotel patrons with the legacy of the 'old-style' female publican, complete with her demure attire, stately comportment and professional air of authority and reserve.

'When we took over the pub, there was definitely a long list of old customers, from the pub's old days, who had the idea of "the matriarch
behind the bar". I didn't embrace that role initially and then I just took it
in my stride.' After eight years in the business, with a string of industry
awards and media accolades behind her, Samantha and her co-licensee,
brother Chris, decided to sell the hotel and step back from 'the public
thing'. Now running a business as a food and fitness consultant, Samantha is 'enjoying just being on the outskirts'. In many ways, Samantha
Gowing is the modern face of female hotelkeeping; perhaps surprisingly,
she articulates her ambitions, motives and satisfactions in much the same
language as her fellow female publicans a century earlier.

Female publicans were never women 'on the outskirts'—lonely,
marginalised, stigmatised or alienated by a culture that privileges male
access to and enjoyment of public leisure spaces. There is no doubt that
Australia is a country that has fostered, and in certain critical ways
still promotes, male-dominated activities and visions to the detriment of
female social participation.[2] Yet the women who have historically run
Australian hotels in large numbers were 'at the centre of the action'. They
played a front-of-house role, highly visible both within the institution of
the pub and through broader forms of social recognition.

Writing the story of female hotelkeeping is by no means an exercise
in 'deviance' studies, a discourse about people with alternative or sub-
ordinated sexual, political or social identities. Australia's female publicans, in the late nineteenth and early twentieth centuries, were at the
heart of an institution that was pivotal to the social, commercial and political economy of the day and has since become part of a dominant discourse about national identity. They were women who were powerful and
respected within their own milieu. They held authority, independence
and self-esteem in the performance and expression of their own lives.
They also had supporters and advocates within mainstream political,
judicial and business circles. They ordered public space. They ordered
men around.

No one factor can adequately explain how women came to occupy
such a prevalent and influential position within the business and culture
of hotelkeeping. Rather, from the earliest colonial times in Australia, the
convergence of structural determinants, ideological discourses, political
allegiances, architectural forms and cultural values worked to enable
women to take up a commanding and discernible role behind the bars of
hotels. Similarly, judging by the motivations for female involvement in
the hotel industry, the pub has been a place that allowed women to

achieve a high level of independence, autonomy and self-fulfilment. This favourable assessment does not mean that all female publicans were *happy* or *nice*, but that as an occupation hotelkeeping has played a positive role in the lives of many women.

As archetypal Australian culture heroines, female publicans have made an impression on—for want of a less clichéd term—the national psyche. This is a tricky subject to address, for it points to the inherent tensions involved in detaching the stereotypical from the real, the fabled from the lived, the fictional from the testimonial. Patently, female publicans aspired to, and were often able to achieve, social mobility, material security and community leadership. But fundamentally, the figure of the female publican was not a cultural pariah because the characteristics commonly ascribed to her—and proudly worn by her—did not offend broadly defined patriarchal, middle-class notions of decent and appropriate womanhood: maternalism, self-control, feminine dignity and sexual restraint. Moreover, in the particular Australian context, her values and attributes conformed to nationalist ideals of character type: self-reliance, independence and social advancement through individual effort *but also* good humour, irreverence towards puritanical constraint and a strong ethic of communal responsibility.

The convergence of these two factors has, if anything, made the female publican a more enduring cultural type than her male counterpart, who is more often seen in literature, from a class perspective, as avaricious, self-interested and untrustworthy. As a surrogate mother figure in a male-dominated popular culture, female publicans are forgiven the 'un-Australian' sin of mercantile ambition. As women entrusted with the job of controlling male excesses, female publicans also fared better than wives in terms of their mainstream popular image: they represented the possibilities of benevolent domesticity rather than a resignation to domestic imperialism. 'The matriarch behind the bar', as Samantha Gowing's old-timers put it, has been an affectionate figure of cultural providence.

Amy Robson, the 31-year-old owner and licensee of the Curry Family Hotel in Collingwood, revels in this leadership role: 'It's mother hen gathering her chicks'.[3] Amy was eight months' pregnant with her first child at the time of our interview. (Coincidentally, I was equally pregnant with my second baby—we looked a sight, hauling our massive bellies up onto bar stools to conduct the interview!) Amy was philosophical about the connection between hotelkeeping and her impending maternity: 'Being a publican is very much like being a kindergarten teacher. That's why I figure I've got great experience for being a mother. Everyone says, "Oh, yes, you're the Mother Theresa of Collingwood. You're every-one's mum".' Amy was educated at a private girls' school but, despite the lure of other professional outlets for her considerable intellect and vigour, she chose to run a pub because it suited a fundamental streak in her personality:

> If my name wasn't Amy, it should be Wendy, from *Peter Pan*. Invariably I'd drag some person I'd just met home who needed help, all these young boys, young kids, so it's a bit like being Wendy and having my lost boys. It's almost a natural progression to have a pub instead of effectively running a half-way house [at home]. It's just a bigger half-way house. It's a huge, huge responsibility.

After ten years of employment as a barmaid, Amy also cites her desire to control her own working life as a reason for buying the Curry Family Hotel (see Plate 27). 'I just basically wanted to run something. I like to say that I run a cruise ship, not a tight ship. I'd rather people enjoyed them-selves. But I have seven rules: No pub TAB, no pokies, no topless bar-maids, no dizzy blonds, no idiots, no arseholes, no junkie scum.' Under her management, Amy has created a family-oriented, old-fashioned local watering hole which is not glamorous or chic but certainly reflects its keeper's values of honesty, responsibility and nurturance. Now a single mother, Amy continues to work tirelessly among her 'extended family' of 'waifs, strays and refugees'.

As the testimonies of Samantha Gowing and Amy Robson affirm, the story of female hotelkeeping is one of continuity in a changing world. It is an occupation that very many women have entered, and for many of the same reasons, across decades which have otherwise seen immense im-provements in the economic, social, welfare and professional opportuni-ties of women. Female publicans could use their skills, temperaments and ambitions to advantage in a job that afforded them independence, the chance to raise a family and work in the same location, and either capi-talise on their personal energies and drives or build on the foundation that marital or other family associations had begun. Female publicans, as an occupational genus if not always on an individual basis, achieved an unusual level of financial self-reliance, cultural agency, control over public space, self-respect and social visibility—all things which women as a whole increasingly claimed for themselves, and won, during the twentieth century. With greater prospects of accomplishing these things through a broader range of occupational and educational choices, women looked less to hotelkeeping to provide them.

27. *Amy Robson in 1997, aged twenty-five, owner and licensee, Curry Family Hotel, Collingwood, Victoria.*

However, as women's social power improved in wider Australian society, the pub became increasingly seen as a masculine space, hostile to female encroachment—from customers, if not custodians. This was so much the case that a symbolic strategy in second-wave feminist activism of the 1970s was for women to chain themselves to a public bar stool, demanding the right to be able to drink with and like men. The irony is that this movement apparently bore no historical memory of the fact that, a century earlier, the hotel had in many respects been gendered female and that women had won their right to control the space through their distinctly 'feminine' characteristics of domestic nurturance, maternal vigilance and moral purity.

Many previous treatments of the Australian hotel and its culture—written from both celebratory and critical perspectives—have failed to invest the pub with any historical specificity. This crucial deficit has meant that knowledge of the tradition of female hotelkeeping, while often stored in the repository of social memory, has been lost to the official historical record. Love it or hate it, as an enduring symbol of the nation's way of life, the hotel has been largely represented as a one-dimensional, unchanging social institution: a male bastion with the pathetic appendage of a Ladies Lounge. The mythologising of the hotel as either cultural pearl or misogynist *bête noire* neglects the physical alterations and ideological shifts that have been wrought on the pub environment, both from within and without. Licensing laws, political agendas, literary currents, architectural fashions and moral concerns have all made the hotel a dynamic institution, constantly responsive to the mood of the day.

In the nineteenth century, the public house was undeniably feminised through legislation, building regulations and common usage that stressed the restorative, civilising virtues of public house home life: shelter, companionship, personal care and connection. After World War I, when the material and spiritual needs of a settler society were replaced by the more formulaic prescriptions of a highly urbanised, industrialised nation, the pub reflected broader trends towards social segregation along class, ethnic, racial and gender lines. As commercial entities, hotels have always traded in the dominant cultural currencies of the times; as social institutions, they have also contributed to the construction of culture through the propagation and perpetuation of certain values, codes and practices.

The idea of the hotel as a male domain—as anti-home, as refuge from female control and influence—only achieved widespread cultural appeal in the period after World War II. While men certainly made up the lion's share of hotel patrons prior to this time, and while it may have been unacceptable among members of polite society for women to drink in hotel bars, the social separation of public house patrons did not, of necessity, make hotels male-dominated social institutions. After 1945, a literary and academic preoccupation with the national way of life, came to replace the erstwhile concept of 'national type'.[4] Prior to this time, the hotel was widely understood to be a place of female management and influence. Burly male publicans offering an unconditional vehicle for masculine indulgence had never made the Australian home-away-from-home.

The hotel was only gendered male in the post-war period, as wider ideas about 'woman's place' in the national way of life became inextricably linked with consumerism, the suburban family home and an exclusively middle-class lifestyle. This movement coincided with the by-now entrenched privileging of masculine drinking practices in the public bar after two decades of the six o'clock swill and the hotel industry's belated transition to modern principles of high finance, company licence-holding and absentee landlordism. There is no doubt that women were adversely affected by this shift away from 'intimate' management ideals (the host–guest relationship) and towards corporate business practices. Salaried nominees of silent company interests were trained in the art of 'disinterested management'—a far cry from the decidedly 'female' basis of traditional hospitality.

When twentysomething Eliza Faull took over the licence to the Sawyers Arms Tavern in Geelong from her grandmother, Eileen Clatworthy, she found that it was advantageous to trade on her Mater's name and reputation as a way of garnering appropriate respect for her position (see Plate 28). Eliza believes it is harder for a young woman to assert her influence in the late-twentieth-century hotel environment because, unlike in her grandmother's day, customers, staff and liquor trade representatives alike expect to find a man in the top position of authority.[5] By the 1990s, the Australian Hotels Association saw fit to create a sub–branch, Women in the Hotel Industry Today (WITHIT), to act as a support network for female licensees who otherwise felt excluded from the boys' club of hotel management.

Ultimately, to represent the hotel as a complex, changing social location is to restore its historical specificity and to overcome the cultural stereotypes that make convenient props for beer advertisements but do little to resolve the tensions and contradictions that lie at the heart of our national icons.

If more evidence is required to convince sceptics that the hotel is an ever-changing social organism, mutating to suit the times, one has only to look at the late-twentieth-century trend towards what I would call the re-feminisation of Australian hotels. In the past decade, inner-city pubs have enjoyed a cultural renaissance, particularly for a legion of professional youth with considerable amounts of disposable income and

28. Eileen Clatworthy (front), her daughter Carmel Cooper (left) and granddaughter Eliza Faull (right). Sawyers Arms Tavern, Geelong, 1999.

leisure time. Hotels have survived the era of the six o'clock swill, and the ensuing phenomenon of the suburban 'beer barn' as home to 1970s and 1980s 'cock rock', to emerge as gentrified spaces for sophisticated dining and mixed-sex sociability.

Many commentators, like *Age* journalist Melinda Houston, have pointed to the resurrection of the 'local pub in the finest tradition': 'Spiritually, a convivial place for mates to get together, have a beer, unwind after work and nut out the big issues; physically, a warren of little rooms and cosy bars that encourage conversation, relaxation, the exchange of confidences'.[6] The return to intimate spaces has been particularly aided by small touches of domestic repose: soft furnishings, linen in the dining room, mood lighting, artwork and collectibles. Current listings of Melbourne's 'best pubs' regularly point to such features of homely adornment. For example, Swallows Hotel, Port Melbourne has been acclaimed for its 'comfortable dining room'. The All Nations in Richmond has 'an open fire' and 'a proper old-fashioned bar', making it the 'the bloke's pub that women enjoy'. The North Fitzroy Star, formerly an old men's boozer, is now touted as 'a very pleasant place—if a bit chintzy— and the locals regard it as an extension of their living rooms'.[7] During a recent (and very pleasant) evening at the North Fitzroy Star, I overheard an enraptured young woman exclaim to her female companions, 'It's just like somebody's house!' The more things change . . .

As the nuclear family continues its demographic decline, more women enter the professions and inner-city property ownership becomes increasingly unattainable, the local pub as home-away-from-home has taken on new meaning. And reclaiming their station behind the bar, swelling the ranks of publican service-providers, are the female hotel-keepers. One recent newspaper article, sub-titled 'The New Publicans', featured several women—some going solo, some in partnership with men, some raising their young children at the hotel—all contributing to the 'significantly more civilised' atmosphere of the fashionably reconstructed hotel.[8] There is, of course, nothing new about advertising women as the civilising agents of this persistently popular cultural institution.

So too, there is a familiar ring to the factors that continue to attract women to hotelkeeping. Lynne Cox has recently taken over the reins of her fourteenth hotel. For Lynne, it's the relationship with her clientele that keeps her coming back for more: 'I get a lot of satisfaction out of it. It's an achievement. They need me because I am their mentor, their coun-sellor, their crisis analyst. You're everything to them. You've broken through their territory. They haven't broken through yours. Quite frankly, I'm a bloody good publican.'

Notes

A Colonial Pub Crawl

1 Freeland, *The Australian Pub*, p. 121.
2 Butler et al., *Hotels in Victoria*, p. vii.
3 Freeland, *The Australian Pub*, p. 129.
4 Public Record Office of Victoria (hereafter PROV). VPRS 7601/P1, Licensing Courts (1853–1982); PROV VPRS 7785 P/1; *Victorian Parliamentary Papers*, 1905, D6 (vol. 1), pp. 41–2. For details regarding the collection of this data, see Note on Sources.
5 *Vigilante*, 1 August 1930, p. 2.
6 For the symbolic importance of shop signs see Garrioch, 'House Names', p. 35.
7 See for example Lawson, 'An Incident at Stiffner's', pp. 309–14; Lawson, 'Jimmy Grimshaw's Wooing', pp. 550–3; Astley, *The Multiple Effects of Rainshadow*; Porter, 'At Mcgarrigle's Inn', pp. 309–21; Pritchard, 'The Mayor of Bardie Creek', pp. 4–5. See also the children's picture book, *The Sea-Breeze Hotel*, which features a cheerful female publican as its central character; Vaughan and Mullins, *The Sea-Breeze Hotel*; the play, *A Quiet Shout* (1999), written by Russell Fletcher for the Melbourne Workers' Theatre; the motion picture, *The Dish* (1999), directed by Rob Sitch for Working Dog Productions; the poetry of Geoff Goodfellow, 'People in Glass Houses', p. 31; and Hannie Rayson's 2003 play, *Inheritance*, for the Melbourne Theatre Company.
8 Freeland, *The Australian Pub*, p. 117; Currey, *The Irish at Eureka*, p. 42; Kenneally, *The Inner History of the Kelly Gang*, p. 209.
9 Of the many populists fuelling the jingoistic myth-making, see O'Grady, *It's Your Shout, Mate!*; Ottaway, *The Pub and I*; Pearl, *Beer, Glorious Beer*; Larkins and Howard, *Australian Pubs*; Hepworth and Souter, *Boozing Out in Melbourne Pubs*; Kelly, *Booze Built Australia*; McKay, *On Tap*. Of the academics, see MacGregor, *Profile of Australia*; Conway, *The Great Australian Stupor*; Fiske et al.,

Myths of Oz. More subtle and critical works still emphasise the sexist nature of pub culture, particularly in relation to barmaids' work. See for example Kirkby, *Barmaids*; Grimes, 'Across the Bar'. Historical treatment of the woman's temperance movements also underscores the theme of the pub as friend to man and enemy to woman. See for example, Dingle, 'Truly Magnificent Thirst', p. 240. See also Powell, *Drinking and Alcohol*, p. 1; Lake, 'Politics of Respectability' p. 122; Pixley, 'Wowser and Pro–Woman Politics', p. 303.

A Monument to Her Enterprise

1 'In Memoriam' speech. Anastasia Thornley file, Foster and District Historical Museum, Victoria. Research notes by Max Downes.
2 Kath Byer, Interview with author, 26 February 1999, Clayton, Victoria.
3 Aveling and Damousi, *Stepping Out of History*, p. 14. See also, Alford, *Production or Reproduction?*, p. 7.
4 Meagher, *Licensing Law in Victoria*, p. xiii.
5 Kirkby, *Barmaids*, p. 13. See also, Kercher, *An Unruly Child*, p. 143; Scutt and Graham, *For Richer, for Poorer*, p. 94.
6 This is a point made by jurists themselves. See *R. v. Licensing Authority of Ipswich, ex parte Conway* (1910), QSR 213 (*R. v. Conway*).
7 Kercher, *An Unruly Child*, p. 143.

Traditions: From 'Shebeen' to 'He or She'

1 Bennett, *Ale, Beer and Brewsters*, p. 12.
2 Ibid., p. 122. For the mythical indistinction between innkeeping and prostitution, see White, *Palaces of the People*, p. 15; Clark, *The English Alehouse*, p. 149; Hanawalt, 'Of Good and Ill Repute', p. 106.
3 Rosenzweig, *Eight Hours for What We Will*, p. 43; Malcolm, 'Ireland Sober, Ireland Free', p. 212.
4 Clark, *The English Alehouse*, p. 84.
5 Ibid., pp. 80–4.
6 Ibid., pp. 282, 7.
7 Burke, *Britain in Pictures*, p. 24.
8 Burke, *The English Inn*, p. 58.
9 Hughes, 'The Brewing Industry', p. 217.
10 Summers, *Damned Whores*, p. 21.
11 Hughes, 'The Brewing Industry', p. 228.
12 Freeland, *The Australian Pub*, p. 20.
13 6 Geo. IV. No 4 (New South Wales) 1825. Cited in *R. v. Conway* (at 216–17).
14 *R. v. Conway* (at 217).
15 Robinson, *Women of Botany Bay*, p. 188.
16 Freeland, *The Australian Pub*, p. 20.
17 See for example, Robinson, *Women of Botany Bay*, p. 190.

18 Bourke and Corridon, *Bourke's Liquor Laws*, p. 69.
19 Atkinson, 'Women Publicans in 1838', p. 92.
20 Robinson, *Women of Botany Bay*, p. 187.
21 Robinson, *The Hatch and Brood*, p. 11.
22 Nichols, *Licensed Victuallers' Consolidation Act*, passim.
23 *R. v. Conway* (at 217).
24 Nichols, *Licensed Victuallers' Consolidation Act*, p. 39.
25 Ibid, pp. 31–2.
26 Matthews, *Good and Mad Women*, p. 8; Finch, *The Classing Gaze*, p. 50.
27 Philips and Davies, *A Nation of Rogues?*, p. 6; Robb and Erber, *Disorder in the Court*, p. 1.
28 *In re the Licensing Court, ex parte Logan & Britten* (1900) 26 VLR 584.
29 *Albrecht v. Patterson* (1886) 12 VLR 597. See also *Ex parte Kinane* (1881) 2 ALT 107; *The King v. Littleton & Others, ex parte Catherine Aldridge* (1907) QSR 146; *Re George Pool* (1885) 14 VLR 519. A detailed analysis of these and other cases is given in my doctoral thesis.
30 Foggo, *Inns and Hotels*, p. 64.

Property and Marriage: An Unholy Alliance

1 *Report from the Royal Commission upon the Operation and Effect of the Wine and Spirits Sale Statute*, Victorian Parliamentary Papers, 1867 (vol. 5), p. 204.
2 Flett, *Old Pubs*, p. 49.
3 Goodman, *Gold Seeking*, p. 149.
4 Flett, *Old Pubs*, p. 86.
5 Ibid, pp. 2–3; McGuire, *Inns of Australia*, p. 211.
6 The question of literary and folkloric representation of female liquor sellers is taken up more fully in Chapter 16 of this book.
7 Cited in Keesing, *Gold Fever*, p. 209.
8 See for example, Twomey, 'Without Natural Protectors', pp. 420–7; Golder and Kirkby, 'Marriage and Divorce Law', p. 155.
9 Flett, *Old Pubs*, p. i.
10 Goodman, *Gold Seeking*, pp. 153–6.
11 Cannon, *Melbourne after the Gold Rush*, p. 1. The Chinese and Aborigines are not included in these statistics.
12 McKean, *Hotel Keepers' Guide*, pp. x–23.
13 Ibid., p. 32.
14 In the metropolitan area, for every single woman there are two whose marital status is unknown; in regional areas, for every single woman there are fifteen whose status is unknown.
15 Atherton, 'Feminists and Legal Change', p. 182.
16 Kercher, *An Unruly Child*, pp. 49–50.
17 Ibid., p. 50.
18 Grimshaw et al., *Creating a Nation*, p. 173.

[19] *Victorian Parliamentary Debates*, vol. 48, 9 July 1885, p. 345.
[20] *Licensed Victuallers' Advocate*, 9 June 1877, p. 8.
[21] The tied-house system, and female publicans' relationship to brewers, is fully discussed in Chapter 9.
[22] Hughes, 'The Brewing Industry', p. 228.
[23] See for example, Atherton, 'Feminists and Legal Change', p. 169; Scutt and Graham, *For Richer, for Poorer*, p. 92.
[24] Chambers, *Married Women and Property Law*, pp. 106–55.
[25] Rahilly, *Liquor Licensing Law*, p. 65. See also Bourke and Corrigon, *Bourke's Liquor Laws*, p. 147; *White v. Thomas* (1932) SASR 66.
[26] *R. v. Conway* (at 221).
[27] Bourke and Corridon, *Bourke's Liquor Laws*, pp. 69–70.
[28] Ibid., p. 219.
[29] Alford, *Production or Reproduction?*, p. 199.
[30] See for example, Vallen, Abbey and Sapienza, *Art and Science*, p. 22.
[31] Cited in Cecil, *The Local Pubs*, p. 18.
[32] Ibid., p. 60.
[33] Atherton, 'Feminists and Legal Change', p. 184.
[34] *Roberts v. Hill* (1889) 10 LR (NSW) Eq. 72.
[35] *In re Martin* (1897) 3 ALR 55. See also *In the Will of Jane Jones Cathery* (1881) 7 VLR 34. For cases which explore the issue of female licensees' legal 'agency', see *R. v. M'Queen, ex parte Hall* (1875) 1 VLR L 18; *ex parte Ivell* (1863) 2 SCR 91 NSW; *Hettenback v. Isley* (1881) 7 VLR L 104; *Reidy v. Herry* (1897) 23 VLR 508; *Ewart v. Fox* (1955) ALR 34.

Person or Woman?

[1] Clark, *The English Alehouse*, p. 79.
[2] Cole Collection, vol. 1–2. Dates of tenure for the licensees listed are: Miss Reynolds 1900–27; Miss Mulhall 1874–98; Miss O'Malley 1895–1919; Miss Hurley 1874–95; Mrs Rahilly 1859–93; Mrs Horton Crundall 1897–1928; Miss Oliver 1866–96; Miss Daisy Cunningham 1898–1948.
[3] PROV, Licences Reduction Board, Maximum Valuation Summaries, VPRS 7722, units 1–3; PROV, Licences Reduction Board, Hotel Licence and Deprivation Files, VPRS 7723, units 1–4.
[4] *Australian Brewing Journal*, 20 August 1914, p. 649.
[5] *Australian Brewing and Wine Journal*, 20 October 1930, p. 70.
[6] Rahilly, *Liquor Licensing Law*, p. 117.
[7] Alford, *Production or Reproduction?*, p. 7; Deacon, *Managing Gender*, p. 131.
[8] Holmes, '"Spinsters Indispensable"', p. 70.
[9] Blainey, 'The "Fallen"', pp. 125–43.
[10] Elder, 'The Question of the Unmarried', p. 153.
[11] Meagher, *Licensing Law*, p. 158.
[12] *Victorian Parliamentary Debates*, vol. 113, 25 July 1906, p. 499.

13 Quick and Murphy, *Victorian Liquor Licence*, p. 93.
14 *Victorian Parliamentary Debates*, vol. 113, 16 August 1906, pp. 635–1303.
15 The architectural, spatial and cultural implications of early closing legislation are discussed in Chapter 11.
16 Rosenzweig, *Eight Hours*, pp. 40–3.
17 Ibid., p. 41. See also, Murphy, 'Bootlegging Mothers', p. 176; Rose, *American Women*, p. 28; Lender and Martin, *Drinking in America*, p. 60.
18 Shields, *American Prohibition Year Book*, p. 41.
19 Haine, *World of the Paris Café*, p. 185.
20 Haine, 'Priests of the Proletarians', p. 25.
21 Quick, 'Colonial Helpmeet', p. 24. See also Hargreaves, *Barmaids, Billiards*, pp. 35–46.
22 Cited in McLaughlin, *The Story of Beer*, p. 115.
23 Hoad, *Hotels*, p. 4.
24 Cited in Sumerling, *Down at the Local*, p. 30.
25 Ibid., p. 30.
26 Smithers, *Licensee's Manual*, p. 146.
27 Gibson-Wilde, *A Pattern of Pubs*, pp. 56–9.
28 Hicks, '"But I Wouldn't Want My Wife"', p. 75. Note that the author is Bronwyn Higgs; her name appears incorrectly in the published article.
29 Alexander, 'The Public Role of Women', cited in Kirkby, *Barmaids*, p. 26.
30 *R. v. Conway* (at 223).

Minogue's Case

1 Grimshaw et al., *Creating a Nation*, p. 196; Davison, *The Rise and Fall*, p. 19.
2 *Age*, 6 November 1884, p. 4.
3 Deacon, *Managing Gender*, pp. 4–11.
4 *Regina v. Nicholson, ex parte Minogue*, 10 VLR (L) (1884) 256.
5 Ibid., pp. 260–3. Bronwyn Higgs has made the point that parliamentarians, in particular, often made assumptions about the character of labour 'judged according to what they would like their female relatives to do'. '"But I Wouldn't Want My Wife"', p. 74.
6 *Ex parte Minogue* (at 259).
7 O'Farrell, *The Irish in Australia*, p. 152.
8 Campbell, 'Irish Lawyers', pp. 40–4. For George Higinbotham, see Macintyre, *A Colonial Liberalism*, p. 4.
9 *Licensing Act* 1876 *Amendment* 48 Vict. No. 803, 2.

The Fallout: Press and Parliament

1 Freeland, *The Australian Pub*, p. 148.
2 Davison, *The Rise and Fall*, p. 9.
3 *Victorian Parliamentary Debates*, vol. 143, 23 August 1916, p. 955.
4 Deacon, *Managing Gender*, p. 131.

⁵ Ibid., p. 73; McCalman, *Sex and Suffering*, p. 77; Grimshaw et al., *Creating a Nation*, p. 157.

⁶ *Age*, 6 November 1884, p. 4.

⁷ *Argus*, 21 November 1884, p. 5.

⁸ Kirkby, *Barmaids*, p. 88; Roe, 'Chivalry and Social Policy', p. 401; Swain, 'Destitute and Dependent', p. 101.

⁹ *Victorian Parliamentary Debates*, vol. 47, 20 November 1884, p. 2244.

¹⁰ Ibid., p. 2245. The description of Service is Geoffrey Serle's: *The Rush to be Rich*, p. 19.

¹¹ Baker, 'The Domestication of Politics', p. 631.

¹² Rahilly, *Liquor Licensing Law*, p. 65.

¹³ *Victorian Parliamentary Debates*, vol. 48, 28 July 1885, p. 345.

¹⁴ Deacon, *Managing Gender*, p. 144.

¹⁵ Ibid., p. 11.

¹⁶ *Royal Commission upon the Operation and Effect of the Wine and Spirits Sale Statute*, Victorian Parliamentary Papers, vol. 5, 1867, p. 256.

¹⁷ Ibid., p. 278.

¹⁸ *Victorian Parliamentary Debates*, vol. 48, 28 July 1885, p. 304.

¹⁹ The concept of a 'statutory number' of hotels was enshrined in the Victorian *Licensing Act* 1885. The number was calculated on the basis of one hotel per 250 inhabitants for the first 1000 inhabitants in a district, then one hotel per 500 inhabitants for every subsequent inhabitant. 'Inhabitants' was defined as five times the number of ratepayers on the electoral roll. Rahilly, *Liquor Licensing Law*, p. 13.

²⁰ Ibid., vol. 113, 16 August 1906, p. 1255.

²¹ Ibid., p. 3287.

²² All references to the work of the LRB relate to the following sources: PROV, Licences Reduction Board, Minute Books, VPRS 7605/P1/P2; Hotel Licence Deprivation and Surrender Files, VPRS 7723/P1/P2; Index to Defunct Hotel Licences, VPRS 8159/P1.

²³ Girouard, *Victorian Pubs*, p. 16. See also Hargreaves, *Barmaids, Billiards*, p. 10.

²⁴ *Victorian Year Book*, vol. 42, 1922, p. 265; Quick and Murphy, *Victorian Liquor Licence*, p. 166.

²⁵ Merrett, 'Victorian Licensing Court', p. 124.

²⁶ Ibid., p. 131.

²⁷ Hicks, '"But I Wouldn't Want My Wife"', p. 71.

²⁸ Statistics based on my own tabulation of data contained in PROV, Licences Reduction Board, Index to Defunct Licences, VPRS 8159, units 1–4.

²⁹ *Victorian Year Book*, vol. 36, 1916, p. 479.

The Licensed Victuallers' Association

¹ The body which represented publicans in Victoria was known by different names at different times, including the noteworthy acronym, VULVA

(Victorian United Licensed Victuallers' Association). To avoid confusion, I use LVA for its clarity and convenience. For a full exposition of the many guises of the LVA, see Higgs, Committees, n.p.

2 *Vigilante*, 29 November 1935, p. 3.
3 *Licensed Victuallers' Advocate*, 8 November 1884, p. 9.
4 Ibid., 22 November 1884, p. 9.
5 Ibid., p. 10.
6 Best, *History of the Liquor Trades Union*, p. 10.
7 Ibid., pp. 85–6.
8 Higgs, Committees, p. 1.
9 *Licensed Victuallers' Advocate*, 6 September 1884, p. 7.
10 *Victorian Parliamentary Debates*, vol. 113, 16 August 1906, p. 955.
11 Connell and Irving, *Class Structure*, p. 91.
12 *Australian Brewing and Wine Journal*, 20 March 1888, p. 154.
13 Ibid., 20 February 1906, p. 281.
14 *Licensed Victuallers' Advocate*, 13 January 1877, p. 6.
15 *Licensed Victuallers' Almanack*, Melbourne, 1864, p. 14.
16 Ibid., p. 99.
17 Ibid., 5 January 1884, p. 9.
18 *Vigilante*, 1 December 1919, p. 20.
19 *Licensed Victuallers' Advocate*, 22 November 1884, p. 6.
20 Ibid., 5 July 1884, p. 10.
21 *Illustrated Temperance Year Book*, Melbourne, 1867, p. 61.
22 *Vigilante*, 29 November 1935, p. 3.
23 Ibid., 17 March 1933, p. 2.
24 *Vigilante*, 1 August 1930, p. 2.
25 *Australian Temperance Year Book*, Brisbane, 1935, no. 16, p. 5.
26 *Licensed Victuallers' Advocate*, 12 July 1884, p. 11.
27 Ibid., 25 April 1885, p. 10.
28 Higgs, Committees, n.p.
29 Ibid., p. 102.
30 *Vigilante*, 1 June 1920, p. 2.
31 Ibid., 24 February 1933, p. 2.
32 Ibid., 17 August 1934, p. 2.
33 Ibid., 28 June 1935, p. 1.
34 *Herald*, 12 September 1940.

The Brewers

1 *Argus*, 26 November 1884, p. 9.
2 Ibid., 28 November 1884, p. 10.
3 Dingle, *The Rise and Fall*, p. 3.
4 Gutzke, *Protecting the Pub*, pp. 7–9, 25; McLauchlan, *The Story of Beer*, pp. 102–5.

[5] Deutscher, *The Breweries of Australia*, pp. 1–9.

[6] *Illustrated Temperance Year Book*, 1877, pp. 61–88.

[7] McLauchlan, *The Story of Beer*, p. 109.

[8] *White Ribbon Signal*, 9 February 1925, p. 69.

[9] Rose, *American Women*, p. 18; Gutzke, *Protecting the Pub*, p. 13; Girouard, *Victorian Pubs*, p. 207; Malcolm, *'Ireland Sober, Ireland Free'*, p. 207.

[10] *Report from the Select Committee on Tied Houses: Together with the Minutes of Evidence*, Victorian Parliamentary Papers, 1905 D6 (vol. 1), p. 28.

[11] Ibid., p. 11.

[12] Ibid., p. 5.

[13] Atkinson, 'Women Publicans in 1838', p. 96.

[14] *Report from the Select Committee*, pp. 22–33.

[15] Ibid., pp. 47–9.

[16] Ibid., p. 22

[17] Ibid., p. 28.

[18] Ibid., p. 38.

[19] Ibid., p. 40.

[20] Ibid., p. 41.

[21] Victorian Parliamentary Debates, vol. 113, 16 August 1906, p. 1016.

[22] *Australian Brewers' Journal*, 21 October 1907, p. 32. Diane Kirkby analyses the visual iconography of anti-WCTU sentiment: *Barmaids*, pp. 103–6.

[23] *Australian Brewers' Journal*, 20 February 1906, p. 283.

Mapping Elizabeth Wright

[1] For all references regarding the coronial inquiry into the murder of Elizabeth Wright see PROV, VPRS 30/P, Criminal Trial Briefs, unit 472, case no. 1, September 1875, Henry Howard.

[2] *Bulletin* (supplement), vol. 11, no. 141, 7 October 1882, p. 2.

'Open House'

[1] Smithers, *Licensees' Manual*, p. 83.

[2] Haine, *World of the Paris Café*, p. 118; Smith, 'Social Usages of the Public Drinking House', p. 383.

[3] Burke, *The English Inn*, p. 17; Duis, *The Saloon*, p. 5; Powers, *Faces Along the Bar*, p. 22.

[4] Dunstan, *The Amber Nectar*, p. 127.

[5] Brennan, *Hotels, Inns and Shanties*, p. 5.

[6] Carter, 'Hotels of Williamstown', p. 83; Freeland, *The Australian Pub*, p. 25.

[7] Giles, *Get Your Fill*, p. 28.

[8] Cole Collection, vol. 2, p. 91.

[9] McGuire, *Inns of Australia*, p. 235; Malone, *Prahran's Pubs*, p. 19.

[10] Freeland, *The Australian Pub*, pp. 26–34.

[11] Clark, *The English Alehouse*, p. 273; Spiller, *Victorian Public Houses*, p. 88.

[12] Gutzke, 'Gentrifying the British Public House', p. 32.

[13] Butler, *Hotels in Victoria*, pp. 12–14.

[14] Robertson, *Hotels and Hotelkeepers*, p. 4.

[15] The phrase belongs to Foggo, *Inns and Hotels*, p. 2.

[16] Freeland, *The Australian Pub*, pp. 145–52.

[17] Spiller, *Victorian Public Houses*, p. 68.

[18] Ibid., p. 23; Girouard, *Victorian Pubs*, p. 40.

[19] Girouard, *Victorian Pubs*, p. 57.

[20] Boys, *One for the Road*, p. 17.

[21] Freeland, *The Australian Pub*, p. 143.

[22] Ibid., pp. 175–6.

[23] Phillips, '"Six O'Clock Swill"', pp. 250–1.

[24] Dunstan, *The Amber Nectar*, p. 138.

[25] Phillips, '"Six O'Clock Swill"', p. 250.

[26] *Age*, 5 May 1955, p. 2.

[27] *Argus*, 21 October 1955, p. 9.

[28] *What's Brewing*, September 1960, pp. 16–17; March 1966, pp. 20–1; March 1965, pp. 20–1.

[29] McGregor, *Profile of Australia*, p. 134.

[30] Kirkby, *Barmaids*, p. x; Summers, *Damned Whores*, p. 82; Matthews, 'Normalising Modernity', p. 6.

The Hotel as Family Home: An Inside Story

[1] For my exploration of women's drinking culture within the Ladies Lounge, based on interviews with female hotel patrons, see Wright, '"Doing the Beans"', pp. 7–17.

[2] Morris, *Wind on the Water*, p. 52.

[3] Anne Parr, Interview with author, 19 February 1999, Melbourne.

[4] Janet Parr, Interview with author, 19 February 1999, Melbourne.

[5] Eileen Clatworthy, Interview with author, 16 March 1999, Geelong.

[6] Anne Parr, Interview.

[7] Gloria Fry, Interview with author, 9 November 2000, Bendigo.

[8] Lillian O'Connell, Interview with author, 28 February 1999, Cheltenham, Victoria.

[9] It is important to note that these perspectives on the 'communal' nature of public housekeeping are expressed from the point of view of women as *employers*. It is beyond the reach of this book to document the experiences of female hotel staff such as cooks, housemaids, barmaids and nannies. Some labour historians have commented on the often acrimonious relationship between publicans and the unions representing hotel workers, including barmaids. See, for example Best, *History of the Liquor Trades Union*; De Mori, 'Time Gentlemen', p. 143; Kirkby, *Barmaids*, pp. 140–6.

[10] Yound and Dalton, *No Place for a Woman*, p. 62.

[11] Van Hek, *The Ballad of Siddy Church*, p. 2.
[12] Edna Jory, Interview with author, 23 February 1999, Brighton, Victoria.
[13] Nancy Reis, Interview with author, 16 February 1999, Brighton, Victoria.
[14] Janet Parr, Interview.
[15] Margaret O'Connell, Interview with author, 28 February 1999, Cheltenham, Victoria.
[16] Van Hek, *The Ballad of Siddy Church*, p. 136.
[17] Ibid., p. 55.
[18] Jory, Interview.
[19] Reis, Interview.
[20] Pam Sleigh-Elam, Interview with author, 23 March 1999, Caulfield, Victoria.

Pub-licity

[1] *Vigilante*, 1 August 1930, p. 2.
[2] Cited in *Vigilante*, 28 June 1929, p. 3.
[3] Kingston, *Basket, Bag and Trolley*, p. 118.
[4] Hanawalt, 'Of Good and Ill Repute', p. 105.
[5] Cited in Campbell and Encel, *Out of the Doll's House*, p. 13.
[6] McGuire, *Inns of Australia*, pp. 14–15.
[7] Ibid., p. 29.
[8] *Licensed Victuallers' Advocate*, 20 December 1884, p. 10, and 30 May 1885, p. 9; *Vigilante*, 5 October 1934, p. 3.
[9] *Argus*, 2 February 1865.
[10] McGuire, *Inns of Australia*, p. 251.
[11] Flett, *Old Pubs*, pp. 104–10.
[12] Ibid., p. 103.
[13] Freeland, *The Australian Pub*, p. 92.
[14] Sutherland, *Victoria and Its Metropolis*, pp. 669–743.
[15] Reproduced in Heber, 'Hotels of Carlton', p. 21.
[16] *Australasian*, 4 July 1903, vol. 24, no. 1220, p. 35.
[17] *Vigilante*, 24 December 1937, p. 3.
[18] Cole Collection, vol. 2, p. 182; *Argus*, 16 December 1872, p. 8.
[19] Jory, Interview; Sleigh-Elam, Interview.
[20] Jory, Interview; Reis, Interview; A. Parr, Interview.
[21] Van Hek, *The Ballad of Siddy Church*, p. 17.
[22] Bourke and Corridon, *Bourke's Liquor Laws*, p. 219.
[23] Girouard, *Victorian Pubs*, p. 28.
[24] Gaunt, *Old Inns of England*, p. 23.
[25] Garrioch, 'House Names, Shop Signs', p. 35.
[26] *Vigilante*, 15 June 1934, p. 4.
[27] See for example, Grimes, 'Across the Bar', pp. 66–75; Bailey, 'Parasexuality and Glamour', p. 151; Cavan, *Liquor License*, p. 97.
[28] Kirkby, *Barmaids*, pp. 45–65.

[29] Girouard, *Victorian Pubs*, pp. 69–73.

[30] Freeland, *The Australian Pub*, p. 55.

[31] Kirkby, *Barmaids*, p. 47.

[32] Haine, 'Priest of the Proletarians', p. 18.

[33] Bailey, 'Parasexuality and Glamour', p. 149.

[34] Lynne Cox, Interview with author, 4 April 2000, Brunswick, Victoria.

[35] *Vigilante*, 28 June, 1929, p. 3.

[36] The phrase is Johanna Clancy's. Johanna gives an account of her life as a publican in my BA Honours thesis, Perry, Real Women Do Shout, p. 27.

[37] Cole Collection, vol. 1, part 2, p. 64.

[38] *Vigilante*, 25 January 1935, p. 3.

[39] Ibid., 1 December 1919, p. 27.

[40] Cole Collection, vol. 2, p. 196a; vol. 1, part 1, p. 160.

[41] Cannon, *The Woman as Murderer*, pp. 11–35. Gedge and Cross were also executed.

[42] *Licensed Victuallers' Advocate*, 16 June 1877, p. 6.

[43] Ibid., 27 January 1877, p. 7.

[44] *Vigilante*, 6 October 1933, p. 2.

[45] Ibid., 3 May 1935, p. 3.

[46] Cole Collection, vol. 2, p. 214.

[47] *Australian Brewing and Wine Journal*, 20 September 1930, p. 699.

[48] The phrase belongs to Charlotte Perkins Gilman. For an exposition of the nineteenth-century American feminist, see Wynn Allen, *Building Domestic Liberty*, pp. 65–83.

Making an Impression

[1] *Vigilante*, 24 December 1937, p. 3.

[2] White, *Inventing Australia*, p. 103.

[3] Cited in Cecil, *The Local Pubs*, p. 38.

[4] *Nathalia Herald*, 16 September 1952. Ellen Gray is the mother of Eileen Clatworthy.

[5] Robertson, *Hotels and Hotelkeepers*, pp. 19–30.

[6] Dormer, *The Bushman's Arms*, pp. 27–8.

Women's Temperance, Class and Social Power

[1] Cited in Dunstan, *Wowsers*, p. 36.

[2] Hyslop, 'Temperance, Christianity', p. 27; Malcolm, *'Ireland Sober, Ireland Free'*, p. 101; Harrison, *Drink and the Victorians*, p. 134.

[3] Dingle, *Temperance Economics*, p. 15.

[4] Epstein, *The Politics of Domesticity*, p. 1; Pargeter, *For God, Home and Humanity*, p. 38.

5 See for example, Tyrrell, *Womans' World, Woman's Empire*; Parker, *Purifying America*; Pixley, 'Wowser and Pro-Woman Politics'; Lake, 'The Politics of Respectability'; Allen, 'Mundane Men'; Baker, 'The Domestication of Politics'.

6 *American Prohibition Year Book* (1915), p. 136.

7 Epstein, *Politics of Domesticity*, p. 1.

8 *White Ribbon Signal*, 1 August 1916, p. 190.

9 Ibid., 1 June 1916, p. 15.

10 *Alliance Record*, 1 October 1902, p. 151. The WCTU's campaign against the employment of barmaids is discussed extensively in Kirkby, *Barmaids*, pp. 92–135.

11 *Alliance Record*, October 1885, p. 3.

12 Tyrrell, 'Women and Temperance', p. 218.

13 Ibid. p. 220.

14 *White Ribbon Signal*, 1 January 1911, p. 60.

15 Baker, 'The Domestication of Politics', pp. 622–5.

16 Koven and Michel, 'Womanly Duties', p. 1079. See also, Hutching, 'Mothers of the World', p. 173; Lake, 'Feminist History', pp. 156–8.

17 O'Farrell, *The Irish in Australia*, p. 152.

18 Powers, 'The "Poor Man's Friend"', p. 3.

19 Cited in Henderson, *The Strength of the White Ribbon*, p. 2.

20 Ibid.

21 Blainey, The 'Fallen' are Every Mother's Children, pp. 128–30.

22 Markey, 'Women and Labour', p. 84; Grimshaw and Willett, 'Women's History', p. 147; O'Farrell, *The Irish in Australia*, p. 152.

23 McConville, *Croppies, Celts and Catholics*, p. 89; O'Mahony, Food and Beverages in Australia, p. 210.

24 O'Farrell, *The Irish in Australia*, p. 153.

25 Compiled from listings in the Cole Collection.

26 Grimshaw and Willett, 'Women's History', p. 135; Campbell, 'Irish Women', p. 35.

27 Cole Collection, vol. 1, part 2, p. 207.

28 Russell, *A Wish of Distinction*, pp. 1–3.

29 Kingston, 'The Lady and the Australian Girl', p. 29.

30 Robertson, *Hotels and Hotelkeepers*, p. 13.

31 Russell, *A Wish of Distinction*, p. 60.

32 Jory, Interview.

33 *Australian Etiquette* (1885), p. 28.

34 Hyslop, 'Temperance, Christianity', p. 41.

35 For the social changes that saw women's temperance activities lose their oppositional strength as drinking became a more heterosocial experience in the twentieth century, see Matthews, 'Normalising Modernity'; Warne, 'Mother's Anxious Future'.

'The Buxom Matron Behind the Bar'

1 Bennett, *Ale, Beer and Brewsters*, pp. 123–36.
2 See for example, Hanawalt, *'Of Good and Ill Repute'*; Martin, *Alcohol, Sex and Gender*; Otto, 'Women, Alcohol and Social Control'; Ettore, 'Women and Drunken Sociology'.
3 Bennett, *Ale, Beer and Brewsters*, p. 134.
4 Grimshaw, '"Man's Own Country"', p. 182.
5 Lake, 'The Politics of Respectability', p. 118.
6 Wannan, *Folklore of the Australian Pub*, p. 32.
7 Edwards, *The Big Book of Australian Folksong*, p. 32. I am grateful to Glen Tomasetti for first introducing me to Big Poll. Glen sings the ballad on her recording *Gold Rush Songs*, Science Museum of Victoria SMV 001 (1975).
8 Edwards, *The Big Book of Australian Folksong*, p. 162.
9 For 'The Flash Colonial Barmaid', see ibid., p. 134.
10 Ibid., pp. 13–14.
11 Cited in Flett, *Old Pubs*, p. 94; Dormer, *Bushman's Arms*, p. 12; Thomas E. Spencer, 'Why Doherty Died' in Scott, *Old Ballads from the Bush*, p. 215; Boree, 'Publicans and Sinners', *Bulletin*, 9 August 1906, p. 43.
12 Anon., 'And He Didn't Get His Drink', *Bulletin*, 28 December 1889, p. 19.
13 Brady, 'Little Bo-Peep: A Bush Version', *Bulletin*, 18 December 1924, p. 38.
14 Cooper, *History of the Overland Corner Hotel*, p. 9.
15 Foggo, *Inns and Hotels*, p. 46.
16 White, *Inventing Australia*, pp. 86–104.
17 Lake, 'The Politics of Respectability', pp. 116–27. See also, Schaffer, *Women and the Bush*, pp. 4–8.
18 F.M., 'Bung in the Bush', *Bulletin*, 30 July 1903, p. 36.
19 Ibid.
20 Lawson, 'An Incident at Stiffner's' in *Collected Stories of Henry Lawson*, p. 309.
21 Lawson, 'Jimmy Grimshaw's Wooing' in ibid., pp. 550–3.
22 Beatty, *A Treasury of Australian Folk Songs*, pp. 173–4.
23 Wannan, *Dictionary of Australian Folklore*, pp. 211–13.
24 Anon., 'On Guard', *Bulletin*, 9 January 1892, p. 15.
25 Cited in Flett, *Old Pubs*, p. 35; *Licensed Victuallers' Advocate*, 5 May 1877, p. 7.
26 Snape, 'Mother', *Aussie: The Soldiers' Magazine*, August 1918, p. 11.
27 Falk, 'At the Loyda Crossin'', *Centennial Magazine*, September 1889, pp. 97–114.
28 Elder, 'The Question of the Unmarried', p. 165.
29 *Vigilante*, 1 December 1918, p. 13.
30 Ibid., 1 December 1919, p. 3.

'Dignity Is the Right Word'

1 See for example, Hey, *Patriarchy and Pub Culture*; Summers, *Damned Whores*, pp. 82–4.

[2] See for example, the anthology, *Debutante Nation: Feminism Contests the 1890s* (Magarey et al., eds).

[3] Chester and Grossman, *The Experience and Meaning of Work*, p. 7.

[4] Russell, *A Wish of Distinction*, p. 92.

[5] Fry, Interview.

[6] Sleigh-Elam, Interview.

[7] Clatworthy, Interview.

[8] The phrases are used by Richard Stivers in his depiction of the phenomenon of 'momism'—the tendency for the mother to take on the roles of both mother and father in frontier and immigrant societies: *A Hair of the Dog*, pp. 131–4.

[9] L. O'Connell, Interview.

[10] Grieve and Perdices, 'Patriarchy', p. 32.

[11] Young and Dalton, *No Place for a Woman*, p. 62.

[12] Lynne Cox, Interview with author, 7 March 1999, Kew, Victoria.

[13] Matthews, *Good and Mad Women*, p. 28; Phillips, *Divided Loyalties*, p. 29.

[14] Cited in Perry, Real Women Do Shout, p. 26.

[15] See for example, Sayers, 'The Need to Work', p. 727; Stewart, 'Discovering the Meanings of Work', p. 262.

The More Things Change

[1] Samantha Gowing, Interview with author, 1 March 1999, Fitzroy, Victoria.

[2] See for example many of the stories told about being footballers' wives or girl-friends in Sheedy and Brown, *Football's Women*.

[3] Amy Robson, Interview with author, 8 March 1999, Collingwood, Victoria.

[4] White, *Inventing Australia*, pp. 156–62.

[5] Eliza Faull, Interview with author, 16 March 1999, Geelong.

[6] Houston, 'Straight Up with a Twist', *Sunday Age*, (Sunday Life!), 28 May 2000, p. 9.

[7] John Hindle, 'Best Pubs', *Age* (Good Weekend), 28 July 2001, pp. 30–1.

[8] Houston, 'Straight Up with a Twist', pp. 7–11.

Bibliography

Note on Sources

The full range of primary sources used to research this book does not appear in this bibliography.

In general terms, I have relied on the archival holdings of the Licensing Courts, Liquor Control Commission, Licences Reduction Board and other agencies responsible for liquor licensing in Victoria. These documents are held at the Public Record Office of Victoria. In particular, I have used the Licensing Registers, 1853–1982 (VPRS 7601/7602) to compile statistical data. Information about other states largely derives from contemporary legal texts, court reports and secondary sources.

I have extensively consulted the unpublished manuscript known as the R. K. Cole Collection, held in the La Trobe Australian Manuscripts Collection, State Library of Victoria (here cited as Cole Collection). This eight-volume manuscript by amateur hotel historian Robert Cole lists every licensee for every hotel in metropolitan, suburban and country Victoria from the 1840s to the 1940s. Some sections are typescript; others are handwritten and virtually illegible.

Statistics based on the Cole Collection and the licensing records are inherently conservative. I have only counted a female licensee where the name or marital status is clearly feminine. (Hence, I have taken an 'E. H. Murphy' to be Edward Henry, not Elizabeth Hannah.) A further structural problem in tracing the gender of licensees in the latter half of the twentieth century is the practice of company licence holding. This method was legally available from 1915 but not commonly utilised for another forty years. In such cases, a company held the licence and appointed a nominee as manager. Although the corporate body could be a family company, with the nominee often a woman, it is not possible to tell from the licensing registers whether the nominee was in fact a salaried manager or a family member. The autonomy of the nominee is thus ambiguous.

Two official printed sources are frequently quoted in this book and thus listed here: 'Report from the Royal Commission upon the Operation and Effect of the Wine and Spirits Sale Statute', *Victorian Parliamentary Papers*, 1867 (vol. 5); 'Report from the Select Committee on Tied Houses: Together with the Minutes of Evidence', *Victorian Parliamentary Papers*, 1905 D6 (vol. 1).

A comprehensive listing of all manuscripts, official printed sources, literary works, newspapers, journals, statutes and court cases consulted can be found in my 2002 doctoral thesis, Beyond the Ladies Lounge: A History of Female Publicans, Victoria, 1875–1945 (held at the Baillieu Library at the University of Melbourne). And if you're really keen, the thesis also contains three times more notes than appear in this book.

Selected Books, Articles, Pamphlets and Theses

Adelaide, Debra. *The Hotel Albatross*. Sydney: Random House, 1995.

Alford, Katrina. *Production or Reproduction? An Economic History of Women in Australia 1788–1850*. Melbourne: Oxford University Press, 1984.

Allen, Judith. '"Mundane" Men: Historians, Masculinity and Masculinism.' *Historical Studies* 22, no. 89 (1987).

Ardener, Shirley, ed. *Women and Space: Ground Rules and Social Maps for Women*. London: Croon Helm, 1981.

Astley, Thea. *The Multiple Effects of Rainshadow*. Ringwood, Vic.: Penguin, 1996.

Atherton, Rosalind. 'Feminists and Legal Change in NSW, 1890–1916: Husbands, Widows and "Family Property".' In *Sex, Power, Justice: Historical Perspectives on Law in Australia*, edited by Diane Kirkby. Melbourne: Melbourne University Press, 1995.

Atkinson, Alan. 'Women Publicans in 1838.' *The Push From the Bush* 8 (1980).

Australian Etiquette: Or the Rules and Usages of the Best Society in the Australasian Colonies. Melbourne: People's Publishing Company, 1885.

Bagguley, Paul. 'The Patriarchal Restructuring of Gender Segregation: A Case Study of the Hotel and Catering Industry.' *Sociology* 25, no. 4 (1991).

Baglin, Douglass, and Yvonne Austin. *Australian Pub Crawl*. French's Forest, NSW: Murray Child, 1977.

Bailey, Peter. 'Parasexuality and Glamour: The Victorian Barmaid as Cultural Prototype.' *Gender and History* 2, no. 2 (1990).

———. *Leisure and Class in Victorian England*. London: Routledge, 1978.

Baker, Paula. 'The Domestication of Politics.' *American Historical Review* 89 (1984).

Barr, Andrew. *Drink: An Informal Social History*. London: Bantam, 1995.

Barrows, Susan, and Robin Room, eds. *Drinking: Behaviour and Belief in Modern History*. Berkeley: University of California Press, 1991.

Beatty, Bill. *A Treasury of Australian Folk Tales and Traditions*. Sydney: Ure Smith, 1968.

Bechervaise, John. *Old Melbourne Hotels Sketchbook*. Adelaide: Rigby, 1973.

Bennett, Judith. *Ale, Beer and Brewsters in England: Women's Work in a Changing World, 1300–1600*. Oxford: Oxford University Press, 1996.

Best, Alleyn. *The History of the Liquor Trades Union in Victoria*. North Melbourne, Vic.: Victorian Branch, Federated Liquor and Allied Industries Employees Union of Australia, 1990.

Betts, Margaret. 'Ladies Lounge.' *Meanjin*, no. 1 (1991).

Birch, Tony. 'Ladies Lounge.' In *Scarred for Life (Republica 3)*, edited by George Papaellinas. Sydney: Angus and Robertson, 1995.

Blainey, Anna. The 'Fallen' Are Every Mother's Children: The Woman's Christian Temperance Union's Campaigns for Temperance, Women's Suffrage and Sexual Reform in Australia, 1885–1905. PhD, La Trobe University, 2000.

Blocker, Jack S., and Cheryl K. Warsh, eds. *The Changing Face of Drink: Substance, Imagery and Behaviour*. Ottawa: Histoire Sociale/Social History, 1997.

Boris, Eileen. *Home to Work: Motherhood and the Politics of Industrial Homework in the United States*. Cambridge: Cambridge University Press, 1994.

Bourke, Brian, and Michael Corridon. *Bourke's Liquor Laws of Victoria*. 4th edn. Melbourne: Butterworths, 1972.

Bourke, Brian, Michael Corridon, and Patrick Tehan. *Bourke's Liquor Laws of Victoria*. 5th edn. Melbourne: Butterworths, 1998.

Boys, Fay. *One for the Road: Condobolin Hotels, Shanties and the Brewery, 1860–1996*. Condobolin, NSW: Fay Boys, 1997.

Brady, Wendy. '"Serfs of the Soddon Scone"?: Women Workers in the Western Australian Hotel and Catering Industry 1900–1925.' *Studies in Western Australian History* 7 (1983).

Brennan, R. M. *Hotels, Inns and Shanties of the Myall and Saltbush Plains*. Warren, NSW: Warren Shire Council, 1979.

Burke, Thomas. *Britain in Pictures: English Inns*. London: William Collins, 1943.
———. *The English Inn*. London: Longmans, Green and Co., 1930.

Burnham, John. *Bad Habits: Drinking, Smoking, Taking Drugs, Gambling, Sexual Misbehaviour and Swearing in American History*. New York: New York University Press, 1993.

Butler, Graeme, Chris McConville, and Vikki Plant. Hotels in Victoria: Thematic Typology. Melbourne: Historic Buildings Council of Victoria, n.d. (c.1990).

Butlin, N. G. 'Yo, Ho, Ho and How Many Bottles of Rum?' *Australian Economic History Review* 23, no. 1 (1983).

Caddie, with an introduction by Dymphna Cusack. *Caddie: The Autobiography of a Sydney Barmaid*. London: Constable, 1953.

Campbell, Dorothy, and Sol Encel. *Out of the Doll's House: Women in the Public Sphere*. Melbourne: Longman Cheshire, 1991.

Campbell, Malcolm. 'Irish Women in Nineteenth Century Australia: A More Hidden Ireland?' Paper presented at the Sixth Irish-Australian Conference, La Trobe University, July 1990.

Campbell, Ruth. 'Irish Lawyers in the Port Phillip District and Victoria, 1838–1860.' Paper presented at the Sixth Irish-Australian Conference, La Trobe University, July 1990.

Cannon, Michael. *The Woman as Murderer: Five Who Paid with Their Lives*. Melbourne: Today's Australia Publishing Company, 1994.

———. *Melbourne after the Gold Rush*. Main Ridge, Vic.: Loch Haven, 1993.

Carstairs, Joan, and Maureen Lane. *Pubs, Punts and Pastures: The Story of Irish Pioneer Women on the Salt Water River*. St Albans, Vic.: St Albans History Society, 1988.

Carter, D., et al. Hotels of Williamstown. BA (Hons), University of Melbourne, 1964.

Cavan, Sherri. *Liquor License: An Ethnography of Bar Behaviour*. Chicago: Aldin, 1966.

Cecil, K. L. *The Local Pubs*. Anglesea, Vic.: Anglesea and District Historical Society, 1990.

Chambers, Lori. *Married Women and Property Law in Victorian Ontario*. Toronto: University of Toronto Press, 1997.

Chester, Nia Lane, and Hildreth Grossman, eds. *The Experience and Meaning of Work in Women's Lives*. New Jersey: L. Erlbaum Associates, 1990.

Clark, Peter. *The English Alehouse: A Social History, 1200–1830*. London: Longman, 1983.

Cohen, Monica. *Professional Domesticity in the Victorian Novel: Women, Work and Home*. Cambridge: Cambridge University Press, 1998.

Collett, Barry. *Wednesdays Closest to the Full Moon: A History of South Gippsland*. Melbourne: Melbourne University Press, 1994.

Collingwood Historical Society. *Hotels of Collingwood*. Melbourne: Collingwood Historical Society, 1989.

Conway, Ronald. *The Great Australian Stupor: An Interpretation of the Australian Way of Life*. Melbourne: Sun Books, 1971.

Cooper, A. A. R., ed. *A History of the Overland Corner Hotel*. Adelaide: National Trust of South Australia, 1986.

Crawford, Alan. *Birmingham Pubs, 1880–1939*. Gloucester: A. Sutton, 1986.

Currey, C. H. *The Irish at Eureka*. Sydney: Angus and Robertson, 1954.

Curtis, John. *The Licensed Victuallers' Act with Remarks Upon the Licensing System and Suggestions for Its Improvement*. Melbourne, 1857.

Damousi, Joy. 'Chaos and Order: Gender, Space and Sexuality on Female Convict Ships.' *Australian Historical Studies* 26, no. 104 (1995).

Davidson, Bonnie, Kath Hamey, and Debby Nicholls. *Called to the Bar: 150 Years of Pubs in Balmain and Rozelle*. Balmain, NSW: Balmain Association, 1991.

Davies, Susanne. '"Ragged, Dirty . . . Infamous and Obscene": The Vagrant in Late Nineteenth-Century Melbourne.' In *A Nation of Rogues? Crime, Law and Punishment in Colonial Australia*, edited by David Philips and Susanne Davies. Melbourne: Melbourne University Press, 1994.

Davison, Graeme. *The Rise and Fall of Marvellous Melbourne*. Melbourne: Melbourne University Press, 1979.

Davison, Graeme, David Dunstan, and Chris McConville, eds. *The Outcasts of Melbourne: Essays in Social History*. Sydney: Allen and Unwin, 1985.

De Mori, Caroline. *'Time, Gentlemen': A History of the Hotel Industry in Western Australia*. Leederville, WA: Western Australian Hotels Association, 1988.

Deacon, Desley. *Managing Gender: The State, the New Middle Class and Women Workers, 1830–1930*. Melbourne: Oxford University Press, 1989.

Deutscher, Keith. *The Breweries of Australia: A History*. Port Melbourne, Vic.: Lothian, 1999.

Dingle, A. E. '"The Truly Magnificent Thirst": An Historical Survey of Australian Drinking Habits.' *Australian Historical Studies* 10, no. 75 (1980).

———. *The Rise and Fall of Temperance Economics*. Clayton, Vic.: Monash University, 1977.

Dixson, Miriam. 'The "Born-Modern" Self: Revisiting the Real Matilda: An Exploration of Women and Identity in Australia.' *Australian Historical Studies* 27, no. 106 (1996).

———. *The Real Matilda: Woman and Identity in Australia 1788 to the Present*. Ringwood, Vic.: Penguin, 1976.

Docker, John. 'The Feminist Legend: A New Historicism?' In *Debutante Nation: Feminism Contests the 1890s*, edited by Susan Magarey, Sue Rowley and Susan Sheridan. Sydney: Allen and Unwin, 1993.

———. *The Nervous Nineties: Australian Cultural Life in the 1890s*. Melbourne: Oxford University Press, 1991.

Dormer, Marion. *The Bushman's Arms: Bush Inns and Hotels of Gilgandra District and the Castlereagh*. Gilgandra, N.S.W.: Gilgandra Museum and Historical Society, 1983.

Duis, Perry. *The Saloon: Public Drinking in Chicago and Boston, 1880–1920*. Urbana: University of Illinois Press, 1983.

Dunstan, David. 'Boozers and Wowsers.' In *Constructing a Culture*, edited by Verity Burgmann and Jenny Lee. Ringwood, Vic.: Penguin, 1988.

Dunstan, Keith. *The Amber Nectar: A Celebration of Beer and Brewing in Australia*. Melbourne: Viking O'Neil, 1987.

———. *Wowsers: Being an Account of the Prudery Exhibited by Certain Outstanding Men and Women in Such Matters as Drinking, Smoking, Prostitution, Censorship and Gambling*. Melbourne: Cassell, 1968.

Edwards, Ron. *The Big Book of Australian Folk Song*. Adelaide: Rigby, 1976.

Elder, Catriona. '"The Question of the Unmarried": Some Meanings of Being Single in Australia in the 1920s and 1930s.' *Australian Feminist Studies* 18 (1993).

Edwards, Anne. 'Women and Deviance.' In *The Other Half: Women in Australia*, edited by Jan Mercer. Ringwood, Vic.: Penguin, 1975.

Epstein, Barbara. *The Politics of Domesticity: Women, Evangelism, and Temperance in Nineteenth-Century America*. Middletown, Conn., and Irvington, NY: Wesleyan University Press, 1981.

Ettore, Betsy. 'Women and Drunken Sociology: Developing a Feminist Analysis.' *Women's Studies International Forum* 9, no. 5 (1986).

Finch, Lynette. *The Classing Gaze: Sexuality, Class and Surveillance*. Sydney: Allen and Unwin, 1993.

Finnamore, John. *A Handy Book of the Existing Publicans' Law*. Melbourne, 1871.

Fiske, John, Bob Hodge, and Graeme Turner. *Myths of Oz: Interpreting Australian Popular Culture*. Sydney: Allen and Unwin, 1987.

Flett, James. *Old Pubs, Inns, Taverns and Grog Houses on the Victorian Gold Diggings*. Melbourne: Hawthorn Press, 1979.

Foggo, Catherine. *Inns and Hotels, 1825–1900: Some Hunter Valley Innkeepers*. Sydney: Harfield Publications, 1990.

Fraser, Dawn. *Dawn: One Hell of a Life*. Sydney: Hodder Headline Australia, 2001.

Freeland, J. M. *The Australian Pub*. Melbourne: Melbourne University Press, 1966.

Friedman, Susan Stanford. *Mappings: Feminism and the Cultural Geographies of Encounter*. Princeton: Princeton University Press, 1998.

Garrioch, David. 'House Names, Shop Signs and Social Organisation in Western European Cities, 1500–1900.' *Urban History* 21, no. 1 (1994).

Geiger, Susan. 'Women's Life Histories: Method and Content.' *Signs: Journal of Women in Culture and Society* 11, no. 2 (1986).

Gibson-Wilde, Dorothy and Bruce. *A Pattern of Pubs: Hotels of Townsville, 1864–1914*. Townsville: James Cook University, 1988.

Giele, Janet Zollinger. *Two Paths to Women's Equality: Temperance, Suffrage, and the Origins of Modern Feminism*. New York: Twayne Publishers, 1995.

Gilbert Murdock, Catherine. *Domesticating Drink: Women, Men and Alcohol in America, 1870–1940*. Baltimore: The Johns Hopkins University Press, 1998.

Giles, Megan. *Get Your Fill at Wattle Hill: The History of the Wattle Hill Hotel, and Surrounding Area*. Skenes Creek, Vic.: Apollo Bay Higher Elementary School, 1991.

Girouard, Mark. *Victorian Pubs*. London: Studio Vista, 1975.

Golder, Hilary, and Diane Kirkby. 'Marriage and Divorce Law before the *Family Law Act 1975*.' In *Sex, Power, Justice: Historical Perspectives on Law in Australia*, edited by Diane Kirkby. Melbourne: Melbourne University Press, 1995.

Goodman, David. *Gold Seeking: Victoria and California in the 1850s*. Sydney: Allen and Unwin, 1994.

Goodfellow, Geoff. 'People in Glass Houses.' In *No Collar, No Cuffs*, edited by Geoff Goodfellow. Adelaide: Wakefield Press, 1991.

Gourvish, T. R., and R. G. Wilson. *The British Brewing Industry, 1830–1980*. Cambridge: Cambridge University Press, 1994.

Grieve, Norma, and Michael Perdices. 'Patriarchy: A Refuge from Maternal Power?' In *Australian Women: Feminist Perspectives*, edited by Norma Grieve and Patricia Grimshaw. Melbourne: Oxford University Press, 1981.

Grimes, Sandra. 'Across the Bar: Women's Work in Hotels.' In *Australian Ways: Anthropological Studies of an Industrialised Society*, edited by Lenore Manderson. Sydney: Allen and Unwin, 1985.

Grimshaw, Patricia. '"Man's Own Country": Women in Colonial Australian History.' In *Australian Women: New Feminist Perspectives*, edited by Norma Grieve and Ailsa Burns. Melbourne: Oxford University Press, 1986.

Grimshaw, Patricia, Susan Janson, and Marian Quartly. *Freedom Bound: Documents on Women in Colonial Australia*. Sydney: Allen and Unwin, 1995.

Grimshaw, Patricia, Marilyn Lake, Ann McGrath, and Marian Quartly. *Creating a Nation*. Ringwood, Vic.: Penguin, 1994.

Grimshaw, Patricia, and Graham Willett. 'Women's History and Family History: An Exploration of Colonial Family Structure.' In *Australian Women: Feminist Perspectives*, edited by Norma Grieve and Patricia Grimshaw. Melbourne: Oxford University Press, 1981.

Groth, Paul. *Living Downtown: The History of Residential Hotels in the United States*. Berkeley: University of California Press, 1994.

Gutzke, David. 'Gentrifying the British Public House, 1896–1914.' *International Labor and Working-Class History* 45 (1994).

———. *Protecting the Pub: Brewers and Publicans against Temperance*. London: Royal Historical Society; Boydell Press, 1989.

Haine, W. Scott. *The World of the Paris Café: Sociability among the French Working Class, 1789–1914*. Baltimore: The Johns Hopkins University Press, 1996.

———. 'The Priest of the Proletarians: Parisian Café Owners and the Working Class, 1820–1914.' *International Labour and Working-Class History* 45 (1994).

Hamilton, Paula. 'Domestic Dilemmas: Representations of Servants and Employers in the Popular Press.' In *Debutante Nation: Feminism Contests the 1890s*, edited by Susan Magarey, Sue Rowley and Susan Sheridan. Sydney: Allen and Unwin, 1993.

Hanawalt, Barbara. *'Of Good and Ill Repute': Gender and Social Control in Medieval England*. Oxford: Oxford University Press, 1998.

Hargreaves, Ray. *Barmaids, Billiards, Nobblers and Rat-Pits: Pub Life in Goldrush Dunedin, 1861–65*. Dunedin North: Otago Heritage Books, 1992.

Harrison, Brian. *Drink and the Victorians: The Temperance Question in England, 1815–1872*. London: Faber and Faber, 1971.

Heber, Hawking. Hotels in Carlton. BA (Hons), University of Melbourne, 1966.

Henderson, Joyce. *The Strength of the White Ribbon: For God, Home and Humanity, 1892–1992*. Perth: Woman's Christian Temperance Union of Western Australia Inc., 1992.

Heney, Helen. *Australia's Founding Mothers*. Melbourne: Thomas Nelson, 1978.

Hepworth, John, and Bloo Souter. *Boozing out in Melbourne Pubs: An Occasional History and Sociological Study of Melbourne as Seen through the Bottom of a Glass*. Sydney: Angus and Robertson, 1980.

Hey, Valerie. *Patriarchy and Pub Culture*. London: Tavistock, 1986.

Hicks [Higgs], Bronwyn. '"But I Wouldn't Want My Wife to Work There!": A History of Discrimination against Women in the Hotel Industry.' *Australian Feminist Studies* 14 (1991).

Higgs, Bronwyn. Committees of the Licensed Victuallers' Association of Victoria, an Index to Committee Members 1840–1920. Melbourne: Australian Hotels Association, 1995.

Hoad, J. L. *Hotels and Publicans in South Australia, 1836–1984*. Adelaide: Australian Hotels Association (South Australian Branch): Gould Books, 1986.

Hodgins, Jack. *Innocent Cities*. St Lucia, Qld: University of Queensland Press, 1990.

Hodgson, Thomas. *Liquor Laws Guide*. Sydney, 1983.

Holmes, Katie. '"Spinsters Indispensable": Feminists, Single Women and the Critique of Marriage, 1890–1920.' *Australian Historical Studies* 29, no. 110 (1998).

Hornadge, Bill. *The Ugly Australian*. Dubbo, NSW: Review Publications, 1975.

Horsfall, David. *The Story of the Shamrock*. Bendigo, Vic.: Clover Hotels, 1997.

Hughes, David. 'The Brewing Industry in Early Australia.' In *The Dynamics of the International Brewing Industry since 1800*, edited by R. G. Wilson and T. R. Gourvish. London: Routledge, 1998.

Hunt, Geoffrey, and Saundra Satterlee. 'Darts, Drinks and the Pub: The Culture of Female Drinking.' *The Sociological Review* 33, no. 3 (1987).

Hutching, Megan. '"Mothers of the World": Women, Peace and Arbitration in Early Twentieth-Century New Zealand.' *New Zealand Journal of History* 27, no. 2 (1993).

Hutter, Bridget, and Gillian Williams. *Controlling Women: The Normal and the Deviant*. London: Croon Helm, 1981.

Hyslop, Anthea. 'Temperance, Christianity and Feminism: The Woman's Christian Temperance Union of Victoria, 1887–97.' *Historical Studies* 17, no. 66 (1976).

Ireland, David. *The Glass Canoe*, Macmillan: South Melbourne, Vic., 1976.

Keesing, Nancy, ed. *Gold Fever: Voices from Australian Goldfields*. Sydney: Angus and Robertson, 1967.

Kelly, Wayne. *Booze Built Australia*. Brisbane: Queensland Classic Books, 1994.

Kenneally, J. J. *The Inner History of the Kelly Gang*. Melbourne: Standard Newspapers, 1929.

Kerber, Linda. 'Separate Spheres, Female Worlds, Woman's Place.' *Journal of American History* 75, no. 1 (1988).

Kercher, Bruce. *An Unruly Child: A History of Law in Australia*. Sydney: Allen and Unwin, 1995.

Kingston, Beverley. *Basket, Bag and Trolley: A History of Shopping in Australia.* Melbourne: Oxford University Press, 1994.

———. 'The Lady and the Australian Girl: Some Thoughts on Nationalism and Class.' In *Australian Women: New Feminist Perspectives,* edited by Norma Grieve and Ailsa Burns. Melbourne: Oxford University Press, 1986.

———. *My Wife, My Daughter and Poor Mary Ann.* Melbourne: Thomas Nelson, 1975.

Kirkby, Diane. *Barmaids: A History of Women's Work in Pubs.* Cambridge: Cambridge University Press, 1997.

———. ed. *Sex, Power and Justice: Historical Perspectives on Law in Australia.* Melbourne: Melbourne University Press, 1995.

———. 'Writing the History of Women Working: Photographic Evidence and the "Disreputable Occupation of Barmaid".' *Labour History* (1991).

Koven, Seth, and Sonya Michel. 'Womanly Duties: Maternalist Politics and the Origins of Welfare States in France, Germany, Great Britain and the United States, 1880–1920.' *American Historical Review* 95, October (1990).

Lake, Marilyn. 'The Inviolable Woman: Feminist Conceptions of Citizenship in Australia, 1900–1945.' In *Feminism, the Pubic and the Private,* edited by Joan Landes. Oxford: Oxford University Press, 1998.

———. 'Feminist History as National History: Writing the Political History of Women.' *Australian Historical Studies* 27, no. 106 (1996).

———. 'The Politics of Respectability: Identifying the Masculinist Context.' *Historical Studies* 22, no. 86 (1986).

Landes, Joan, ed. *Feminism: The Public and the Private.* Oxford: Oxford University Press, 1998.

Larkins, John, and Bruce Howard. *Australian Pubs.* Adelaide: Rigby, 1973.

Larkins, John, and Don Muir. *Victorian Country Pubs.* Adelaide: Rigby, 1980.

Lawson, Henry. 'A Bush Publican's Lament.' In *Collected Stories of Henry Lawson.* Melbourne: Viking O'Neil, 1987.

———. 'An Incident at Stiffner's.' In *Collected Stories of Henry Lawson.* Melbourne: Viking O'Neil, 1987.

———. 'Jimmy Grimshaw's Wooing.' In *Collected Stories of Henry Lawson.* Melbourne: Viking O'Neil, 1987.

———. 'The Shanty-Keeper's Wife.' In *The World of Henry Lawson,* edited by Walter Stone. Sydney: Paul Hamlyn, 1974.

Lender, Mark, and James Martin. *Drinking in America: A History.* New York: Free Press, 1982.

Lewis, J. Parry. *Freedom to Drink: A Critical Review of the Development of the Licensing Laws and Proposals for Reform.* London: The Institute of Economic Affairs, 1985.

Lewis, Milton. *A Rum State: Alcohol and State Policy in Australia.* Canberra: Australian Government Publishing Service, 1992.

Low, Charles. *Digest of Various Acts of Parliament Containing Penal Clauses Effecting [sic] Those Engaged in Business as Licensed Victuallers: Also, Some Recent Important Decisions.* Sydney, 1909.

Macintyre, Stuart. *A Colonial Liberalism: The Lost World of Three Victorian Visionaries.* Melbourne: Oxford University Press, 1991.

Magarey, Susan, Sue Rowley, and Susan Sheridan, eds. *Debutante Nation: Feminism Contests the 1890s.* Sydney: Allen & Unwin, 1993.

Malcolm, Elizabeth. *'Ireland Sober, Ireland Free': Drink and Temperance in Nineteenth-Century Ireland.* Dublin: Gill and MacMillan, 1986.

Malone, Betty. *Prahran's Pubs, 1852–1988.* Prahran, Vic.: Prahran Bicentennial Community Committee in conjunction with the City of Prahran, 1988.

Martin, A. Lynn. *Alcohol, Sex and Gender in Late Medieval and Early Modern Europe.* Hampshire: Palgrave, 2000.

Matthews, Jill Julius. 'Normalising Modernity.' *The UTS Review* 6, no. 1 (2000).

———. *Good and Mad Women: The Historical Construction of Femininity in Twentieth-Century Australia.* Sydney: Allen and Unwin, 1984.

McConville, Chris. *Croppies, Celts and Catholics: The Irish in Australia.* Melbourne: Edward Arnold, 1987.

———. 'Rough Women, Respectable Men and Social Reform: A Response to Lake's "Masculinism".' *Historical Studies* 22, no. 88 (1987).

———. 'The Location of Melbourne's Prostitutes, 1870–1920.' *Historical Studies* 19, no. 74 (1980).

McDowell, Linda, and Joanne P. Sharp, eds. *Space, Gender, Knowledge: Feminist Readings.* London: Arnold Hodder Headline, 1997.

McGregor, Craig. *Profile of Australia.* London: Hodder and Stoughton, 1966.

McGuire, Paul. *Inns of Australia.* London: Heinemann, 1952.

McKay, Mark. *On Tap: A Calvalcade of Trivia and Tall Stories Celebrating 200 Years of the Australian Pub.* Kent Town, SA: Wakefield Press, 1999.

McKean, James. *Hotel Keepers' Guide: The Licensing Act 1876.* Melbourne: George Robertson, 1877.

McLauchlan, Gordon. *The Story of Beer: Beer and Brewing, a New Zealand History.* Auckland: Viking Penguin, 1994.

Meagher, J. S. *Licensing Law in Victoria.* Melbourne: Melville and Mullin, 1908.

Merrett, D. T. 'Stability and Change in the Australian Brewing Industry, 1920–94.' In *The Dynamics of the International Brewing Industry since 1800*, edited by R. G. Wilson and T. R. Gourvish. London: Routledge, 1998.

———. 'The Victorian Licensing Court, 1906–68: A Study of Role and Impact.' *Australian Economic History Review* 19 (1979).

Mitchell, Susan. *Public Lives, Private Passions.* Sydney: Simon and Schuster, 1994.

———. *The Matriarchs: Twelve Australian Women Talk about Their Lives.* Ringwood, Vic.: Penguin, 1987.

Modjeska, Drusilla, ed. *Inner Cities: Australian Women's Memory of Place*. Ringwood, Vic.: Penguin, 1989.

Morris, Myra. *The Wind on the Water*. London: Thornton Butterworth Ltd, 1938.

Monckton, H. A. *A History of the English Public House*. London: The Bodley Head, 1969.

Murphy, Mary. 'Bootlegging Mothers and Drinking Daughters: Gender and Prohibition in Butte, Montana.' *American Quarterly* 46, no. 2 (1994).

Nichols, G. R. *The Licensed Victuallers' Consolidation Act*. Sydney: William Moffitt, 1838.

Nicholson, Linda. 'Feminist Theory: The Private and the Public.' In *Defining Women: Social Institutions and Gender Divisions*, edited by Linda McDowell and Rosemary Pringle. Milton Keynes: Polity Press, 1992.

Noel, Thomas. *The City and the Saloon: Denver, 1858–1916*. Lincoln: University of Nebraska Press, 1982.

Norris, Merle. *Brisbane Hotels and Publicans Index, 1842–1900*. Kelvin Grove, Qld: Brisbane History Group, 1993.

O'Driscoll, Jack, and Kevin Anderson. *Meagher's Licensing Law and Practice*. 4th edn. Melbourne: Law Book, 1952.

O'Farrell, Patrick. *The Irish in Australia*. Sydney: New South Wales University Press, 1986.

O'Grady, John (Nino Culotta). *It's Your Shout, Mate! Aussie Pubs and Aussie Beers*. Sydney: Ure Smith, 1962.

O'Mahony, Barry. Food and Beverages in Australia: An Irish Perspective. PhD, University of Melbourne, 2003.

Ottaway, Noel. *The Pub and I: The Experiences of a Sydney Publican*. Sydney: Horwitz, 1967.

Otto, Shirley. 'Women, Alcohol and Social Control.' In *Controlling Women: The Normal and the Deviant*, edited by Bridget Hutter and Gillian William. London: Croon Helm, 1981.

Pargeter, Judith. *For God, Home and Humanity: National Woman's Christian Temperance Union of Australia: Centenary History, 1891–1991*. Golden Grove, SA: National Woman's Christian Temperance Union of Australia, 1995.

Parker, Alison. *Purifying America: Women, Cultural Reform, and Pro-Censorship Activism, 1873–1933*. Urbana: University of Illinois Press, 1997.

Pateman, Carole. 'Feminist Critiques of the Public/Private Dichotomy.' In *The Disorder of Women: Democracy, Feminism and Political Theory*, edited by Carole Pateman. Cambridge: Polity Press, 1989.

Pearl, Cyril. *Beer, Glorious Beer: With Incidental Observations on Great Beer Myths, Pubs and Publicans, Barmaids and Breathalysers, Mum, Flip, Beer Bards, and Beer in the Kitchen, Etc., Etc*. Melbourne: Nelson, 1969.

Peiss, Kathy. *Cheap Amusements: Working Women and Leisure in Turn-of-the-Century New York*. Philadelphia: Temple University Press, 1986.

Perrott, Monica. *A Tolerable Good Success: Economic Opportunities for Women in NSW, 1788–1830*. Sydney: Hale & Ironmonger, 1983.

Perry [Wright], Clare. Real Women Do Shout: Women's Narratives of Pub Culture. BA (Hons), University of Melbourne, 1991.

Philips, David, and Susanne Davies. *A Nation of Rogues? Crime, Law and Punishment in Colonial Australia*. Melbourne: Melbourne University Press, 1994.

Phillips, Anne. *Divided Loyalties: Dilemmas of Sex and Class*. London: Virago, 1987.

Phillips, Walter. '"Six O'Clock Swill": The Introduction of Early Closing of Hotel Bars in Australia.' *Australian Historical Studies* 19, no. 75 (1980).

Pickett, Charles. *Brewing and Pubs*. Ultimo, NSW: Powerhouse Museum, 1989.

Pixley, Jocelyn. 'Wowser and Pro-Woman Politics: Temperance against Australian Patriarchy.' *Australian and New Zealand Journal of Sociology* 27, no. 3 (1991).

Porter, Hal. 'At Mcgarrigle's Inn.' In *Hal Porter*, edited by Mary Lord. St Lucia, Qld.: University of Queensland Press, 1980.

Powell, Keith. *Drinking and Alcohol in Colonial Australia, 1788–1901 for the Eastern States*. Canberra: Australian Government Publishing Service, 1988.

Powers, Madelon. *Faces Along the Bar: Lore and Order in the Workingman's Saloon, 1870–1920*. Chicago: University of Chicago Press, 1998.

———. 'The "Poor Man's Friend": Saloonkeepers, Workers, and the Code of Reciprocity in U.S. Barrooms, 1870–1920.' *International Labor and Working-Class History* 45 (1994).

———. 'Decay from Within: The Inevitable Doom of the American Saloon.' In *Drinking: Behaviour and Belief in Modern History*, edited by Susanna Barrows and Robin Room. Berkeley: University of California Press, 1991.

Prichard, Katharine Susannah. 'The Mayor of Bardie Creek.' *Bulletin*, 28 July 1937, p. 45.

Quick, Sandra. The Colonial Helpmeet Takes a Dram: Women Participants in the Central Otago Goldfields Liquor Industry 1861–1901. MA, University of Otago, 1997.

Quick, Sir John, and Luke Murphy. *The Victorian Liquor Licence and Local Option Laws, Charles Maxwell*. Melbourne, 1920.

Rahilly, J. F. *The Liquor Licensing Law of the Colony of Victoria: Comprising 'the Licensing Act, 1885', Notes of English and Colonial Cases, Copious Explanatory Memoranda: Also the Amending Licensing Acts Nos. 886, 949, 1007: With Comparative Notes and Analytical Index*. Melbourne: C. F. Maxwell, 1890.

Reekie, Gail. 'The Sexual Politics of Selling and Shopping.' In *Debutante Nation: Feminism Contests the 1890s*, edited by Susan Magarey, Sue Rowley and Susan Sheridan. Sydney: Allen and Unwin, 1993.

Reynolds, G. T. *Hotelkeepers—Innkeepers—Publicans: An Alphabetical Index of Hotelkeepers—Innkeepers—Publicans in the South-East Corner of New South Wales, 1894–1903*. Batemans Bay, NSW: Possum Printing, 1993.

Roberts, Mick. *The Local: A History of Hotels and the Liquor Industry in the Far Northern Illawarra of N.S.W.* Bulli, NSW: M. R. Roberts, 1992.

Robertson, Andrew. *Hotels and Hotelkeepers of the Blackwood Goldfields*. Melbourne: C. C. Jones and H. M. Robertson, 1978.

Robinson, Portia. *The Women of Botany Bay: A Reinterpretation of the Role of Women in the Origins of Australian Society*. Sydney: Macquarie Library, 1988.

———. *The Hatch and Brood of Time: A Study of the First Generation of Native-Born White Australians, 1788–1828*. Melbourne: Oxford University Press, 1985.

Roe, Jill. 'Chivalry and Social Policy in the Antipodes.' *Historical Studies* 22, no. 88 (1987).

Rose, Gillian. *Feminism and Geography: The Limits of Geographical Knowledge*. Cambridge: Polity Press, 1993.

Rosenberg, Rosalind. *Beyond Separate Spheres: Intellectual Roots of Modern Feminism*. New Haven: Yale University Press, 1982.

Rosenzweig, Roy. *Eight Hours for What We Will: Workers and Leisure in an Industrial City, 1870–1920*. Cambridge, Mass.: Cambridge University Press, 1983.

Rowe, David, and Geoff Lawrence. *Sport and Leisure: Trends in Australian Popular Culture*. Sydney: Harcourt Brace Javanovic, 1990.

Rumbarger, John. *Profits, Power, and Prohibition: Alcohol Reform and the Industrializing of America, 1800–1930*. Albany: State University of New York Press, 1989.

Russell, Penny. *A Wish of Distinction: Colonial Gentility and Femininity*. Melbourne: Melbourne University Press, 1994.

Sayers, Sean. 'The Need to Work: A Perspective from Philosophy.' In *On Work: Historical, Comparative and Theoretical Approaches*, edited by R. E. Pahl. Oxford: Blackwell, 1988.

Schaffer, Kay. *Women and the Bush: Forces of Desire in the Australian Cultural Tradition*. Cambridge: Cambridge University Press, 1988.

Scutt, Jocelynne, and Di Graham. *For Richer, for Poorer: Money, Marriage and Property Rights*. Ringwood, Vic.: Penguin, 1984.

Serle, Geoffrey. *The Rush to Be Rich: A History of the Colony of Victoria, 1883–1889*. Melbourne: Melbourne University Press, 1971.

Shapcott, Thomas. *Hotel Bellevue*. London: Chatto and Windus, 1986.

Shaw, Barry. *A Brisbane Historical Pub Tour*. Kelvin Grove, Qld: Brisbane History Group, 1995.

Sheedy, Kevin, and Carolyn Brown. *Football's Women: The Forgotten Heroes*. Ringwood, Vic.: Penguin, 1998.

Smith, Michael A. 'Social Usages of the Public Drinking House: Changing Aspects of Class and Leisure.' *British Journal of Sociology* 34, no. 3 (1983).

Smithers, Charles. *The Licensee's Manual: Being a Guide to the Liquor Laws of New South Wales*. Sydney: Law Book Company of Australasia, 1932.

Spain, Daphne. *Gendered Spaces*. Chapel Hill: University of North Carolina Press, 1992.

Spencer, Thomas E. 'Why Doherty Died.' In *Old Ballads from the Bush*, edited by Bill Scott. Sydney: Angus and Robertson, 1987.

Spiller, Brian. *Victorian Public Houses*. Newton Abbot: David and Charles, 1972.

Stewart, Abigail. 'Discovering the Meanings of Work.' In *The Experience and Meaning of Work in Women's Lives*, edited by Nia Lane Chester and Hildreth Grossman. New Jersey: L. Erlbaum Associates, 1990.

Stivers, Richard. *A Hair of the Dog: Irish Drinking and American Stereotype*. University Park: Pennsylvania State University Press, 1976.

Sumerling, Patricia. *Down at the Local: A History of Hotels in Kensington, Norwood and Kent Town*. Adelaide: Wakefield Press, 1998.

Summers, Anne. *Damned Whores and God's Police: The Colonization of Women in Australia*. Ringwood, Vic.: Penguin, 1975.

Sutherland, Alexander. *Victoria and Its Metropolis: Past and Present*. Melbourne: McCarron Bird, 1888.

Tennant, Kylie. 'Jim.' *Bulletin*, 2 December 1942.

Tighe, W. H. *Inns and Hotels of Old Bathurst Town: Their History and Locations*. Bathurst, N.S.W.: Bathurst Family History Research, 1992.

Twomey, Christina. *Deserted and Destitute: Motherhood, Wife Desertion and Colonial Welfare*. Melbourne: Australian Scholarly Publishing, 2002.

———. 'Without Natural Protectors': Histories of Deserted and Destitute Colonial Women in Victoria. PhD, University of Melbourne, 1997.

Tyrrell, Ian. 'Women and Temperance in International Perspective: The World's WCTU, 1880s–1920s.' In *Drinking: Behaviour and Belief in Modern History*, edited by Susanna Barrows and Robin Room. Berkeley: University of California Press, 1991.

———. *Woman's World, Woman's Empire: The Woman's Christian Temperance Union in International Perspective, 1880–1930*. Chapel Hill: The University of North Carolina Press, 1990.

———. *Sobering Up: From Temperance to Prohibition in Antebellum America, 1800–1860*. Westport, Conn.: Greenwood Press, 1979.

Vallen, Jerome, James Abbey and Dunnovan Sapienza. *The Art and Science of Managing Hotels, Restaurants, Institutions*. New Jersey: Hayden Book Company, 1968.

Van Der Wagen, Lynn. *Professional Hospitality: An Introduction*. Melbourne: Hospitality Press, 1996.

Van Hek, Lin. *The Ballad of Siddy Church*. Melbourne: Spinifex, 1997.

Vaughan, Marcia, and Patricia Mullins. *The Sea-Breeze Hotel*. Hunters Hill, NSW: Margaret Hamilton Books, 1991.

Walker, Louise. Beers, Bed and Board: Industrial Behaviour around the Victorian Hotel and Liquor Industry Wages Boards, 1900–1914. BA (Hons), Monash University, 1995.

Wannan, Bill. *Folklore of the Australian Pub*. Melbourne: Sun Books, 1975.

———. *A Dictionary of Australian Folklore: Lore, Legends, Myths and Traditions*. Melbourne: Viking O'Neil, 1970.

Ward, Russel. *The Australian Legend*. Melbourne: Oxford University Press, 1958.

Warne, Ellen Mary. The Mother's Anxious Future: Australian Christian Women's Organisations Meet the Modern World, 1890s–1930s. PhD, University of Melbourne, 2000.

Warsh, Cheryl K., ed. *Drink in Canada: Historical Essays*. Montreal: McGill–Queen's University Press, 1993.

White, Arthur S. *Palaces of the People: A Social History of Commercial Hospitality*. New York: Taplinger, 1968.

White, Richard. *Inventing Australia: Images and Identity, 1688–1980*. Sydney: Allen and Unwin, 1981.

Woolmer, George. *Overland Corner: A History of Overland Corner and Its Hotel*. Barmera, SA: Barmera Branch of the National Trust of South Australia, 1986.

Wright, Clare. '"Doing the Beans": Women, Community and Drinking in the Ladies Lounge.' *Journal of Australian Studies* 76 (2003).

Wynn Allen, Polly. *Building Domestic Liberty: Charlotte Perkins Gilman's Architectural Feminism*. Amherst: University of Massachusetts Press, 1988.

Young, Mayse, with Gabrielle Dalton. *No Place for a Woman: The Autobiography of Outback Publican, Mayse Young*. Chippendale, NSW: Pan Australia, 1991.

Index